Better to Be Lucky than Smart!

Better to Be Lucky than Smart!

A Memoir

Bill Mares

Montpelier, VT

Better to Be Lucky than Smart! ©2024 William Mares

All Rights Reserved.

Release Date: September 24, 2024

Published by Rootstock Publishing,
an imprint of Ziggy Media LLC
info@rootstockpublishing.com
www.rootstockpublishing.com

Printed in the USA.

Paperback ISBN: 978-1-57869-283-5
Library of Congress Control Number: 2024913120

Cover and book design by Eddie Vincent, ENC Graphics Services. Interior photographs provided by the author, used with permission. Author photo by Jan Peyser.

For reprint permissions or to schedule a reading, contact the author at bill.mares@gmail.com.

To Chris, for all and ever.

Foreword

Bill Mares? That mischievous Texan? That smug, wannabe comic who wrote *Real Vermonters Don't Milk Goats* with Frank Bryan? Well, in 1983, I WAS that back-to-land hippy who DID milk goats. I was trying my darndest to fit into my adopted Vermont. Bill comes along and scarfs up fame and riches peddling 70,000 cheap shot books making fun of invaders like me who thrived on growing kale and milking goats in our rural Vermont utopia.

Full disclosure. I've known Bill Mares for only forty years. So I don't know everything about him—just enough to be dangerous. Most of what he says in this book can and will be held against him. An MC introducing Mark Twain in some forlorn, frontier outpost a century ago quipped, "I only know two things about Mr. Twain: One. He ain't never been in jail. And two, I don't know why." Feels like Mares to me.

We expect Bill, as storyteller and fisherman, to stretch the truth. But in this aptly named memoir, "Lucky Bill" forgoes the tempting whopper, eschews hyperbole, and mostly sticks to the truth. Which is good news for us. Undistracted by the need to sift humor from insight, we can curl up by the woodstove and absorb the wisdom Bill has gleaned from his excellent, full-throttle life.

Bill is not the iconic, laconic Vermonter he reveres. Instead, he is a closet-driven Calvinist. But his unpretentious, understated persona saves his creds. He knows he was born on second base and he doesn't squander his lead-off double. During his childhood family travels, not a moment was wasted as Bill devoured a smorgasbord of history— the French, Russian, and Chinese Revolutions, Indian Independence, etc. Harvard only exacerbated his scholarly curiosities.

Outrageously productive in all he decides to undertake, there's an authenticity about Mares he just can't cover up. When Bill does a thing, he does it fully homeworked, legs pumping, brain grinding, annoyingly quickly. Bees, brookies, beer...they're all gorgeously on display here, as Mares trots out this marathon of his life, singing bass every step of the way.

In January of 1985, when Bill and I met for the first time, we were freshman legislators in the State House in Montpelier. He from lofty Burlington, I from hayseed Brookfield. That chill January morning, the Burlington Free Press ran a puffy, front page "gotcha" story on how many odd ducks populated the incoming crop of lawmakers. The Free Press predictably saluted humorist Mares for writing Goats while indicting me for milking them. But, being people of immense goodwill, we submerged our divergent worldviews and became fast friends.

Now churning through his ninth decade, and fulfilling the hypothesis that "an unexamined life isn't worth living," Bill is "tidying up" in his twentieth book. From his father, Bill inherited the phrase, "The steam that toots the whistle never turned a wheel." Perhaps that explains Bill's reflexive modesty.

Bill's fluency makes storytelling look easy. He has a gift for showing, not just telling. Heartily believing the adage "there's no such thing as writing, only rewriting," I congratulate Bill on the meticulous hard work that produced this enthralling odyssey.

In many collections of his poetry, Robert Frost entices his readers to join him as he moseys out "to clean the pasture spring." Frost suggests he'll "only stop to rake the leaves away (and wait to watch the water clear, I may). I sha'n't be gone long. You come too." With this memoir, I think

Bill is cajoling us each to explore our own pasture spring. Try some self reflection. Tidy up. Along the way, he demonstrates the fun and joy of reliving some experiences that really are memorable. It's not so hard. You come too.

—Don Hooper, January 31, 2024

Introduction

It's 5 a.m. Street light slices through the blinds. My coffee steams at the ready. I've finished the morning Spanish language exercise and my diary entry. Outside, the occasional car, truck, or snowplow rumbles by. The computer hums and the radiator clanks. A few weeks ago, I finished writing a history of Vermont humor with Don Hooper, a former fellow legislator. It was fun to collaborate for three years. We happily fed off each other—he the artist, I the writer.

But now, for the first time in fifty years, I don't have a book to work on. Ordinarily the early morning is my golden time for two or three hours of concentrated, uninterrupted work. No music, no news, no food, and no email; just me, caffeine, the work at hand, and the coming dawn. This room, my office, is twelve feet by twelve feet. It was perhaps a child's bedroom in 1865, when the house was built. It has two desks, one utilitarian for the computer, and the other a nineteenth-century rolltop we bought fifty years ago in a West Virginia antique store. Both have swivel chairs from where I can survey my domain. Bookshelves line all four walls. Their volumes—hundreds of them—are of all sizes and ages. Thirty or so are autographed by such people as Bill Mauldin, John Hersey, Jared Diamond, Andreï Sakharov, and John le Carré. Two of them are by my mother. Eighteen others are by me, some solo efforts and the rest with nine different collaborators. In one bookcase there are miscellaneous prayer books, bibles, and diaries. On other shelves are scores of current fiction and nonfiction books, some bought for my Big Boys Book Club, a local Burlington men's reading group I've been with for thirty years, and others recommended by friends and book reviews. One whole shelf contains World War I histories and novels, background for one of my books. There's also my mother's college yearbook from Bryn Mawr and a scrapbook my father kept on a 1923 trip he took to Europe.

Atop one bookcase is a miscellany of small statues, a photo of our son

Nick leaping across a World War I trench in France, and another of my first beekeeping mentor, Arnold Waters.

On the walls hang another gallery of my life. There are photos of George Orwell and Reinhold Niebuhr, my greatest intellectual heroes. Several fishing and hunting prints and a couple of duck decoys beckon me to rod and gun memories. An eighteenth-century map of Arabia and a photo of me in the Saudi desert share space with my Harvard diploma. The roll top desk with its red-leather writing surface is where I hunch over to write all my first drafts on yellow pads with a fifty-year-old Cross pen. Crowning the desk are family photos, rocks from fishing trips to Montana and Quebec, a beehive tool, and a brass coffeepot from Saudi Arabia.

Next to the computer another bookcase holds phone books, an array of beekeeping books, manuals, and catalogs, two encyclopedias, four dictionaries (one in Spanish), a thesaurus, *Bartlett's Quotations*, and my favorite reference work, *Brewer's Dictionary of Phrase and Fable*.

High on the largest bookcase is a solemn bronze bust of my father, which Mom commissioned in the 1930s. I've brought him down to earth by hanging most of my marathon medals around his neck and crowning him with a Marine Corps drill instructor's campaign hat from Parris Island.

For the last two years, I've lived at least six hours a day in this cell "scribbling, scribbling," like Mr. Gibbon, but also attending frequent board meetings, talks with Hooper, book club gatherings, and church services using the near-indispensable Zoom. I've even lectured and preached this way.

Now that Hooper and I are done with our collaboration, however, I've begun to feel the familiar shortness of breath, muscle ache, and fever of my literary double pneumonia. "I'll never write another book!" I say, and a moment later, "What's the next one?" Why this urge to fill, as they say in libraries, "one linear-foot" of my own books? Recurring anxiety? Simple ego? Curiosity? Wanderlust? Companionship? Maybe all of the above. I didn't plan it this way. I was always hesitant to call myself a writer. The books came serendipitously, a professional voyage boosted by generous gusts of luck. They were always hard work.

In his 1946 essay "Why I Write," George Orwell says: "Writing a book is a horrible, exhausting struggle, like a long bout of some painful illness. One would never undertake such a thing if one were not driven on by some demon whom one can neither resist nor understand. For all one knows that demon is simply the same instinct that makes a baby squall for attention."

I remember my father telling me as I went off to college: "Do whatever you want as an individual, but be a professional, an expert, in one thing." Then I went off to do the reverse, a number of things modestly well, but nothing really grand. I wish we could have joked about this before he died, because he also loved to say "An expert is a person who avoids all the minor errors as he sweeps forward to the grand fallacy." I just kept collecting friends, experiences, and books.

"What else can I write about?" I ask myself. In this Covid-19 era, I have little desire for serious travel. I have no talent for fiction or poetry, and no interest in blogging or tweets or other social media. My eyes turn to two waist-high black filing cabinets. In them sit the "Mares Papers." There's three- to four hundred pages of diaries, background work on various books, family histories, teaching assignments, letters, radio commentaries and newspaper columns, travel files, etc. Before Covid-19 arrived, I offered them to the University of Vermont Archives. In part, this was my thank-you for use of the university library on several of my books. They had said yes, if I would write an accompanying twenty- to thirty-page autobiography. I was flattered. Yes, of course. I could write such a descriptive essay.

But then, I began to wonder: Could I, should I write more? Dare I enter the terra incognita of a whole book about me? As I looked through some of those UVM-bound papers, I thought: My polymathic schooling, which began at home and continued through college and the world, had made me a perpetual (lifelong) student in a real-world university! Could such a student write an autobiography, or a memoir? The process would be threading the needle of writing in the first person about the third person who is the first person. Such literary gymnastics might be fun, being inside and outside the story simultaneously, all the while sailing between the Scylla of Bragging and the Charybdis of False Modesty. At what depth and detail would this be? The great existential philosopher Søren Kierkegaard's aphorism gave me some support when he wrote, "Life can only be understood backwards, but it must be lived forwards."

Well, a memoir was probably easier than an autobiography, which is based on hard facts. In a memoir you get to "invent the truth," in the felicitous phrase of Prof. William Zinsser (*On Writing Well*). You fill in the gaps with honest speculation. My father-in-law had written a memoir he called *By*

Memory Alone.

I thought back to a question posed by my good friend John Donnelly, a longtime reporter and fellow marathoner: "What are the threads that tie your life together, that made you into a writer?"

Well, I thought, I only had to look around this room and see the reflection of my life's passion and work. Let me see. I suddenly thought of the famous Escher etching of the hands drawing each other.

I grew up in a house of books and ideas. And here I was in a similar setting.

Dad's grounding in science and technology combined with Mom's deep interest in history and the humanities and her vast correspondence and their friendships from around the globe brought the world to us, and then us to the world. The second great gift from my parents was a love of travel, starting with trips to the American East and West, then to Europe. After that, my brothers and I launched our own boats to Latin America, Asia, and Africa. For us all, travel was always more than physical movement or relaxation; it brought education and action. Then there were the people along the way. I loved meeting people everywhere, strangers on the road, at schools, workplaces. I could get along with just about anyone, even jerks, in part because I felt I could almost always learn something from others. They, in turn, led to more friends and more ideas. I picked up the ancient Chinese custom of guanxi from my Chinese-speaking Harvard roommate. The term means to have a favorable balance in human relationships. You want the other fellow to owe you just a little more than you owe him, and thus you always have chits you can call in. It's an Eastern version of the West's Golden Rule. As I was a reasonably curious boy, journalism gave me some advanced tools of inquiry, to slice and dice knowledge and ignorance, to ask good follow-up questions.

Teaching taught me to turn around and share what I knew, not so much to stand and deliver, but to intrigue, entice, arouse students (and others) to put on their own thinking caps, to ask themselves questions. For twenty years my license plate was THINK, which my son Nick has now adopted. Outside the classroom, almost all of my writings, speeches, commentaries, books, and sermons were also forms of teaching, of posing the diffident reflection "I've been thinking…"

Finally, religion has been the moral glue holding the other threads together. Through formal church and private practice, I have tried to follow one injunction from St. Luke: "To whom much is given, much will be required" (Luke 12:48), a favorite biblical quote of my mother's which she recited to us often. I wouldn't pretend to Orwell's political purpose in what I wrote, but I have tried to follow his advice consistently to efface my own personality and wipe clean the reader's "windowpane." I took my marching orders from the sixteenth-century polymath Francis Bacon, whose words Dorothea Lange put on her darkroom door: "The contemplation of things as they are, without error or confusion, without substitution or imposture, is in itself a nobler thing than a whole harvest of invention."

OK, enough talk. Let's get started!

My Literary Evolution by my high-school classmate Roger Lewis

Chapter One

The Beginning (1940–1952)

> "The only things worth spending money on
> are travel and books."
> —J.R. Mares

I was born on November 8, 1940, as Nazi bombs rained down on Coventry Cathedral during the Battle of Britain. At least, that's what my mother told me later. In fact, the cathedral was destroyed on November 14, a week later. Her confusion was not hard to explain. For all her three pregnancies, she refused newspapers and radio news during her stays in the hospital, the easier to stay calm, for she was, in fact, a passionate interventionist during the years before the US entered World War II. For her, the right message she wanted to convey was the link between my birth and history.

~

My mom was born in Binghamton, New York, in 1905. Her father was a Harvard-educated high school principal who, with her Radcliffe-educated mother raised, five children. Her Anglo-Saxon ancestors came to America in 1630 and produced a mixture of farmers, ministers, teachers, missionaries, and one notable warrior.

That person was Gen. William Shepard (after whom I was named), who fought all through the French and Indian War, then farmed in Western Massachusetts. He was a member of the Committees of Correspondence, joined the militia as a colonel, and served at Washington's side through the battles of Long Island, Trenton, Princeton, and Valley Forge. He served three terms in Congress, and died at the age of eighty.

My mom enjoyed school, for she did well, which was very important in her family, with schoolteachers on both sides. "However, I must have been a mixed blessing to my teachers," she told me. "For although I did my work faithfully and usually knew the answers, I was assertive, competitive, and, in the words of a classmate, stuck up. Most of my teachers were tolerant, probably because they knew and liked my gentle mother."

She enrolled in Bryn Mawr, where she again did well, graduating first in her class of 1926. She majored in modern European history. After graduation, when she had a fellowship to study in France and Austria. She took a keen interest in the intellectual currents of Central Europe and met such people as the novelist Robert Musil and social reformer Rudolf Steiner.

Sometime during her Bryn Mawr years she fell in love with a Haverford student named Ames Johnson, whom she later married. On a second year abroad, when she worked in the ministry of education in Austria, she could see how fragile democracy was in both Austria and Germany, made worse by the worldwide depression, which began in Austria. She watched the growth of nationalistic groups like the Stahlhelm (steel helmet) and the Nazis in Germany and the Heimwehr (home guard) in Austria. She came back from her fellowship and taught in two different Philadelphia-area Quaker schools for the next six years. She loved teaching, but the marriage foundered. She never spoke of it except to say that 1932 was the "worst year in my life."

Determined to leave both her husband and the Philadelphia area, she applied to schools around the country and found salvation teaching history and German at the elite John Burroughs School in St. Louis, Missouri. The school was full of bright students, some the sons and daughters of several Swiss immigrant chemists who worked for Monsanto Chemical Company. Sometime in 1934, the couple Jules and Helen Bebie thought she would like to meet the head of the company's patent office, a tall, taciturn, rangy man named Joe Mares, and invited them both to a dinner party.

My father, Joe Mares, was born in Helena, Montana, in 1903, the first of three children to Josef and Antoinette Mares, who emigrated from the Bohemian town of Zemberk, one hundred miles east of Prague in the present-day Czech Republic. Trained as a shoemaker, Josef first came to Eastern Montana in the 1880s, to work as a cowboy, then moved to the mining town of Marysville, to make boots, saddles, and harnesses. Through a lucky grubstake with a solitary miner, he got early word of a silver strike at the famous Drumlummon Mine. In twenty-four hours he scoured up perhaps five hundred dollars to buy as much stock as he could. With the earnings from this investment, Josef was able to move to Helena and set up with two brothers, Frank and Wesley, what became one of the largest retail and wholesale meat businesses in the state, the Helena Meat Company. Josef and Frank went back to Zemberk to marry two sisters and brought them to Montana. The three children were Blanche, Joe, and Ernest. Sketchily, Dad recalled:

> Our household was one of hard work and enterprise. Our parents never said 'you can't do this or that.' They told us what we were expected to do. When we did it, we were largely free to plow our own furrows. You ate what was on your plate or you didn't eat.
>
> Father and Mother didn't read a lot but they kept up with the news. They talked only Czech to each other. But we children were Americans and spoke English. Education was very important to them. The house was like an inn with people coming from all over the state to eat dinner or even stay the night. Many business deals were conducted over the dining room table, and we children were invited to sit and listen to the adult conversations.

Dad's high schooling was rigorous. His senior year he took physics, calculus, English, European history, French, and German. The principal, Mr. A. J. Roberts, who had been educated in Europe, was a great influence on Dad, who said that Roberts "badgered us to decide what we wanted to accomplish, to think for ourselves. What was our ambition? Start planning for it in high school!"

In 1920, Dad went off to Montana State College to major in chemistry. During the next two summers he walked house to house and farm to farm in the Bitterroot Valley of Montana selling agricultural almanacs and encyclopedias about World War I. Impressed by his work, several of his professors encouraged him to transfer to the Massachusetts Institute of Technology. He was accepted, and by taking seven courses a year graduated with the class of 1924.

In the summer of 1923, he worked his way to Europe by working as a stock tender and coal shoveler on a live-cattle boat. Two weeks in Germany in the tumult of their hyperinflation had a lasting effect on him. (I inherited several fifty-million and one-hundred-million-mark notes he brought home as souvenirs.) After college he worked as a chemist for Goodyear Tire and Rubber Company in Akron, Ohio, and at Willy's Overland Auto Company. Along the way he took enough law school night classes to pass the bar exams in two states. That extra work paved the way for him to be hired as the first patent attorney for the Monsanto Chemical Company in St. Louis, Missouri. (He would eventually earn over fifteen mechanical and chemical patents in his own name.)

His circle of friends revolved around the company, but it was quite a cosmopolitan group. In particular, there were four chemists, three Swiss and one Greek, with whom he shared evenings and ideas. One couple, the Bebies, invited him to a fateful dinner party in part to meet a teacher of their children at John Burroughs School, one Delia Smith.

The match worked and they were married in August 1935. Here, our family story gets hazy. We boys simply never queried our parents about their courtship and marriage. We knew that Dad and his brother Ernest lived together as bachelors when they both worked for Monsanto. We know that Mom and Dad were married in New Jersey and honeymooned in Mexico. And the next year she stopped teaching history.

But from then on, she joked, she was teaching life and death. While a schoolteacher she had joined the St. Louis League of Women Voters and its commitment to public issues. She told me:

> Ignorant of St. Louis and Missouri politics, I chose foreign policy as my preferred topic and swiftly became the chair of that department. I was responsible for assembling facts on a previously chosen item, for communicating those facts to the entire League in study groups or by written materials, for directing any action the League voted to take, and for helping formulate new program items.
>
> I watched in dismay as the toothless League of Nations failed to end aggressions of Italy, Germany, and Japan. The Franco

Grandparents Joseph Mares and Antoinette Yama, married in 1901

invasion, aided by German and Italian warplanes, was my first realization that Germany's tragedy was to be a threat to all Europe. Joe brought me a radio in the hospital when Jan was born. But most people in America were too concerned with domestic economic crisis to care about aggression and totalitarianism abroad. With the Austrian Anschluss in the spring of 1938 and the rape of Czechoslovakia at Munich the following fall, Joe and I became wholly committed interventionists, among a handful in St. Louis.

Once the war in Europe began, and impatient with the League's more measured stance, Mom joined the openly interventionist Committee to Defend America by Aiding the Allies, which included people like President James Conant of Harvard, the theologian Reinhold Niebuhr, and the Kansas newspaper editor William Allen White. They went toe to toe with isolationist groups such as the German American Bund and the America First Committee, which wanted the country to stay out of Europe's fight. While Charles Lindbergh may have been one of the great heroes of the twentieth century, in our house his name was mud. (My mother would continue her foreign policy work after World War II, as she engaged in the Cold War with a small book about the threats of Communism, *Know Your Enemy*, while also fighting against both the McCarthyites and their kindred spirits, like the John Birch Society.)

With modest hyperbole, I would say my parents formed a literal marriage of the American West and East, two of the great strands of the American experience. Both were always proud to be Americans, but were plenty conscious of the nation's flaws. We lived in a three-story frame house at the corner of Swon and Gray Avenues in the leafy St. Louis suburb of Webster Groves. There was a big L-shaped yard with enough space for baseball and war games. Three blocks away was our school, Bristol Elementary. The three of us came along in metronomic succession: Jan, in December 1936, named after Jan Masaryk, foreign minister of Czechoslovakia; Tom, in January 1939, named after ToMáTomáš Masaryk, the first president of Czechoslovakia; and me, in November 1940, named after my mom's ancestor, Gen. Shepard. My first memories were of Mom reading to us boys. For me, of course, it was only sounds: *brrrrrrrr, psssssst, ta-pocketa-pocketa, Stickly-Prickly, Rikki-Tikki Tavi* ...

Gradually, the words became common speech and uncommon rhyme, coming in luxuriant profusion—"The great grey-green greasy Limpopo river,

My Parents Delia and Joe Mares, Kowloon, c. 1959

all set about with fever trees," (from *Just So Stories* by Rudyard Kipling). Before I was allowed in the yard, I accompanied some of Aesop's animals on their journeys. I ventured into the jungle with Mowgli, Kaa, Shere Khan, the Kolokolo Bird, Yellow-Dog Dingo, the Bi-Coloured-Python-Rock-Snake. I joined Toad and Rat and Badger in their battle against the hated stoats. The books became tales of adventure. *Captains Courageous*, *Kim*, *Toby Tyler: Or Ten Weeks with a Circus*, *Treasure Island*, *Last of the Mohicans*, *Stuart Little*. There was no pallid *Dick and Jane* for us!

Our house was full of books. We had the famous eleventh edition of the

Encyclopædia Britannica, books of politics, science, and sociology, current affairs, the Harvard Classics, novels, and plays in profusion. My father loved to sit in an easy chair and listen to the music of Eduardo Lalo, Antonin Dvořák, Beethoven, and Gilbert and Sullivan, rising every four minutes to turn over the big 78 rpm records. A piano, which my mother played fitfully, filled half of the living room. Prints of the Impressionists and Winslow Homer adorned the walls. On one bookshelf, there was a bronze bust of Dad, which my mom had commissioned.

From print, our adventures turned to radio. There was *The Lone Ranger*, with the stirring background music of Rossini, Liszt, and Rimsky-Korsakov, *Sergeant Preston of the Yukon*, *Sky King*, *Boston Blackie*, and *The Shadow*, whose voice intoned: "Who knows what evil lurks in the hearts of men? The Shadow knows!"

Our outdoor games took on a more martial tone. Dusk was the time for great roaming bands of ten to twenty kids to swarm around our big house and yard, kick the can, capture the flag, reenact real battles of far away. In one episode, I fell out of a tree while on a spy mission and sliced open an elbow on a broken bottle. In another encounter, my brother Tommy and I had a spectacular collision as we rounded the same corner and knocked each other out.

The war came closer, adding fact to fiction. Mom had come back from visiting her mother to report she had seen ships sunk off the New Jersey coast. While one of her brothers, too old for the draft, continued to teach in a New Jersey college, the other, a brilliant linguist, became an army code breaker. Our father, also too old to serve, spent a year working on radar technology at the Massachusetts Institute of Technology.

Our local heroes were now in the North Atlantic, the South Pacific, on beaches, at North Africa, Italy, and Normandy, in planes over Germany.

We tried to do our bit. We collected cans and newspapers. We scouted out tinfoil on gum wrappers, made balls of metal that we could take to the salvage shop for payment. I became a literal poster child for canned vegetables at a local market, while Tommy promoted war bonds.

Our fantasy wars turned somber when our neighbors' kin began dying. One son was killed in a bombing raid over Germany. Another son died at Anzio in Italy. And our doctor's beloved only son, a marine lieutenant, was killed on Iwo Jima.

Vaguely do I remember radio reports of Roosevelt's death and the atomic bomb. At the war's end, the town hosted a traveling exhibit of war equipment, newsreels, and photos of cheering crowds, leveled cities, and stacks of bodies in concentration camps while huge search lights played tag in the skies above.

Of school, I remember almost nothing about my years of kindergarten and first grade, except that I was an acceptable student who didn't stand out.

Explosion

When I was six years old and in the first grade, Dad, by then Monsanto's director of development, was transferred to Texas City, Texas, to manage their plant of some five hundred workers making ethylene, polystyrene, and butadiene for the nascent plastics industry. On April 16, 1947, I walked home to lunch from school to find my brother Jan at the door. "There was a huge explosion at the Monsanto plant in Texas where Dad works," he told me. "But he is safe!" Phew!

On the previous night, he had worked at the plant until 3 a.m. when they were trying to get the polystyrene line onstream. The next morning he decided to drive to work about an hour later than normal. As his rented car drove across the three-mile-long Galveston causeway leading to Texas City, at 9:15 a.m. there was a huge explosion five miles away in the direction of his plant. In seconds the noise and shock wave hit his car, and a huge cloud spread across the city. He stopped, found a phone, and made an urgent call to the home office in St. Louis. He then drove on to what remained of the plant, and the city. The "Texas City disaster" was one of the worst industrial accidents in American history. An ill-fated freighter, the SS *Grandcamp*, had been docked next to the Monsanto plant with a cargo of twenty-five hundred tons of ammonium nitrate. Irony of ironies, this load of fertilizer was destined for French and Belgium farmers in the war's wake. Now it had become an instrument of death for almost six hundred people, including the entire Texas City Fire Department of twenty-seven men. The company dead reached 145, with almost every other working employee injured. Mom would tell us later that Dad felt most sharply the deaths of fifteen young chemical engineers, including the father of one of my second-grade classmates. While Dad worked on in Texas, the family stayed in St. Louis through the school year and through a nationwide polio scare. With Mom's long-distance support, Dad looked for a house and found one about ten miles away in the town of Dickinson. In August, we drove the eight hundred miles south from St. Louis to our new home on the Texas Gulf Coast.

Dickinson (1947–52)

On our first hot, sticky night in Texas, screams suddenly blared through our porch windows. "Awwwrr, awwwrr, awwwrr!" It sounded as if someone was being strangled. Then, just as suddenly, they stopped. The next day, a neighbor told us, laughing, that the "screams" were really the cries of a flock of peacocks belonging to the Catholic bishop of Galveston, who lived about three hundred yards away. This was our introduction to what Mom called "the wild south of Texas."

In our second week in Texas, my father took us on a tour of Texas City and the Monsanto plant destroyed four months earlier. Back in St. Louis we'd seen aerial photos of the smoke, others of piles of cars and debris, the rows of bodies on the high school gym floor, the wounded being treated. But this was in our faces. We drove through the city half flattened by the blast, where whole blocks were broomed clean as if by giants. At the company gate, a guard waved us through. Then, inside, we drove slowly through the maze of damage and new construction. Piles of rubble were juxtaposed with naked girders clawing the sky. Construction workers were everywhere. The scenes were like those from newsreels of bombed-out London or Tokyo or Berlin. Dad showed us where his office had been. The only memento he recovered was a blue wool cardigan sweater riddled with glass shards, which he wore until moths performed their own final rites on its fibers. For the next two years, Dad would continue to work six and sometimes seven days a week overseeing the plant's reconstruction in this, his war zone, so that on the second anniversary, April 16, 1949, the plant was back onstream. For the rest of our lives, that event was the "9/11" to all our friends. The code words for that day became "Texas City," "the Explosion," or just "the Blast."

Dickinson lay roughly halfway between Galveston's fading economy of cotton and tourism and Houston's explosive growth fifty miles inland. Galveston had over thirty miles of beaches, an active underground gambling industry, and the University of Texas Medical School.

Slicing the town from west to east was Dickinson Bayou, a tidal stream that started fresh in the rice fields to the west of us and was salt by the time it reached Galveston Bay, twenty miles to the east. The town had a modest economic base in rice, cattle, and oil. It was not exactly a commuter town, although many of its four thousand residents drove to other parts of the surrounding counties for work. It had been settled over the years by small waves of immigrants from East Texas and the Rio Grande Valley, and from Sicily and the North—the "damn Yankees," we were told.

Yes, the town was split into white and Black neighborhoods, towns, schools, churches. The only connections were largely in maid service and sweat labor.

Downtown ran three blocks from State Highway 3 to the Missouri Pacific Railroad tracks. In the center of town was Nick Liggio's Humble Oil gas station, the Red Pheasant Inn, which ran a low-grade gambling operation, and the large white stucco Shrine of the True Cross Catholic Church. On the main street were a feed-hardware store, two groceries, the Citizens State Bank, a five-and-dime, Klecka's Department Store, several beauty parlors, a Ford dealership, and even a small hotel by the railroad tracks. We could walk or bike to church, school, and the Hollywood Theater and almost to the Little League field. However, there was no library. Mom loved to tell of walking into the town's only drugstore to ask where to find a bookstore. "What kind of books you looking for, ma'am," asked the clerk, "readin' books or picture books?" (Eventually, she would help endow a town library.)

My friends were a mix of white, middle-class Americans, sons and daughters of farmers, ranchers, a banker, clerks, letter carriers, oil field workers, chemical engineers, and doctors, but no lawyers. Our family was among the upper class in the town, but, my mother warned, we should never show it.

Our House

Our lot was almost eight acres of live oak, cedar, and pine trees. A gravel driveway led fifty yards from State Highway 517 Pines Road to the house, then around it. No one ever visited unannounced, for the gravel, like watch geese, crunched a warning that sounded right down the hedges toward the house. Four of the acres were grass and trees, surrounding the house, and four were woods where we played war games and I kept a horse for a couple of years. The property bordered on Dickinson Bayou. At our house, the bayou was thirty to forty yards across, wide enough for two motorboats to pass. The oaks and cedar were hung with hoary Spanish moss, and if you tried, you could imagine yourself in semi jungle, but not quite *Heart of Darkness*. The water had fish, crabs, and the antediluvian alligator gar, and, we told our friends breathlessly, some people have seen alligators there.

Built in 1912, the three-story frame house swallowed up visitors and road noise. On one side of the driveway was a primitive tennis court where my mother taught us to play with rackets that went back to her youth, thick wooden things with handles bigger than hoes. But the court never stayed true, and balls kept getting caught in the Spanish moss. None of us boys or neighbors stuck with the sport. We turned our attention to baseball and football, which we played with the neighbors on an all-purpose trapezoidal space on the other side of the driveway, where Dad fashioned a makeshift basketball court by putting a hoop ten feet up an oak tree. A family tradition developed to play a pickup game on Christmas Day—barefoot!

The house had high ceilings, four rooms downstairs, and four upstairs. There was a grand concrete front porch for greetings and farewells and for sharing evenings with the mosquitoes. Without air-conditioning, we kept the house cool with high ceilings and thick canvas awnings, which were rolled down to keep direct sunlight out of the rooms.

For hide-and-seek games, the favorite spot was the attic, except in the summer when it was well over one hundred degrees. There were wasp nests in the eaves. We had huge steamer trunks, camping gear, containers of disintegrating movie film, toys, magazines, books. On one shelf was my father's old pipe collection, which proved irresistible to small boys. Inevitably, my father caught us once when he smelled the smoke. He was enraged. I think it was the closest he ever came to striking us. Later, I realized that he was far more worried about burning the house down than our youthful transgression.

We three boys slept on a three-sided sleeping porch with windows that brought peacock and owl calls by night, and mockingbirds, robins, and woodpeckers by day.

One of the more bizarre memories of those days is the early morning *chug, chug, chug* of a truck driving around the house spraying clouds of oily, sweet, white smoke into the trees and through the windows of our sleeping porch. At breakfast my mother explained that in the post office, she had overheard the director of the Galveston County Mosquito Control district telling someone that their biggest problem was their inability to drive off the main roads to do their spraying. "Well," said my mother, anxious to do her civic duty, "you may certainly come to our house. Just come down the driveway and drive around the house and spray all you want." So three or four times a year, the tanker truck would bring us DDT with our pancakes and toothpaste.

A favorite summer room for our parents was the glassed-in downstairs porch with windows on three sides. This porch contained hundreds of windowpanes, 572, to be exact. How did we know? A housepainter told us that the 1915 hurricane blew out every one, and he had replaced them!

Warfare

While Mom fought the Cold War and the McCarthyites in print and speech, we boys fought among ourselves. Then we called a truce and began alliances in the neighborhood. These were more elaborate battles than in Webster Groves. And what games we invented! Up to twenty boys spread across ten acres and three properties. We had bamboo thickets, pine trees, hedges, fishponds, buildings, sheds, ditches. We built lookouts in trees and turned ditches into moats. We tried signal fires only once and earned the same rebuke from my father as when he caught us smoking. This time he worried about grass fires. Tommy drew up elaborate rules of war, with treaty obligations, treatment of prisoners, boundaries, when you could reenter the fray after being killed, and more. World Wars I and II merged in a flurry of dirt, water, mud balls, water pistols, and bags of sand. Firecrackers sometimes substituted for hand grenades. Once one went off in my hand. Boy, it stung, and I had a good story until the next year, when one of the kids in my class went one worse and blew off part of a finger with a cherry bomb.

On the bayou's bank, Tommy and I played out the Battle of the North Atlantic. Packing stiff mud around a cherry bomb, we would launch these depth charges into the water, waiting breathlessly for the waterproof fuse to bubble to the surface. Then the water pimple erupted into a foot-high geyser. Anxiously, we peered down to see the flotsam of a Nazi U-boat in the form of dead or stunned fish.

A satisfied Tommy would say, "Very good, Lieutenant, return to the convoy." And back we would go for more mud.

To the imagined dangers of World War II, nature added a bit of real local peril—venomous snakes. In our first year in Texas, we killed six copperheads. By the time I had graduated from high school, the body count was sixty-two copperheads and eight coral snakes. My mom became so blasé about the snakes that when we once hired a local man to cut the grass, she told him, "If you see a snake, just pass over him with the mower, twice if you don't get him the first time."

Schools

I don't remember much of the schools. The students were mostly white with a sprinkling of Hispanic kids. I played the clarinet in the school band. One year I was president of my class, whatever that meant; I was not a leader.

Blissfully, I sailed through the early grades. How could I fail? No homework, no failure. My report cards were full of "gentleman S's," for satisfactory. One thing drove Mom batty—corporal punishment. The practice was still legal, and swats from the principal were delivered with the authority of an Old Testament prophet. The two licks I received for fighting in the cafeteria brought tears to my eyes and fire to my mom's. She dressed down the principal in scalding terms. "The power to hit kids makes sadists of us all!"

I did have one good teacher. In the fifth grade it was Elaine Mantooth, who had always wanted to be a doctor but went into teaching to send her husband through college. She was the first person outside my family who said I should stop playing to the crowd and get to work. (Later, she was able to go to medical school and returned to Dickinson as a general practitioner.)

Our Real Education

In retrospect, I think Mom saw the local school as an interruption in our education. She was never publicly critical, but she saw big gaps, and she was determined to fill those potholes. Again and again, she pounded on us this double drumbeat of being superior in gifts but servants in fact. It was a kind of double-edged sword of Christianity and our democracy. "To whom much is given from him shall much be required" was a favorite aphorism.

The family air crackled with ideas. We competed in checkers, gin rummy, some chess. On car trips we begged Dad to ask us history questions. We had our own version of twenty questions. We loved to listen to the quiz shows *Twenty Questions*, *Truth or Consequences*, *The Cliché Club*, and *Quiz Kids*.

Our parents' friends were an amazing collection of academics, scientists, engineers, civil servants, industrialists. My mother kept up a vast correspondence with people in a score of countries. My parents loved to travel to Africa, Asia, Latin America. Between them, they could talk to anyone about anything. But they had blind spots. She couldn't resist finishing her boys' sentences, and Dad jumped to conclusions, as when presented with a new dish for dinner, he growled, "I don't want any; what is it?"

The first movies I ever saw were shown at the University of Texas Medical School in Galveston, in a film series that included a man in a pit playing a piano for three silent films in the group: Eisenstein's *Battleship Potemkin*, Flaherty's *Men of Aran*, and Griffith's *The Birth of a Nation*. Others included *Henry V* with Laurence Olivier, *How Green Was My Valley*, and *Great Expectations*. (Forty years later, I showed parts of *Henry V* and *Potemkin* to my European history students.)

My parents drove us into Houston for performances of *South Pacific*, *Oklahoma*, and *Carousel*. We saw our first operas, *La bohéme* and *Pagliacci*, and occasionally the Houston Symphony. For cultural balance, my father bought season tickets to Rice Institute (now University) football games. While the family maintained its enduring loyalty to the St. Louis Cardinals, Tommy and I played Little League baseball. Here, we benefited from the work of dozens of dads who built the park, coached the teams, umpired games, fitted the uniforms. Tommy and I were on different teams. I wasn't terribly good, but I did hit a home run in my last game.

Books and More Books

Neither parent ever said, "Get your face out of that book!" I read everything: newspapers, dictionaries, encyclopedias, novels, all the Hardy Boys mysteries, *The Saturday Evening Post*, *Life* magazine, short stories, *Boys' Life*, *Popular Mechanics*, map legends, advertising fliers, cereal boxes, catalogs, postal fliers, and comic books we could sneak into the house, as well as *Mad* magazine. A more bizarre comic was a book called *Texas History Movies*, written in the 1920s. This graphic history of Texas winning its freedom from Mexico was full of cannibals, racism, Texan heroics, and Mexican perfidy.

I read dictionaries, and loved the etymological growth of words, from G to L to OE to ME. I loved mouth-filling words like "salubrious," "antediluvian," "eponymous," "irascible," "pedantic," "rapscallion," "inculcate," "amorphous," and "parsimonious."

My favorite books were Frank Buck's *Bring 'Em Back Alive*, John Hunter's *Hunter*, and Roy Chapman Andrews's *Quest in the Desert*, about a boy on an archaeological dig in China in the 1920s. I read the entire Sherlock Holmes collection in one summer.

I took books with me everywhere, on trains, in the car, to bed, in sickness and in health. I took them to doctors' offices, to dentists' chairs. On the few cold mornings in winter when we turned on our wall gas furnace, I would go downstairs and lie with my feet against the register and read.

We were also allowed more plebian entertainment. Although we didn't have a television until I was a senior in high school, we were allowed to go to the neighbors' to watch programs like *Mr. Peepers* and *The Honeymooners* and occasional sporting events. The movies at the local Hollywood Theater were of a considerably lower niveau than *Potemkin*, etc. The theater was a white stucco pile next to the Dairy Queen between the high school and Highway 3. Movies were twelve cents until I was twelve, when they cost twenty-five cents. There we saw *Francis the Talking Mule*, Abbott and Costello, Martin and Lewis, The Three Stooges, plenty of Westerns, some detective dramas. I would have seen more, but my father was stern. We had to ask permission, and the school buzz on movies often ran up against my father's mood. My brother Tom and I even composed songs to ask permission, to appeal to his sense of humor. They worked about half the time, and half the time we got a "No, no, *no!*" You could walk to the theater, along the main highway, then up Yupon Street under the power lines, across the old interurban tracks. The owner of the theater, Sam Termini, never failed to ask you how old you were.

A memorable graffito on the men's bathroom wall, "Don't piss on the floor—the next person may be barefooted," was practical advice to many boys.

Animals

Wild animals were everywhere on our property—raccoons, possums, rabbits, and squirrels. We had a succession of dogs. Red, a Chesapeake Bay retriever, would retrieve thrown sticks from the bayou until our arms hurt. We had one Dalmatian with the racehorse-like name of Pokey-Jinks, and two Weimaraners, both named Lady. And all died of the ubiquitous heartworm.

After Tommy raised several batches of chickens for layers and broilers, Dad decided that we would kill and pluck them ourselves. The line "like a chicken with its head cut off" suddenly had real meaning when we didn't cleave the neck at first whack. After two batches of local executions and feathers galore, we took subsequent flocks to the local slaughterhouse.

Several of my friends had horses, which were actually working ponies, for their fathers were small ranchers. I began pestering my parents for one. What a great place to keep it, on our back four acres. My parents tried to dissuade me. "You'll never take care of it. It will get away. You'll forget to feed her. Who will fix the fence?" Then, fortuitously, a ten-year-old blue roan, unsurprisingly named Blue, was advertised in the local paper. And my parents surrendered. I helped my father repair the fence and fix up a feeding station. For about six months, I rode almost every day. I ventured out onto the town roads, but that made us both nervous. Pleasant, amiable Blue was, but she had an independent streak and became adept at finding unlocked gates and weak fence.

More than once I was called home from school to help my mother go fetch Blue, who had wandered off to another part of town. We made quite a conveyance, Mom driving car, boy sitting on tailgate with bridle, horse following docilely and fed with occasional cubes of sugar.

Fortunately, P.J., a boy from our church, asked if he could buy the horse from us. Over dinner we discussed it. I was going off to a new school, and my parents persuaded me that I would have less time to care for her, and P.J. really wanted Blue. So we just gave the horse to him.

Travel

Starting in 1946, our family took one major trip every summer. For three years my mother piled us in the car and took us to the YMCA camp in Estes Park, Colorado, for hiking, crafts, and meeting people from across the country. One year we took the train east to visit her home and a bevy of cousins in New Jersey. On that trip, we spent several days in the mountains and valleys and New York City museums skyscrapers, ferries, and Circle Line tours. In 1951, in the middle of the Korean War, she drove us three boys down the Texas coast to Brownsville, Matamoros, Puebla, Mexico City, Acapulco, and home, all with very modest linguistic ability. That linguistic skill did not go unnoticed by her children. When she carelessly stepped into a Mexico City street, Jan spoke out, "Watch out, Mom. We need you for your Spanish."

Twice, my father took us west in our lumbering station wagon. The first time was the Grand Circle Tour of the national parks of the Painted Desert, Grand Canyon, Bryce and Zion, Yellowstone, and Glacier Parks. Another was specific to his boyhood haunts of Helena, Bozeman, Great Falls, the Bitterroot Valley, and the mining camp of Marysville, where his father had worked. On one we took a five-day horse-borne pack trip into the Bob Marshall Wilderness for the adventure and some spectacular trout fishing.

For six summers we attended the residential Camp Fern in East Texas. Divided into two "tribes," the boys competed in everything from crafts to archery, track and field, canoeing, horseback riding, rifle shooting, swimming, etc. My first year, I was a momentary center of attention when the saddle of my horse broke and I fell off and got kicked in the head on the way down. I was knocked out and had to get four stitches. The owners of the camp took their Christianity seriously, and we had a service on Sunday and exhortations in the dining hall, like "God is first; others are second; I am Third," and "Don't wait to be a great man; be a great boy." Not from our counselors, we learned some doggerel, like "Peanut sitting on a railroad track, heart was all aflutter. Round the bend can 110, toot, toot, peanut butter." And the more scandalous folk song, "Morphine Bill and Cocaine Sue."

Hunting and Fishing

I think it was my ninth Christmas, our third in Texas, when we came down that morning to find the tree festooned with balls, lights, and tinsel, and around its base, packages of all sizes. Most distinctive were three boxes about four feet by six inches by four inches. Wrapped professionally, they had identical cards reading To Dad, From the Boys (one of his jokes). The three mysterious boxes contained a .30-06 rifle, a pump twelve-gauge shotgun, and a .22 caliber pump rifle.

~

By this time Dad had established a Christmas regimen. We would have an immense breakfast of huevos rancheros—ranch eggs with onions, tomatoes, celery, and cayenne pepper—fried oysters, sausage, and English muffins. Then, before we could open presents, we had to clean the dishes. Talk about deferred gratification!

As a boy, my father had hunted and fished. At friends' houses nearby, we learned to shoot at clay pigeons. For the rest of our Texas life, we would hunt ducks and geese with Dad's business friends along the Gulf Coast. Although I didn't kill my first buck until I was fifteen, I still enjoyed the times with my father in a deer blind, waiting for the dawn, hearing turkey calls, sucking on chocolate bars and licorice sticks, and peering out for deer.

There was fishing off our dock, ugly catfish, a few perch, and crabs, which we kept for Mom to cook. We moved on to more serious fishing. Usually, once a year in late summer, we would drive to Port Aransas, two hundred miles down the coast, to go deep-sea fishing for tarpon, kingfish, mackerel, and sailfish. We stayed at a famous hotel called the Tarpon Inn, which displayed in its lobby scales from tarpons caught by hundreds of guests, including one Franklin Delano Roosevelt. We caught a modest number of fish under the guidance of Elmer Towne, our favorite guide, but our larger success was in conquering seasickness and drowsiness and the fraternal high jinks of jabbing the rod of a dozing brother.

Mom and the Cold War

Even before World War II was over, Mom joined Churchill in worries about the USSR and Stalin's murderous streak. She became an unabashed cold warrior, of the more moderate streak. She continued her League of Women Voters speaking, but now with two different targets, Soviet Communism and domestic know-nothings like the John Birch Society. She decided to write a book, really a primer, about Communism, built around Marx, Lenin, and Stalin. She aimed it at the high school level. She persuaded Gen. William Donovan, first director of the CIA, to write the forward. With the red-meat title *Know Your Enemy*, it went through several printings. In addition to high schools, a more grateful buyer was the United States Information Agency,

Me and My Horse Blue

which translated the book into a dozen languages and put copies into their libraries around the world.

Modest fame from this book brought her an invitation to join the first television news discussion show in the country, *University Forum*, at the University of Houston TV station. I would sometimes sit in the control room and watch her more than hold her own with the likes of Gen. Mark Clark and Eleanor Roosevelt.

Mom subscribed to the Sunday *New York Times*, *The Christian Science Monitor*, *Foreign Affairs*, *Encounter*, *Christianity and Crisis*, *The New Leader*, and both local papers. My first paid job, at age seven, was to take a big set of shears and cut the clippings she had marked with a black grease pencil. At first I just stacked them, but then I was deputed to put them into accordion files properly labeled. For each I was paid a nickel.

Church

When we moved to Dickinson, my mother chose the local Episcopal parish for us because there was no Presbyterian church in town, and it was the only one where she could be assured the clergy had a college degree. (According to her, the Catholic Church was beyond the pale.) Trinity Church's board-

Family Trip West, 1949, somewhere in Colorado

and-batten structure had been built by a retired sea captain after the 1900 Galveston hurricane. It was tucked away on State Highway 3 amid oak and oleander trees and jasmine bushes.

The church became an extra family, because our blood relations were thousands of miles away. A number of the kids were school classmates; they were a cross section of white, middle-class postwar America—the families of ranchers, farmers, clerks, feedstore owners, workers, and engineers who were employed in the growing petrochemical industry. Diversity was limited to one Japanese American family, the Kobayashis.

I became an acolyte and would often walk the mile to church through thick humid air to serve at the eight o'clock service, then stay for the ten o'clock service with music. I liked the rituals of robes and carrying the cross, lighting and putting out the candles. The church smelled of candle wax, mildew, furniture polish, oleander from the bushes outside, the priest's sweat inside. There was no air-conditioning in those days. I grew to love the rich language of the Book of Common Prayer, and especially the phrases from the General Confession: "We have strayed from thy ways like lost sheep. We have followed too much the devices and desires of our own hearts. We have offended against thy holy laws. There is no health in us."

Our hymns were "The Church's One Foundation," "Jesus Christ is Risen Today," "Holy, Holy, Holy," "We Gather Together to Ask the Lord's Blessing." We reached out to the Baptists with "That Old Rugged Cross" and to the Lutherans with "A Mighty Fortress Is Our God."

My mother was not a churchgoer, but she did participate in after-service discussions.

My brothers and I joined the children's choir, at about the age when I could read the hymns. I was the only one of us who stuck with ritual and music. The children's choir practiced on Saturday afternoons. Attendance varied from six to ten, mostly boys, for some reason. After church most Sundays we poured on out to someone's house to play football or baseball.

The church's one big fundraiser was a strawberry festival in May, when we passed the collection plate to the entire community. People came from across the county. We blocked off the lawn in front of the church and lined its edges with food and midway-like booths for knocking over bottles, barbeque, coin toss. The pièce de résistance was the strawberry shortcake with berries parishioners had picked in nearby fields. A perennial visitor was state senator Jimmy Phillips, who passed out cardboard pistols, which cracked when you flicked them at other kids. With a string tie and ample brisket, he was the quintessential Southern politician, although his exhortation to "Vote for Jimmy!" paled by comparison with that of a sheriff's candidate who asserted that "Honesty is no substitute for experience."

One of Many Family Hunting Trips on the Texas Gulf Coast

A New School

Worried about the quality of the Dickinson public schools, my mother began a long-game plot to get us into a better school. Over the years my mother had learned that getting Dad to do something took at least two days—rejection first and acceptance later. This time it took a year.

It came about in this way. When I was in the sixth grade at Dickinson Elementary School, Tommy was in the eighth grade. (Over growls from my father, she had persuaded him to let Jan go to St. Louis, to John Burroughs School, where she had taught, and board with the family of one of her former students.) Now she wanted us three to enroll in a six-year-old private day school in Houston. Angrily, my father replied. "Dee, you and I went to public schools and did quite well. Why can't our kids do the same? How will they get there? What kind of example is that when the plant manager takes his kids out of the local schools?"

Mom didn't confront that directly. She just kept chewing at the edges. She began tutoring me and Tom. She said she could do the driving, and even offered to teach part-time (which she later did). Several months later, she drove us up to the Houston school for entrance exams. There was no explosion from Dad. In May 1952, we were admitted to St. John's School. Dad said nothing.

After he died, my mother told me that during the first year at St. John's, my father hardly spoke to her, except in our presence.

"Wow! Did you think of divorcing him?" I asked.

"No," she said. "I'd been through that once before and I didn't want to do that again."

Two shocks in one minute—a yearlong silent treatment and an unknown previous marriage! She never brought up either subject again.

Chapter Two

A Teenager in Texas (1952–58)

"Only two things to spend money on—travel and books."
—Joe Mares

"Ah, books, the next best thing to friends."
—Delia Mares

"Better to know some of the questions than all of the answers."
—James Thurber

"Daylight in the swamps! Man the pumps!" came my father's voice at 5:30 every school morning. Groggily, we boys rolled out of bed in light or dark, took turns in the bathroom, dressed, and rode the banister of eggs and coffee smells down to breakfast, which my mother was cooking. We ate in silence. By 6:30, we were away, packed into the car with books, notebooks, jackets, athletic gear, and musical instruments.

Out of our driveway we turned west on Highway 146 to drive a mile to pick up the newly built freeway, the I-45, which would carry us the thirty-five miles to Houston and our new school. When we began school at St. John's in the early 1950s, those first twenty miles were still prairie, shared by cattle and oil wells. While Mom or Dad drove, each of us slumped into our respective corners (with one in front and two in back) to sleep or study. At 7 a.m. we all listened to the gravel-voiced CBS anchor Martin Agronsky, who told us the latest world woes from Korea, Europe, the Middle East, and Washington.

Downtown Houston came into view about ten miles out, around the air force's Ellington Field. Then we joined the growing Mississippi of traffic flowing past burgeoning shopping malls, cloverleaf intersections, two vast cemeteries, and an army proving ground for tanks headed for the Korean War, through two Black neighborhoods, along a score of synchronized traffic lights to glance off downtown Houston, through lower middle-class white neighborhoods, into the ritzy Spanish-style River Oaks Shopping Plaza, and on into River Oaks for the last three miles to school.

Some days, I would idly count the number of Cadillacs along those three miles. The highest total was close to sixty. We poked out onto River Oaks Boulevard, which the wags said had a country club at both ends, the River Oak Country Club and the public Lamar High School.

Across the street from Lamar was the almost-cathedral-sized sandstone St. John the Divine Episcopal Church. And next to it was our destination, St. John's School. When we entered St. John's in 1952, the school was six years old. It was founded by a group of wealthy Houstonians who wanted their kids prepared for Ivy League colleges without sending them east to boarding school. A core of parents belonged to the St. John the Divine Episcopal Church, and they provided the biggest bloc of endowment money. But from the start, the school was consciously nondenominational. It accepted Baptists, Methodists, Catholics, Jews, and agnostics alike, though no people of color. Innovative the school was, but not revolutionary.

The school held a weekly nondenominational chapel service with prayers from the Book of Common Prayer and speakers from across the religious spectrum, except the Catholics, who declined invitations to preach. Students were acolytes, sang in the choir, did some of the readings. The seventh grade offered a course on religious history. The school worked to blunt the temptations and display of wealth by decreeing a sartorial democracy of uniforms. Boys would wear khaki pants and shirts (with black ties during the winter quarters) and girls would wear blue-and-white dresses or red jumpers. About my third year, the school allowed boys to wear white shirts as well.

It was a brilliant way to reduce clothes competition in this wealthiest of city districts. A few people groused, but for most, the uniforms made life much simpler. Personally, I was happy to know that every morning I didn't have to think about what to wear, beyond finding clean trousers or shirts. Uniformity of dress meant that people stood out for their accomplishments, not for their regalia.

St. John's was academically rigorous. Unfortunately, as my report cards said, during my first two years, rigor was not for me. The nadir of my school career (for my parents as well as me) was getting a C-minus in my mother's own class. She taught a class called Language, which was etymology for kids, to introduce us to the joys of words and prepare us for Latin. I actually liked the substance of cognates, inflections, derivations, and syntax. But I was in high rebel mode, far more enamored of girls, Elvis, and blue suede shoes than of schoolwork. My brothers, meanwhile, did quite well.

The grade reports would come in creamy, high-class envelopes adorned with the St. John's seal of a red-and-black lamp of knowledge and the motto "Faith and Virtue," and be placed like Christmas cards on the mantelpiece above the fireplace. In those first years, the teachers' comments were variations on the theme "Billy has the potential to do honors work. He simply chooses not to." My parents would read them to themselves and then out loud to me, or they would just hand them to me and wait for my (always lame) promise to do better. After two or three weeks, the reports disappeared into a brown folder labeled Boys' Marks.

Teachers

Throughout my St. John's years, most of my teachers were heroic males. While my father had been too old for World War II service, most of these men were veterans. One had been on Tarawa in the marines; another was an intelligence officer who interrogated German prisoners; another was in the air force. One was a retired army colonel who had taught physics at West Point. My Latin teacher had been in the British Army and won a Military Cross in Burma.

As I look back, the most influential teacher I had was in seventh-grade English, Ernest Wright. He was a tall, gangly man with horn-rimmed glasses who walked with a limp and carried a briefcase as big as an airline pilot's. The limp was from a war wound he'd suffered in the Italian campaign. for which he won a Bronze Star. He made us write oddball essays, like describing a pencil. He hardly smiled, never laughed, and was always serious. We read great short stories that year by Dorothy Parker, James Thurber, Stephen Crane, O. Henry, Bret Harte, Saki, Mark Twain, Ring Lardner. We learned grammar the old-fashioned way—memory and repetition. He gave us an enduring definition of humor, the "juxtaposition of the incongruous." To illustrate this he had us read some Thurber classics, like "The Catbird Seat" and "The Secret Life of Walter Mitty." He got me to enter a citywide writing class with a short story about a cousin of my grandfather who burned up in a Montana mining accident. I won second prize. Getting a B in Wright's class made me prouder still.

A Most Memorable Family Vacation

In early 1954, my father left Monsanto Chemical Company to go into business as a chemicals consultant. Using her incomparable power of suggestion at dinner one evening, my mother proposed that we take a family trip to Europe before Dad settled into his new work. We boys—ages thirteen, fifteen, and seventeen—jumped at the thought. Jan was headed for college in the fall, and I had loved history all my life. Tommy was willing to forgo a slot of counselor in training at our summer camp for an intercontinental adventure. For once my father was silent. No instinctual "No" came from his end of the table. The next day, he was on board.

At first my parents thought of going by plane, but when they counted that cost and the rented cars, they decided to take our own 1953 four-door Ford station wagon. Therefore, in mid-June we drove north and east to New York, and boarded the twelve-hundred-ton Cunard liner SS *Parthia* to join its three hundred passengers. It was small by liner standards but gargantuan compared to the Texas fishing boats and ferries we knew.

Along with our clothes and toothbrushes, Mom gave us each an eighty-page school notebook. "This is your diary for your impressions and only yours. Fill it up. Doodle on the pages. Write every day, even if it's only a few sentences. Create your own shorthand note-taking. Imagine you are writing a postcard to yourself every day. This will be your record of this trip." It only took a few days' reminders to settle into this habit. The grind became a delight, as the words became sentences and the sentences paragraphs. By the end of the trip, these notebooks had become as precious as the Swiss watches Dad bought for us in Zurich. Without knowing it, I was practicing my first journalism.

After two days of nausea and throwing up all our food, we got our sea legs, and, in our minds, the ship was transformed into the HMS *Compass Rose*, the first corvette in Nicholas Monsarrat's *The Cruel Sea* novel, then film, of the boredom and terror of convoy duty in the same North Atlantic we sailed.

We landed in Liverpool, which was still showing the bombed blocks from the Blitz. Driving on the left side in Britain and Sweden, and the right side everywhere else, our trip took us across Northern England and Scotland, by ferry from Manchester to Bergen, Norway, then in an arc north to Loen, down to Lillehammer, Oslo, across to Stockholm, on to Copenhagen, and down into Germany. From Hamburg and Bremen, we drove on to Amsterdam, then back to Frankfurt, Heidelberg, Strasburg, Ulm, Munich, Innsbruck, Zürich, Geneva, Dijon, and Paris. At Calais we flew across the Channel, car and all, to land at Lympne, one of the secondary RAF airfields during the Battle of Britain, fourteen years before. Then it was on to Canterbury, London, Oxford, and back to Liverpool for the trip home.

That trip was life-changing for me. Even after fifty years, my skin tingles with its stiletto images. We all had our jobs as we motored across the continent, only nine years after Patton's tanks had done the same. My father did all the driving, left side, right side, roundabouts, mountain defiles, German autobahns, Parisian alleys. He also did most of the photography. Good with maps, and aided by a dictionary-size British Automobile Association road guide, my mother did the navigating. Not only had both parents been to Europe before, they had numerous friends there and contacts through friends in Houston. In almost every country there was at least one family we knew or met, who deepened and broadened our stays. Jan, the oldest brother, kept the books, a stream of receipts, bills, and postcards, in eight currencies. Neat and organized, he would proudly offer them to the customs agent at trip's end only to have the man wave us through as honest looking and unworthy of inspection. Tommy, the middle brother, the only one of us with any artistry, snatched quick charcoal visual impressions, and occasionally would take an afternoon for a watercolor of an abbey or castle or even chimney pots. Being quite able to read in a car, I was the trip historian, that is, the one who searched our accompanying guidebooks, histories, and brochures to prepare the family for forthcoming sites and describe places we had already seen, all too briefly.

Family Trip to Europe, 1954

And what a history it was, starting with World War II! For us teenagers, it was a kind of diorama, a 3D movie. We boys had read countless books on the war. I had read *The Young Lions, A Bell for Adano, Into the Valley, Hiroshima.* We pored over *Life's Picture History of World War II.* But even for us boys, the war was only one draw. History was everywhere. In Oslo, we could touch the fragile strength in the Gokstad ship, imagining its intrepid Norsemen plowing those North Atlantic waves over which I had just come. Next door was Thor Heyerdahl's fabulous *Kon-Tiki* raft, which he and his companions had sailed from Ecuador to Melanesia just seven years before. In Innsbruck, we stayed in a hotel that trumpeted the unverifiable claim that Mozart had slept there, "and they haven't changed the sheets since," growled my father at breakfast. Sailing into Bergen, we could see the gingerbread-like medieval storefronts of the Hanseatic League businessmen. To walk across a castrum in England and see gravestones of Roman soldiers born in Spain or walk Hadrian's wall gave us a sense of Rome's mighty extent. We shivered as we climbed the stairs of the Tower of London to see the crown jewels but also to think of the scores of criminals and innocents executed there. In Vézelay, France, we could stand on the hilltop and listen to St. Bernard call the faithful to launch the Second Crusade. The year before, my class had seen a movie about Luther's life, so when we stopped in Worms, I could hear Luther's stirring call for religious freedom: "Here I stand! I can do no other. God help me!"

And in Mannheim, our parents took us to see a version of Beethoven's *Fidelio* set not in a Spanish prison but in a Nazi concentration camp with all the prisoners in the stripes of Buchenwald or Flossenbürg. In Versailles's opulence we could glimpse some origins of the French Revolution, especially in that Hall of Mirrors, where the treaty's vindictive clauses helped launch World War II. On a stone slab in Durham Cathedral was the familiar name Washington, the president's ancestors. By family agreement, we only visited three museums collectively. The first was the Louvre, which disappointed us in its crowds. Only the Venus de Milo and Winged Victory were soaring, headless in that chill space. At the Rijksmuseum in Amsterdam, we saw not only the portraits of the rich, smooth, and smug burghers at the height of Dutch world power, but the magical Rembrandt genius for drawing ethereal light from the depths of mere canvas. At the Deutsches Museum in Munich, we pored over the scientific equipment of early experiments in physics and chemistry, saw the first equipment that split the atom, and studied technological displays in transportation, mining, construction, and smelting. My parents also encouraged us to strike out on our own. In London, we boys tried to cover the entire city by underground in a day, but after three-quarters of a day pacing through Waterloo, Paddington, Covent Garden, Wembley, etc., we gave up. We roamed the back streets of Innsbruck and Zurich and parks in Paris. Bored with the horizontal, we turned to the vertical. We raced each other up the stairs of the Eiffel Tower, and ran up hillsides in Switzerland, Britain, and Germany. Eschewing great feather beds in the Swedish farmhouse of our parents' friends, we slept in the hayloft, and itched for two days. We used the acrid-smelling pissoirs on Parisian streets even when we didn't have to go. In a Swiss bookshop we filched some Chinese communist propaganda booklets to take back to our cold warrior mom. Roughhousing in our Durham hotel room, we broke a bed slat. Too embarrassed to tell our parents, we pooled our spending money and pinned a five-pound note to the underside of the bed with an apology for our misdeed. At the Follies Bergère in Paris, we sat between our parents in the third row and gazed in embarrassed fascination at the bare-breasted chorus line.

Some of the adventures were solo. In Munich one afternoon, rather than go back to the Deutsches Museum, I packed up ten marks, a chocolate bar, a bottle of apple juice, a small street map, and two German phrases, "Entschuldigen Sie, bitte" ("Excuse me, please") and "Wo is die Stadtmitte?" ("Where is the city center?"). I went to the main train station and picked the first streetcar that came by. From my map it looked like about five miles to the end of the line. I'll just ride there and walk back, I said to myself. Off I went past bombed blocks, past the last apartment houses, to a few houses standing alone, and the line ended in weedy desolation. As I walked back, people and smells multiplied—diesel and coal smoke, cabbage, cigarettes, and paving tar. No one paid me much attention. After half an hour, I noticed a large park along the tracks. According to my map, this was the sprawling Englischer Garten. I peeled off and wandered through its ponds and paths, a zoo, gazebos. I passed mothers or nannies with children in strollers, retirees and their canes, grandmothers on benches, a few schoolkids with neat backpacks kicking soccer balls. After an hour or so, I realized I was lost. The map gave me no details of park services. In the gray afternoon, there was no sun to guide me. It was past 4 p.m. My feet were getting sore. What to do? Time for my German. I looked for the friendliest face among grandmothers sitting on a bench. "Entschuldigen Sie, bitte, Frau. Wo its die Stadtmitte?" With a stream of German, she pointed in several different directions. This isn't working. "Strassenbahn?" I asked brightly. "Ach, so!" she said, and pointed definitively. "Da drueber!" ("Over there.") I followed the paved walkway as straight as possible for perhaps ten minutes and then there was my same streetcar line. Suddenly starving, I plumped down on the bench at the stop and devoured my chocolate and apple juice. I took the next tram and in fifteen minutes I was back at the Hauptbahnhof, from where I walked to our hotel, just as my parents were starting to worry. I was exhilarated.

The Food

"A boy is just a piece of skin stretched over an appetite," my mother loved to say. We brothers joked about Tommy not eating, just inhaling, food. We ate everything except kippers and a few of the smellier cheeses. Every day there were new foods, varieties of bread, shrimp, soups, and cheeses without number. We learned to eat European-style with knife and fork, not putting the knife down. And on very special occasions, we had our first tastes of alcohol. While Mother went off to Berlin to visit a friend, Dad took us through the upper Rhine wine country. He permitted us each a small glass of wine for dinner. At one inn in Deidesheim, the owner took us down into the cellar, and said with some pride, "The American soldiers took most of my wine," but then, pointing to a dusty, cobwebbed alcove worthy of Poe's "The Cask of the Amontillado," he said, "They left a few bottles. It was my best. Would you like some?" My father said it was quite fine. For us, utter novice tipplers, it could have been vinegar, we didn't care. It was almost illicit. By family agreement, the most remarkable meal was at an Indonesian restaurant in Amsterdam, where a half-Dutch, half-Indonesian headwaiter told us how he escaped from a Japanese prison camp, between courses of ever-spicier foods that made Mexican food taste like weak oatmeal. (The next year I won another citywide prize for a description of this meal.)

Coming Home

Our car was loaded with twenty-two different pieces of luggage. We brought a few gifts, a few articles of clothing, but for the rest, we had a small mountain of programs, diaries, posters, guidebooks, postcards, beer coasters, and shell casings from the battle at Overloon, all priceless to us, but not of much value to the taxman. Jan spent hours on board collecting and collating the receipts for this mountain of what the museum people call ephemera.

When we docked at New York, while the car was being unloaded, Jan presented his four-page list to the customs officers, who looked at our young faces, the stacks of nondescript luggage, and the car, and said, "Oh, just go on!" I think Jan was a little disappointed.

That trip was life-changing in its cornucopia of sights, ideas, culture, and history. I felt a year older in three months. The world was in my eyes and hands. Foreigners were real people. Stones became flesh. We had traveled with heroes and villains, across landscapes and ages. We were not just in history but of it. Mother's tutelage and focus on current events had abiding context. This trip locked in a lifelong interest in the actions of humans through time.

This world maturity and curiosity showed up in my schoolwork. From the ninth grade on, my grades improved, I made the honor roll every year, and won several history prizes. Along with the athletics, I served on the student council and became head prefect, or student body president, in my senior year.

Some of the student papers I remember best were on honeybees, Grant's Vicksburg campaign, Lend-Lease, a comparison of *Darkness at Noon* and *Animal Farm*, and reports on *Crime and Punishment* and *Pride and Prejudice*.

My teachers were all solid, competent, and demanding. But there was very little student participation. They stood and delivered. There were occasional memorable observations, as when our US history teacher described life for the Plains farmers: "They planted their wild oats on Saturday night, and prayed for crop failure on Sunday." Our job was to sit quietly and take lots of notes. My English papers were competent, but not terribly creative or very original. I didn't write for the newspaper, literary journal, or yearbook. One teacher, surprised at a lively essay about Austen's great novel, wrote in the margin, "You've changed trains from freight to an express. Keep it up!" But by and large my prose was stolid; I did my work dutifully. Writing itself held few special charms. As would happen at Harvard, I got much intellectual stimulation from my fellow students. There was no wall between jocks and nerds. The girls were collectively as smart as the boys. Outside of class, we talked of books and ideas, and sometimes acted on them. In that spring of 1958, after the launch of Sputnik, several of us mixed solid fuel and launched one rocket about five hundred feet into the air. The second one blew up on the pad and brought the police.

Sports

During my six years at St. John's, I played three sports every year. This being Texas, football was king. Mother half joked that you could drive across Texas on Friday nights without headlights, using the illumination of high school football fields. Even at a high-end prep school, football held pride of place; with minor exaggeration, a winning season could define class success. For these gladiatorial contests on hard Texas turf, we armed ourselves in pads, cleats, jockstraps, and helmets, though no face guards. We prepared in August with a week of twice-daily practices in heat and humidity and *no* water breaks. How we raced for the water cooler at the end of practice! Until my senior year, I was a so-so running back. Then the coaches switched me to tackle (at 165 pounds) and I earned all-conference honors. But I suspect that award was some kind of coaches' trade-off. I wasn't that good. My "Friday night lights" were those in the infirmary of the team doctor, Dr. John Broyles, who sewed up my war wounds. In four games out of eight my junior year, I either was cut on the face or broke my nose, or both. By the end of the season I'd had over forty stitches in my face, and my nickname became Little Scar.

To my retrospective embarrassment, our nickname was the Rebels, and the mascot, I kid you not, was a life-sized colonel, "Johnny Reb." Not until 2004, long after Black people were admitted to the school, did St. John's change the name to the Mavericks. I played basketball well enough to become captain my senior year. And the third sport was track, where I came under the influence of Bill Wallace. When the school dumped baseball in my junior year, a group of teachers decided to substitute track. Thus, a week after the end of basketball season, thirty-five to forty of us gathered on the weedy dirt track surrounding the football field and waited like recruits at boot camp. The teachers went down the ranks like drill instructors sizing the material. "Ginther, you'll sprint. Steward, you gangly horse, will do hurdles. McMahon, you'll throw the shot. Mares, you'll do the distances. You're too slow for a sprinter." I had never run more than a mile before, but I was game. The distance coach was a newly hired mathematics teacher from Yale. Bill Wallace was short and compact and brought to mind a young James Cagney with a nasal New England voice that carried the length of the straightaway. He smoked almost two packs a day, a habit that, at the time, seemed only mildly odd. Many of our teachers smoked, just not in the classroom. Indeed, in the spring 1957 issue of the *St. John's School Review*, I and another runner are shown on the cover launching ourselves and the track team into existence, while on the back a full-page ad exhorted readers to smoke Winstons.

A former college runner himself, Wallace knew how to get inside runners' heads and push us until our own motivational engines kicked in. My first race under his coaching set the tone. We had gone to a meet for the Houston-area runners who had never competed before. He entered me in the half mile and sent me off around the track. I did respectably, finishing midway in a pack of fifteen. *That's fine, a good start*, I thought. *Now, I'll go watch the other events and*

High School Track, 1957

cheer on my buddies. But Wallace had other ideas. "I won't force you, Mares, but you owe it to yourself to run the mile. They are the normal pair of races," he said. For twenty minutes I walked around in refusal. Then for five minutes I muttered "maybe," and five minutes after that I was at the starting line with a score of gangly runners. The gun went off. At the end of the first lap, I was dead last. But there was Wallace, yelling me on. By the end of the second lap, I was in the middle of the pack and Wallace kept urging me on. On the third lap, I moved into third. More Wallace shouts. I kept gaining, and at the end I won the stretch sprint by a yard. I staggered to the infield and threw up. But the victory's sweetness washed away the bile. As I knelt on the grass, Wallace growled, "Good start. And you know what, Mares? I was so sure you would run the mile I entered your name at the beginning of the meet." Bill Wallace was the first person outside the classroom who pushed me into terra incognita beyond what came easily.

Social Life

Before Christmas of my first year at St. John's, two of my classmates' families adopted me, and invited me to stay the night with their boys for some school activity or other. My mother would make up an overnight bag, and I kept a second set of clothes at each house. At Penny Ruthven's I had my own room, which I didn't have at home. He was an avid hunter and fisherman. We went to deer camps in West Texas and Port Aransas on the coast for fishing. My most vivid memory there was the dinners his mother cooked for us on Friday afternoons before football games: green beans, steak, potatoes, milk, and apple pie, while we watched *Howdy Doody* on a grainy twelve-inch black-and-white TV.

Terry Thomas was another all-around boy whose family adopted me. He picked up a love of classical music from his parents, and he and I would argue about which was the better book, Aaron Copeland's *What to Listen for in Music* or Leonard Bernstein's *The Joy of Music*. Terry's mother was on the Houston Symphony Orchestra board and told us a wonderful story of how she solicited donations from a Texas oilman so persistently that he finally gave in. "OK, I'll give you five thousand dollars if you don't make me go!"

This was still a time of lavish debutante parties, of wealthy parents introducing their daughters to society at local country clubs. At one, the parents hired both Fats Domino and Cell Block 7 for the entertainment. Another girl received a Chevy convertible every year from her car-dealership-owning father. Other parents were doctors, lawyers, and professors at Rice Institute. At St. John's, I joined that unhealthy system of pairing off. Kids were obsessed with who you were "going with." You sort of marched through the school year, in couples, meeting out for lunch, sitting together in class, watching to see who else talked to her or him. The relationships were casual, even when some could surely fog up car windows. In those pre-pill days most boys and girls found the faith and fear to pull back from the brink of intercourse.

Once I had a legal driver's license (at age fourteen, mind you), the wide-open spaces grew wider. By fifteen, I was sharing the driving to school. By sixteen, I was driving the hour alone. You could pick up a date. My only accident was when driving around a corner with my arm around a girl when a woman at a convenience store backed into our car. No injuries and the cops found more fault with her. I never got a speeding ticket, but I did a few foolish things, like study German vocabulary over the steering wheel as I drove to school. Around my sophomore year, my dates became more and more cultural—the symphony, local plays, even an opera or two. I think now that despite the commuting, and the daily worry about traffic accidents, living in Dickinson was a healthy antidote to Houston's material excess. It kept our family tight and the competition with classmates was intellectual and athletic.

Music

Some musical background at home was reinforced at schools. Between the fourth and eighth grades I played the clarinet in school bands, but that didn't survive the braces that came in ninth grade. That year, I joined the all-school chorus. It was an easy thirty minutes twice a week to skylark and tease the girls. I don't remember that we learned any formal musical appreciation, but I do remember that it was music that was acceptable to everyone.

Of popular music, I wasn't averse to Bill Haley and His Comets, Buddy Holly, the Everly Brothers, Fats Domino, and Elvis, but my preferences were classical. The first LPs I ever bought were the *Messiah*, Rachmaninoff's *Rhapsody on a Theme of Paganini*, Berlioz's *Symphonie Fantastique*, and lots of Bach's organ music. When we bought a recording of Bach's *St Matthew Passion* done in 1939, my mom, always anxious to clothe experiences in the raiment of history, said, "You can hear the foreboding of the coming war in their voices." The only time I ever skipped class was to sneak out and listen to the great E. Power Biggs himself practice for a concert at St. John the Divine Church next door.

For five or six years the St. John's School headmaster and music director wrote, composed, and directed their own musicals each spring. They were impressive productions, which involved almost a quarter of the high school student body in some way—acting, singing, stagecraft. I played in the orchestra and sang in the chorus until I was a senior, when the two got tired of the work of creation and switched to Broadway. They mounted *The Desert Song*. I got the second male lead as Claude, the French captain who loses his girl to the Riff chief. It turned out that I was wretched as soloist and actor alike and so stiff that in the middle of a rehearsal, they cut one of my duets and half a page of my dialogue.

But I didn't abandon singing. The summer before college, I took half a dozen voice lessons from a local church organist in Dickinson. Even more exciting, I heard about The Gilbert & Sullivan Society of Houston, who were to perform *The Mikado*. On a lark, a friend and I went to audition. Short of men, they found us acceptable. It was my first bite in a lifelong feast of G&S's tuneful witty genius. (Later, in Vermont, I would get to sing almost all their operettas.)

Me as Chorus Singer (Dead Center) in "The Mikado" 1958

Summer Jobs

A blue-collar summer job was a status symbol for my classmates, and for me, the dirtier the better. We all said this was to get ready for football, but we could have done that with running. I wanted the physical labor, the chance to sweat and spit and swear with ordinary people—a break from the cerebral.

Summer Construction Work, 1957

The sexiest jobs were working on oil rigs or on ranches or shrimp boats or in construction. But digging ditches was not bad. And my mom put a noblesse oblige cast to work. "You are more privileged than most people but you'd better not show it," she'd said. I enjoyed packing my own lunch box and going off to work, leaving the tiny cares of the day behind and thinking of nothing but that welding torch, that shovel, that jackhammer.

I liked dressing in Levi's, a dungaree shirt, an aluminum hat, and steel-toed boots and going off to the steam, hiss, and hoot of three different chemical plants. I earned money and even earned overtime and double time. I hung out with guys who talked about their kids, their affairs, their drinking, their wartime experiences. For one summer I worked as an apprentice in a local pipe fitters' union. I learned a bit about welding, marveling at the bead work (or the pass made by the welding torch or electrode along a joint) of these guys and their ability to weld almost upside down.

Yes, I went to a fancy prep school, but I could still work in the ditches with people of all ilks and economic status. They would keep me from flying too high and, Icarus-like, losing the wax wings of pride. I was part of the gang.

Junior Year

My junior year at St. John's was full of glory. My grades jumped upward. I lettered in three sports, I was elected captain of the basketball team and president of the student body, and I won the *Time* current events prize. I had a steady girlfriend, and the use of my brother's car.

Life at home, however, was more complicated. In that year, both brothers were away at college, so we were now three at the dinner table two or three nights a week when I wasn't still in Houston at some game or school function.

My dad, having survived a bout of cancer, was just building up his consultant's business. Mom was deep in the Cold War, writing the third edition of her book on Communism, *Know Your Enemy*. World events took up most of our conversations. Just that fall, the Hungarians had revolted against the Soviets. France, Great Britain, and Israel had invaded Egypt to protect the Suez Canal. At home, she was fighting the McCarthyites and John Birchers through her work with the League of Women Voters. The second presidential contest between Eisenhower and Adlai Stevenson was upon us. Integration battles were beginning across the South. There was lots to talk about, and for my parents, lots to disagree about. With Dad supporting Eisenhower and Mom supporting Stevenson, dinners were lively affairs. My father liked to bait my mom in a loving way, and she admitted to being "God's gift to the practical joker." She more than held her own. Some topics were heated, and some were humorous.

It was time, my parents thought, for me to get serious about my future. They had been warned, going back three years to a family visit to an English country teahouse with friends of our parents, the Griffiths.

Wanting to engage us boys in the conversations, the Griffiths asked Jan what he planned to study in college.

"Chemical engineering, like Dad."

"And you, Tom?"

"Oh, I think medicine."

"Now, Bill, how about you?"

"Oh, I think I will live off my brothers!"

Mrs. Griffith choked on her biscuit, and her husband spilled his tea.

~

After the school fight, the next-most heated battle was over a television set. My dad wanted to watch major league baseball games and college football. So one Saturday morning we snuck out of the house to drive into Houston to an appliance store, where we bought a twelve-inch GE TV set. My mom was livid. My mom thought that TV was the great evil of our society. We reminded her that she had been on University Forum, the TV news panel show. She still railed against the "idiot box."

As for my future, I felt I had to choose something. I nosed around for something to do with history. My best grades were in history and German. I could write competent papers, but every one of them was hard.

Somewhere, I'm still not sure how, the idea of the Foreign Service crept into the discussion. Maybe it was all the current events I followed. Maybe it was the succession of foreign visitors we had at the house. Maybe it was residual interest from our great European trip. To say I would major in something like Soviet studies sounded sexy. My mom was all for it. My dad was more cautious. "A career has to be your choice." My mom fed me more and more articles. She found a set of Russian-language 78 rpm phonograph records.

Then came Tommy's death, and my career goals froze in place. On the afternoon of July 12, 1957, I was on a pipe-laying crew at a local chemical plant when the foreman came to me and said my brother Tommy had been in some kind of accident. I should take my gear and drive to the Dickinson Country Club, where he worked as a lifeguard.

I drove to the club in a daze. An ambulance and a county sheriff's car were parked near the pool, where a small crowd gathered. Neither of my parents was there. The silence was thick as smoke. I could see a body lying on the concrete apron. The club manager guided me to a chair across the pool and whispered that my brother had apparently drowned about an hour earlier.

No, this couldn't be! I protested, "He was as healthy as a horse. He just finished his freshman year. He wrestled and played lacrosse!"

"We don't know what happened, but we'll sure find out," the manager whispered.

"Where are my parents?"

"They've gone home. I can have someone drive you home if you want."

"No, let me sit here for a few minutes." Sweaty and lonely and lost, I stayed for ten to fifteen minutes, long enough to watch the ambulance attendants carry away the body. Then I drove the four miles home as through a suddenly foreign country.

The next days were a blur. Jan was working in Germany. We reached him that night by phone and agreed that he would stay there rather than come home.

After a small service, my parents had Tommy cremated, and his ashes we sprinkled on the bayou out back where we used to fish. Visitors came by the dozens, sympathy letters by scores came from around the country and the world. We spoke of our gratitude for his full life, especially his last chapter a full freshman year at Williams College. A later autopsy revealed a congenital heart defect, which, the doctors said, had it been detected would have made him a cardiac invalid for the rest of a short life. Mom's favorite eulogy was: "He belongs to the company of the eternally young."

I felt lonely, even abandoned, but then angry at myself for feeling that way. "What about me?" I thought. But that made me feel more guilty. Who was I now, one son or two? Part of me felt obliged to make up for that loss to my parents, to live two lives. But until his death, Tommy and I had been mostly rivals, not friends. We had competed in sports, hunting, even once for the same girl. There was no one to talk to, not my friends, not my parents, not our priest, not even Wallace, who was of the "tough it out" school. I wandered around the house for a week, and then went back to work. It gave my days structure.

A few days later, I came home from work, threw my sweaty work clothes in the closet, changed into running gear, and fled the still-gloom-filled house. I took my normal route, dodging traffic and road trash for a mile, out beyond the roar and speed of the interstate. From the main road there branched off a spiderweb of unpaved roads made of crushed oyster shells and gravel. I took one of these, and ran across the bayou, past a cemetery, past several small cattle ranches and a few oil derricks. Dogs barked furiously at this unexpected biped. Cars and trucks sped by, spewing funnels of choking dust. I hardly noticed. Halfway home I was running faster than when I began.

I was trying to not think at all, to just put my mind in neutral. It got easier the longer I ran. When thoughts came, I pushed them away, like vines on a forest trail. I became oblivious to the curs who barked from the other side of the cyclone fences. On I ran, past the Little League ball field, back across the bayou, past our church. I hardly felt the ground. Rather, I felt a little high I circled back into town and took the main road where we lived. Thoughts gradually reappeared, the dusk, sore legs, thirst, dinner. I reached our long driveway and walked down it to cool off. After what I figured were about eight or nine miles, I was exhausted, but the fever of grief had broken. The running seemed to have cushioned my mind like a shock absorber. A pleasant exhaustion came over me.

I did not run that far again for twenty years, but the habit of meditative exercise was established. I had a new friend, my body, which would accompany me anywhere and offer both engagement and release. Running could clear the mental and emotional decks, for at least a while, each day. Even in storms, I would always be able to find these fair winds.

Meanwhile, my mother did three things to work through her grief. She republished a book of prayers sent to her by a friend who had lost her husband and two sons in a sailing accident in the 1930s. She persuaded my father to adopt a refugee from the failed Hungarian Revolution the year before and used Tommy's college money to send him through Rice Institute. And third, she wrote a book about Tommy's life, which she called *An American Boyhood*. What could have been gushy and self-pitying became (for us, anyway) a lively and fairly objective family history, one that surely neither I nor Jan would have assembled.

One other local event had a profound ameliorating effect on my parents. It was the political pork barrel that brought NASA's Manned Spacecraft Center (now Johnson Space Center) to Clear Lake, Texas, only ten miles from their home. The center brought a flood of new employees to the region. My parents soon befriended the families of engineers, managers, and a couple of astronauts. My mom adopted a number of those young NASA wives to be the daughters she never had. They even attended the 1969 launch of Apollo 9, on which their friend Russell Schweickart would be one of the first to walk in space. (Three years later he would come to my wedding.)

I think that's when I decided that I would be a Foreign Service Officer, or work elsewhere in the government. I liked history and current affairs. Such a career would please my mom. My father was more circumspect. "Be sure you are right, and then go ahead," he said. Bill Wallace worried that I might feel too obligated to my mom. "You have to run your own race!"

Looking back across sixty years, and after writing scores of college recommendations for my students, I'm stunned at how easily came my admission to Harvard and Princeton and Williams. I don't think I even wrote an essay. In my favor, I was a legacy at Harvard, thanks to my brother, one cousin, two uncles, and one grandfather. Harvard also had a very energetic recruiter for boys from the Southwest, that is, Texas, Oklahoma, and New Mexico. Diversity was geographic, not racial. After visits to all three, I chose Harvard over Princeton and Williams, which was Mom's hope.

~

The next two summers I literally dug ditches as a member of the Hod Carriers labor union. The first summer, I was the only white man on a crew of Black and Latino men. We dug ditches, carried pipe, ran jackhammers; this was true grunt labor.

My closest friend was a Black man named Ernest Tibbs, who weighed a good 250 pounds, gargantuan by the standards of the day, with the appropriate nickname of Tiny. His prominent facial feature was two gold front teeth with stars cut into them. "That's to get the ladies' attention," he explained.

Tiny showed me how to pace the work. "Sure, you can fling sand and dirt like a Tasmanian devil, but you'll wear yourself out. How do you think we survived slavery?" he said. On a late August day we were sitting at lunch, and he asked, "Now, Bill, tell me, you're not going to do this for a lifetime, are you?"

Oh, here we go. "Well, no, I'm actually going off to college."

"Well, that's great! Keeps you out of these damn ditches. Where you going?"

"Er . . . *Harvard*," I choked.

He looked at me curiously. "Isn't that a colored school?"

"Uh, I think you mean Howard University, in Washington, DC."

"Oh, yeah," he boomed.

Chapter Three

The Best Place in the World to Feel Stupid
(1958–1962)

"**Fifty years ago, along** with a thousand other raw youths, I arrived in the Square with a piquant mixture of entitlement, wonder and doubt . . ." So began my Harvard fiftieth-class-reunion report.

During my four years in Cambridge, I wandered through a thicket of emotions. "I must be a hot shit: they admitted me!" "Holy moly! This is such an amazing place, why did they admit me?" "Can I survive this pressure?" My brother Jan had just graduated and was down Massachusetts Avenue at MIT getting an MS in Chemical Engineering, after which he would return to Harvard for law school, two years hence.

For my freshman year in Lionel Hall, abutting the Square, I joined three roommates from Oklahoma City, Wellesley, Massachusetts, and Louisville, Kentucky. All were out for freshman football and were confidently headed (it seemed) for careers in medicine, law, and business. I did know three of my thousand classmates. I had played football against my Oklahoma roommate, and there were twin brothers from Brookline, Massachusetts, who had been on our return voyage of the trip to Europe four years earlier.

That first year I took all the required general education courses as well as Russian literature in translation, a notorious "gut" populated by many football players. The best class was the Enterprise of Science, a history of the scientific method taught by chemistry professor Leonard Nash, who had worked on the atomic bomb. He gave us a memorable encapsulation of a scientist's vital intellectual tool: "to put on a different thinking cap" in treating the same information rather than viewing from a single perspective.

At Harvard, ideas were the coin of the realm. "Only connect," remarked one freshman friend who had read E. M. Forster's *Howards End*. "That's all you need to know from that book." Another glib judgment was making the rounds: A Harvard freshman thinks he knows everything; the sophomore knows he knows everything; the junior isn't sure; and the senior knows he knows very little. At only a short distance, we were surrounded by some of the great minds in their fields: Henry Kissinger and Zbigniew Brzezinski, Arthur Schlesinger, Paul Tillich, Hamilton Gibb, Sam Beer, James Watson, Archibald MacLeish, and on and on.

Many more of our discussions were among ourselves, over meals at the Freshman Union (now known as the Baker Center)—politics, economics, literature, sports, and the quality of local dates. I loved to spoon up the intellectual soup: one friend's scatological poems from classical Latin writers; another's study of the Chinese army in Korea; a third's ideas on staging Bertholt Brecht plays. It seemed that everyone was reading or had read *Young Man Luther*, by Prof. Erik Erikson, in which he developed his theory of an identity crisis. One future roommate, Jack Downing, taught me to prowl the bookstores around the Square, including the Coop, of course, and Grolier, Schoenhof's, Pangloss, and the Harvard Bookstore. Our high jinks were, well, pretty sophomoric, like filling a bathroom sink with gin, and painting graffiti on construction fencing. But one performance had an audience of thousands. In May of 1959, Fidel Castro, fresh in power, came to Harvard to give a speech, which was held out of doors across the river near the football stadium. One of my roommates and I bought some army surplus fatigues and caps, fake beards, and big cigars. We paid standing-room-only fee. Then just before the introductions began, we lit the cigars, donned our beards, and went racing up and down the aisles yelling "Viva Castro!" Triumphant, we were ushered out.

The Glee Club

When I was admitted to Harvard, my brother told me I should get into some extracurricular activities to counterbalance the intellectual intensity of the place. He suggested that I join the freshmen glee club, but I wanted something physical. Too small for football, too slow for cross-country running, I decided to try out for the crew.

In working construction that summer before college, I bulked up my weight to 160 pounds to get ready for the rowing, but for a backup plan, I took half a dozen singing lessons from our church choir director. Good move. When I arrived in Cambridge that fall, the obligatory physical exam picked up a heart murmur. Because of Tommy's death the year before, I was pulled from crew tryouts. While the doctors probed further, I wandered into Sever Hall for a few glee club practices. Almost anyone could get into the freshmen glee club, but to make the varsity, one had to perform well in a quartet trial, which mixed veterans and novices. Why not try it? Several dorm mates intended to.

Thus, I joined my bass voice to the baritone of another freshman and the tenors of two veterans in two quick rehearsals. The trial pieces were something religious and Thomas Morley's lively motet "Say, Dear, Will You Not Have Me? The veterans were blasé, while we two freshmen fidgeted as we appeared before the student judges and conductor, Eliot Forbes, in a stuffy music room that felt more like a jail cell.

We got through the pieces. I hit all the right notes, but my voice seemed strained and shrill. I was surely the weakest of the group. A week later, however, a postcard arrived with the cryptic message that my quartet grade of seventy-seven (on a scale of seventy to eighty) was good enough for the varsity. I was both disbelieving and ecstatic. Have they no standards? Maybe it was the very blandness of my voice that got me in—I didn't stand out, but I didn't lay any eggs either. Well, if they made a mistake, I wouldn't tell. Meanwhile, the doctors cleared me to row. But now, with a varsity singing slot, I knew I couldn't do both. So I opted for singing and recreational running until I began playing rugby the next year.

The glee club changed my life, musically at least. There in Sever Hall, three times a week over four years, I learned to read music, to make music, to sing a cappella, to watch conductors like a hunting dog on point, to listen to other parts. "If you can't hear the fellow next to you, you're singing too loudly," said one of the seniors. Singing was both an escape and an opening. It was collective and individual. I sang with my own voice but the whole was greater than the sum of the parts. We practiced hard. One of the music majors quoted the pianist Wanda Landowska approvingly: "I practice fanatically, so that I may play with abandon."

Singing was a balm for the rash of intellectual inferiority I felt so much of the time. The glee club made me a competent, well-trained choral singer who could in the future join almost any amateur group. It gave me an instrument to play anywhere in the world. In addition, it solidified my love of classical sacred and secular music.

And what great music it was! Over four years, I sang much of the great choral literature of Western Civilization, from the sixteenth-century motets of des Prez to Schütz, Bach, Handel, Mozart, Brahms, Schubert, Poulenc, and Stravinsky. We sang choruses from operas like *The Magic Flute, Fidelio,* and *Boris Godunov.* We even sang some songs written for the glee club, including the poem "God's Grandeur" by Gerard Manley Hopkins set to music by the club's assistant conductor, Bruce Archibald. In the fall on football weekends we sang joint concerts with Princeton and Yale and offered dueling medleys of rousing fight songs, like "Ten Thousand Men of Harvard." Twice a year with the Radcliffe Choral Society, we sang works like Fauré's Requiem and Brahms's *A German Requiem*. On other occasions, a select group traveled to Wellesley and Smith for joint concerts. In the spring, we took tours to cities like New York, Chicago, Atlanta, and Cincinnati.

Most of my classes were lecture driven. I didn't mind. I wasn't up to the hand-to-hand mental combat of most seminars. Besides, I was picking up a second education by osmosis in the dorms and at the dining tables. To my demerit, I was so fixed on my course of Russian studies and so needful of requirements in my field of history that I didn't ever take the great survey classes, such as Music 1 or Fine Arts 12, known by its nickname, "Darkness at Noon."

My sophomore year I took intensive Russian, which counted as two courses because it met eight hours a week. Oh, did my head ache with Russian history and grammar.

The Libraries: Reading and Romance

For three years, I went almost every weeknight to Lamont, the undergraduate library for serious study in an antiseptic, slightly carbolic, sweaty atmosphere amid the buzz of florescent lights and laboring air circulation. I moved my work around to different corners and alcoves, because then I could take down different random books and read for relaxation. I found Dorothea Lange's photographs, Kurt Vonnegut's novels, Dostoyevsky, Adam Smith, and early volumes of what would become Holocaust studies.

I was so dutiful, and yet at the same time so envious of one roommate who never went to the library until reading period, that week before exams. After a few desultory hours, he would come back and say, "Boy, I'm not in such bad shape after all." And then he would pull out all B's. Grrrrrr!

Later, I discovered the social bibliophilia of Widener Library's atmosphere. Built in memory of Harry Widener, who drowned on the *Titanic*, the library sat like a huge bullfrog right in the middle of the campus, across from Memorial Church. The space in between was called Tercentenary Theater, where graduations were held. The tourist guide's line was that if all Harvard were destroyed except Widener, the university would survive. There were two parts to Widener—the playground and the workroom. The workroom was the stacks. Twelve floors, or levels (six of them below ground), wire partitions, then holding over six million volumes, which gave the hint of a prison, but only a hint. That's where the real work happened, where honors candidates, graduate students, and professors did much of their research, and where I would work on my senior thesis. You got a special pass, went through a gate, and used the staircase or a tired elevator seemingly installed just after the *Titanic* sank.

The Widener playground was the cathedral-size Reading Room, a place to gawk at others and be seen by them. Twenty or thirty oak tables seated eight people each. Regulars had their favorite seats and could get petulant if someone else sat there. Along the walls was a vast number of dictionaries and encyclopediae. Smoking was permitted. Conversations were almost constant, but whispery. It was like a European sidewalk café. Some of the most beautiful (I thought) 'Cliffies (or Radcliffe students) studied nowhere else. There were also some Cambridge residents with no apparent university connection who came to sit for hours. Sprinkled among the rows of socializers were some people actually studying.

From Russia with Regrets

My difficulties with Russian and my modest grades in Russia-related courses began to eat away at my interest in the field. I could do no better than a C in my intensive Russian class. My father suggested that I go have a look. "I'll grubstake you for a trip this summer!" With that generous offer, I looked for short-term language classes in the USSR but found none. I learned I would also have to join preapproved government Intourist tours. But my Russian language professor said, "Go anyway. If you're clever, you don't have to stick with the tours all the time."

Nothing ventured, nothing gained. I signed up for back-to-back package tours of Moscow. Then I added a three-stop air tour to Leningrad, Kyiv, and Yalta. I made the plans in February and March. In May 1960, Gary Powers and his U-2 spy plane were shot down over Sverdlovsk, and Nikita Khrushchev pounded his outrage on the United Nations podium with his shoe. The trip turned doubtful.

By early June, however, Intourist was again welcoming visitors on their strictly supervised programs. I landed at the newly opened Sheremetyevo Airport, into the belly of the beast. Miles and miles of housing blocks and few private cars. Stores with numbers—Bookstore #4, Bakery #7—no advertising posters, but lots of political exhortations. The hotels were Soviet Gothic monstrosities, with an unsmiling woman at the elevator exits on every floor checking you out and in. After seeing the sights, Red Square, the Kremlin, and the Tretyakov Gallery (with its unforgettable Ilya Repin painting of Ivan the Terrible and his son, whom he has just murdered), I went to the Bolshoi Theatre to a stirring performance of the opera *Boris Godunov*, the coronation chorus of which we sang in the glee club.

On several days, I slipped away from the guided tours. I took a train out to Peredelkino, to visit the home of Nobel Prize–winning Boris Pasternak, author of *Doctor Zhivago*, who had died the month before. Through my mother's cousin Joe Harrison, who worked at *The Christian Science Monitor*, I met their Soviet correspondent, Edmund Stevens, who lived in one of the few privately owned houses in Moscow. I lunched with him, his Russian wife, and their independent red-haired daughter, who showed me some of her Moscow.

Rather self-consciously, I went to an exhibition about the U-2 Incident in Gorky Park, with Powers's equipment laid out in excruciating detail. I was feted by some Georgians at a fancy restaurant, who asked about changing rubles for dollars (which I declined) and who then disappeared . . . after paying the bill. I did take advantage of the black market. (My Harvard

Russian professor had said, take Levi's and Marlboros, they're worth more than gold. He also suggested a Polaroid camera. He was right.)

Another *Twilight Zone* moment was a two-hour half-English, half-Russian conversation with a Russian man who in retrospect reminded of Aleksandr Solzhenitsyn. He had been a tank commander in the war, been arrested for anti-Soviet remarks, jailed, then released, and now taught high school. I didn't know what to make of him. We talked about the Cold War, his teaching, and my own education until suddenly, he was up and away. Two days later, I saw him again in a park. He appeared more nervous and declined to chat. He gestured toward two dark-suited men and whispered, "KGB," and then disappeared.

I suppose I was followed on my hooky adventures down back streets, but I never saw the tails. At several different hotels I had calls to my room from women who wanted to visit me. I had the smarts and caution to say no to those entreaties.

The most memorable day was the eight hours outside the tomb of the embalmed saints Vladimir Lenin and Joseph Stalin. After I had joined the line of visitors past the waxen bodies in their air-conditioned crypt, I stood near a wall forty yards from the tomb entrance. In jeans, T-shirt, and baseball hat I stood out like, well, a tourist. When I struck up small talk with a couple of visitors, I became the clover to other bees. They peppered me with questions about education, my father's job, our cars, the price of gas, size of our house, entertainment, American jazz.

With the Polaroid, I took two dozen portraits of some of my conversation partners. They were enchanted. "And how did you get here?" In my now-punchy state, I blurted out "An OO-DVA!" (a "U-2.") A few laughed nervously; others choked. The only unpleasantness was from a party official who berated me for American spying and my lèse-majesté in front of the Communist shrine. To cap the day, I had one of the people take a photo of me standing on my head in front of the tomb.

Despite adventures like these (or maybe because of them) I felt my interest in Soviet affairs draining away. I was seeing for myself, as my father had suggested, but what I saw was simply less appealing. Some of it was the open (and covert) repression; some was the stultifying uniformity of the culture; some was the ubiquitous propaganda. The language remained tough; Pushkin and Yevtushenko were not bedtime reading for me. On my way home, I spent a week in Mannheim, Germany, with friends of my parents and then a week hiking in Switzerland. When I returned from Europe, my sophomore grade report greeted me with straight Cs, and selection out of the honors program in Russian history.

That next fall, now my junior year, I was of two minds. I could try to persuade the Russian studies department to give me another chance. Or I could say, "To hell with honors." Have a good time. Try the full range of Harvard classes beyond my field. Get a general education with my gentleman Cs. Did I really need an honors degree to get into the Foreign Service? I could take courses about the rest of the world. Go broad rather than deep. Who knew where the Foreign Service might send me? Thus I chose two more survey courses, one on the Far East and one on the Middle East. Both had the potpourri of scholars who gave some lectures on history, culture, and geography, and then turned the day-to-day teaching over to section leaders, who were graduate students and PhD candidates.

Well, a funny thing happened that fall as I ate of this intellectual smorgasbord. My grades improved. I made the dean's list for the first time, with my best grades coming in the Middle East course, although I was more interested in China and Japan. I petitioned the History Department for readmission to the honors program, in Middle Eastern studies, and was provisionally accepted.

They put me into a junior tutorial with a young, intense assistant professor of history and Arabic, William R. Polk, who had already written two books, and who seemed to know everyone in the Middle East. Among my fellow seminarians was John Damis, a rugby-playing friend from freshman year, and Frankie Fitzgerald, who would go on to write a Pulitzer Prize–winning book on Vietnam, *Fire in the Lake*. Polk gave us good readings and lively debates over the major conflicts of the day. But he always seemed in a hurry, always edgy to be away. Halfway through the semester, he told us he had been tapped to run the Middle East desk of the Policy Planning Staff of the State Department. He left before commencement, but he would reappear in my life. I finished the year solidly ensconced in the honors program. Now all I needed was a thesis topic.

Outside of academics, I had a wonderful time at Harvard. For athletics I ran alone along the Charles. Then one of my dorm mates introduced me to rugby, the macho club sport of "football without pads." It was a scratch collection of Americans, Brits, Aussies, South Africans, and Melanesians that practiced twice a week and played various Ivy League and New England squads. I loved the camaraderie with its blood, sweat, and beers, and had the satisfaction of scoring a try (goal) against Yale in a snowstorm in New Haven. For more cerebral delight, my brother Jan, I and two friends shared two season tickets for the Boston Symphony Orchestra.

Harvard Rugby Match

I fell pantingly in love with a 'Cliffie, Nora McKeon, the raven-haired daughter of a philosophy professor at the University of Chicago. We roamed around Cambridge for concerts, walks, football games, plays, and hours of restrained passion in my dorm room and car. On campus, I heard sermons at Memorial Church by Dr. Martin Luther King Jr., Reinhold Niebuhr, Paul Tillich, and others. When Niebuhr spent a semester at Harvard, he and his wife Ursula gave teas for undergraduates on Tuesday afternoons. I literally sat at his feet listening to the master.

I joined the crowds at the Bogie festivals at the Brattle Theater. These were sequences of major Bogart films repeated during exam period twice a year. You found yourself sitting next to people who had memorized the dialogue and who mouthed famous lines like "I don't need no stinking badges!" "Play it, Sam," and "Just whistle." Legitimate theater downtown brought Miller, Sartre, Ionesco At a hole-in-the-wall Cambridge club called 47 Mt. Auburn, a little-known folk singer named Joan Baez was just beginning to perform.

To the Far East with Song

In my junior year I was among fifty glee club singers chosen to tour the Far East for two months, singing thirty-six concerts in sixty days in eight countries. Coincidentally, my Far Eastern civilization course, then called "Rice Paddies," was a wonderful intellectual preparation for the trip. It was taught by the two giants of the field, John K. Fairbank on China and Edwin Reischauer on Japan.

The Far Eastern Tour became the second great trip of my life. For the first time, I felt the power of performance as a gift. As we traveled from Japan to Korea, Taiwan, Hong Kong, the Philippines, and Thailand, then to India, we

Harvard Glee Club Far Eastern Tour at Dinner in Sapporo, Japan, with Mares Leading the Toast, 1961

stayed with local families about half the time. The tour concluded in Greece as part of the Athens Festival.

Musically we prepared four different programs, mixing sacred and secular music. The range was great: des Prez, Gabrieli, Weelkes, Bach, Mozart, Beethoven, Mussorgsky, etc. In addition, we prepared at least two folk songs for each of the Asian countries. I still sing a few lines of them when I meet people from those countries: "Oh Edo Nihon Bashi," "Arirang, Arirang," and "Kan Ting Love Song." In those cities where the local Harvard club helped sponsor us, we ended with a medley of football songs and, of course, the shivery "Fair Harvard."

Over the two-month trip, we came, we sang, we conquered, singing thirty-six formal concerts and numerous informal ones in Japan, Korea, Taiwan, Hong Kong, the Philippines, Thailand, India, and Greece. We sang before crowds of five to six thousand, for impromptu groups on street corners, in train stations or private homes, on college campuses, and at local churches. We serenaded the wives of American ambassadors in Tokyo and New Delhi. When we sang the folk songs, the applause was tumultuous. We were the perfect traveling hybrid—performing tourists. It was better to give than receive. I stayed with a Korean professor whose home had a dirt floor, and with a Japanese dentist, an American journalist, and an Indian businessman.

I tried to write a postcard home every day as a diary substitute or supplement, depending upon time and mood. From Bangkok, Thailand, on August 1, 1961, I wrote:

> A GREAT DAY! Took a klong tour at 7:30 a.m. Hundreds of sheet-metal-covered barges sit low in the water. Saw the floating market and the Emerald Buddha. Climbed the stairs of Wat Aroon temple. On a crazy impulse, went running three miles around a lake near host's house. Temperature 93 degrees. (My host is a Harvard educated civil engineer who is a court chamberlain and fills dual post of teaching and diplomacy.)
>
> In afternoon went shopping to buy some Thai silk and bargained instead for a samurai sword left over from the Japanese occupation.

I would transport that sword home in my carry-on luggage for some ten thousand miles and a dozen flights, wrapped in two pillowcases.

We spent the night in a Zen monastery. In Hiroshima, I stayed with a college student who told me that his aunt and uncle had been killed in the atomic bomb, but he had volunteered out of curiosity to host a pair of us Americans.

The normal tourist photos of the Taj Mahal bring back our trip out to Agra (some of us riding atop the bus), where we sang inside the building and measured the echo at fifteen seconds. The Japanese concerts were all at 6:30 p.m., which was too early to have a meal beforehand. We had to have something in our stomachs. The solution? Our hosts produced great tin pots of green tea and bowls of rock sugar. Caffeine and carbohydrates, just right to keep our pitch up. Then we could feast afterward and drink not a few Asahi, Kirin, or Sapporo beers.

One of our singers, Pat Pepe, was blind. We all took turns accompanying him through the day, explaining what we were seeing. It was good practice for our own attention. One had to describe how an airport arrival felt, the faces of an audience responding to a concert, what a pagoda was like, what the North Korea guards looked like at Panmunjom.

We lived in our art. We were good enough to be taken seriously. We were amateurish enough to mix high music with high jinks. We were kids, after all, an intense, witty, enterprising gang of young men who thought they had the world by the tail. The musical climax was being a part of the Athens Festival. In a feast of cerebral and sensory overload, we sang Stravinsky's *Oedipus rex* in The Odeon of Herodes Atticus theater while looking up at the light-bathed Parthenon.

A review by "Our Western Music Critic" in the *Indian Express* in New Delhi read:

> There are few things in life so beautiful as standing in the silence of a cathedral as the sunlight streams through the stained glass. Great choral music, properly sung, can be like that—luminescent, deeply moving, able to lift the soul heavenward.
>
> It is the sincerest tribute I can pay to the Harvard Glee Club

that listening to it on Friday at the C.J. Hall, I only had to shut my eyes to have the cathedral illusion come to life. A choral group as good as this needs no sentimental glossing, however; behind the superbly musical rendering of the Harvard men lie talent, dedication and countless hours of hard work.

Distant Ambitions

Senior year, I finished a round of courses on Islam, the Ottoman Empire, and modern Egypt and then wrote my honors thesis on the arcana of Anglo-French Relations in Lebanon and Syria, 1941–43. It did receive a Magna/Magna Minus, equal to a B+ in less-august colleges. I was pleased and proud. Surely, this would help me get into the Foreign Service.

In April, I took and passed the Foreign Service written exam, which was essentially a tougher SAT. Then in May, I went down to the State Department in Washington, DC, to sit for the oral exam. On a sunny day, three relentless and unsmiling officers fired questions at me: How should the US treat President Nasser of Egypt? What were the Molly Maguires? Why have third political parties struggled in the US? What are the principal exports of Paraguay and Pakistan? Should the US defend the nationalists on Taiwan? On what page is the index in *The New York Times*? Etc., etc.

My answers were embarrassingly weak, at best.

"And what will you do if you flunk?" they asked finally. I gulped. "Get my military service done," I said.

When they came out of their judicial conference, they were pleasant, but blunt. "Go to grad school. Learn more US history. Do the military, if you wish. Then come back and take the test again."

"Are you just being polite?" I asked.

"No, we think you have some potential. You're just a little . . . green."

I carried that half loaf back to Cambridge, where I finished my exams, hung out with classmates, and mulled my next move. The draft, as Samuel Johnson said of hanging, concentrated the mind wonderfully. Should I go to officer candidate school in one of the services? There was the nascent Peace Corps. Both army and marines had programs of six months' active duty and five and one-half years in the reserves. That appealed. I could do six months, then go to graduate school to bulk up on American studies and reapply to the Foreign Service. Spurred on by the example of my roommate, Jack Downing, I opted for the marines. I said farewell to Nora, who was off to Paris for graduate study. And four days later, I headed for boot camp at Parris Island, South Carolina.

Chapter Four

From Parris Island to Parris Island (1962–69)

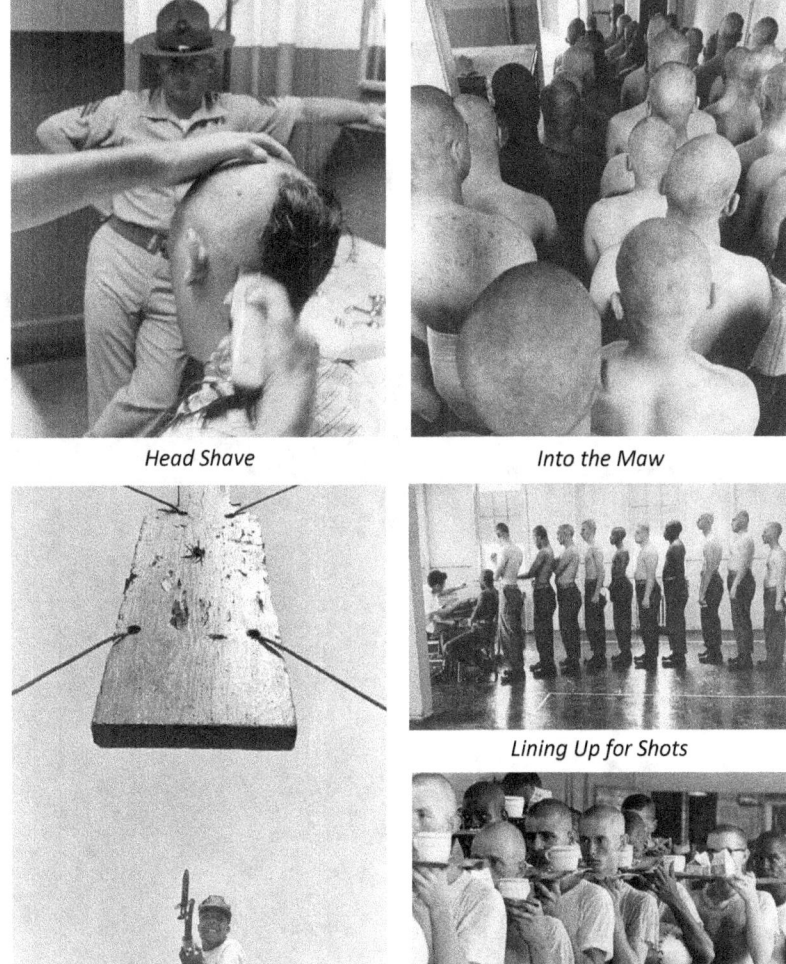

Head Shave

Into the Maw

Lining Up for Shots

Bayonet Practice

Chow Hall

Ropes Course

Platoon Tug of War

Strength Battalion

Looking Down the Muzzle

Rifle Training

In 1962, at the end of my senior year at Harvard, I was in "high cotton." With my honors degree, the only boll weevil was failing the Foreign Service exam. But even there, the examiners had been encouraging. "You need some seasoning," they said. "You haven't even taken a college-level US history class. Go learn something more about your own country. Go to graduate school. Go into the military. Work for a year or two, and come back."

Well, the military draft wonderfully concentrated the mind. What, then, would it be? Air force, navy, army? Three years? Six months' active duty? Wait to be called up for two years of conscription? What would be the biggest contrast to Harvard? Parris Island. My roommate, Jack Downing, was headed for marine officer training. But the marines also had a six-month active-duty program, with a further five and a half years in the reserves. I could find something to do with the other six months and then go off to some graduate school, the better to prepare for a second application to the Foreign Service.

And so, four days after graduating from Harvard, I carried a seabag across the hot parking lot of Marine Corps Recruit Depot, Parris Island, South Carolina, to join seventy-five other young men as a member of Platoon 360.

The first two weeks were a shitstorm of flies, heat, yelling, insults, scorn, drills, threats, and physical training. The swearing was so frequent, so extravagant, and so constant that ultimately it lost its force. But at first, we were terrified. The word "fuck," which I generally avoid, was used as every part of speech, including prepositions and syllables, as in "Out-fucking-standing, Private Mares!" Humiliation, harassment, and hurry were the early watchwords of training. Generally, to my credit and benefit, I could do just about everything required. The words of my Tarawa-veteran high school teacher Jim Goodrich helped me: "Don't argue, don't think! Some orders will seem picayune, petty, silly, even mean. Just go along. Play the game. There's method to that madness."

Our head drill instructor, Sergeant John Kent, was a bulldog figure who had fought at the legendary breakout from the Chosin Reservoir in North Korea in 1950. He never smiled, and he gave a whole new meaning to the phrase "in your face." Like everyone, I had my screwups, as when I once could not get the canvas strapping into a brass belt buckle. Kent exploded with scorn. "You must have gone to college to be such a fuckup! Well did you?"

"Yes," I peeped.

"Where?"

"Harvard," I whispered.

Kent roared. "Come here, Sergeant Davis, Sergeant Weatherall. See what a real Ivy League pussy looks like up close. What a loser!" I wanted to crawl under a bunk. Then he went on to another target.

Fortunately, that was almost my only exposure to the tender mercies of the drill instructors. I could do all the physical activities to perfection. I became the battalion chin-up champion. I was the fastest runner in my platoon in combat boots. In fact, I was actually surprised that the physical training was so relatively easy.

As the weeks progressed, we recruits learned a few furtive facts about each other. Standing in the interminable lines, shining shoes, in the mess hall, at the rifle range, we could compare notes. I was amused to see that we fulfilled the qualities of the standard war movie: Jews, Italians, farm kids, Black men, a New York City cop, and other white college kids from Fordham, Hofstra, and Princeton. A few youngsters had been given the choice of jail time or the marines.

My closest friend became Win Hodges, a newly minted Princeton graduate who had a hobby of reading military history. He was headed for a job at the publishing house Doubleday and Company. He pointed out that the marine definition of discipline was the key—"Instant willing obedience to orders." That, and group punishment—you pay for your buddy's screwups. The unit was all. Win said, "That lets them get away with anything, in the name of esprit de corps and unit discipline. That's why we compete with other platoons in field meets and marching. That's why they encourage us to carry out some of the discipline."

Gradually, I felt the platoon coming together, coalescing as a single unit. I could see the pounds disappear, the tans deepen, and join the collective cheers in the intrabattalion tug-of-war. It was most audible in the marching, to hear the gradually uniting crunch of seventy-five pairs of boots on the graveled parade field, to the musical crow caw of drill instructors' commands.

There was physical training, or P.T., every day, and lots of it. Lectures on how to do laundry, on communism, and on sex hygiene. Bayonet practice with padded substitute weapons, and a week of mess duty.

We spent three weeks at the rifle range, all geared toward one goal: to "make every marine a rifleman," as the recruiting exhortation had it. Because we were under the rifle instructors' command for much of the day, drill instructor pressure lightened up. We even watched a movie the night before we fired for qualification. Fittingly, it was *The Sands of Iwo Jima*, with John Wayne.

I was good at all the physical training. I shot Sharpshooter (but not Expert) at the rifle range. I won the Dress Blues Award, as the best recruit in my platoon, and left Parris Island with a promotion to private first class, in its own way, another cum laude degree.

In the fall of 1962, we moved on to advanced combat training at Camp Lejeune, North Carolina. In October came the Cuban Missile Crisis, the nearest the world had come to Armageddon. I remember watching President Kennedy's October 21st speech on a grainy ten-inch TV screen in the laundry room while the Four Seasons' "Big Girls Don't Cry" blared in the other corner. Like everyone else, we lived in a bubble of fear and impotence. But then, in two weeks, it was over with a sigh of relief heard round the world.

I finished my six months' active duty in December and got permission from the Marine Corps to go abroad for six months to study in preparation for the graduate school that would, I trusted, get me into the State Department. I applied to Johns Hopkins in Baltimore, Georgetown in Washington, and the Fletcher School of Law and Diplomacy in Medford, Massachusetts. Then I took off for Germany to do two months of intensive German at the Goethe-Institut in Murnau, Bavaria, about an hour's train ride to Munich. Mixed classes with Greeks, French, Spanish, Americans, and Japanese boosted my high school German to a low-grade fluency. Besides skiing and hanging out in the local Bier-stube (pub), I made trips into Munich, and once, in a fateful portent of future singing, I heard the famous Karl Richter conduct Bach's *St Matthew Passion*.

Then I moved on to Heidelberg, the fabled university town of *The Student Prince*, undamaged in the war and full of beer halls and legions of American tourists. I enrolled in university classes in economics, history, and poetry. I joined a local rugby club and played in tournaments in Germany and France. With another Goethe-Institut classmate who had bought a VW, I took a three-week trip through Yugoslavia to Greece, and another trip to France, first to the castles on the Loire river and then to several World War I battlefields in Picardy.

Returning to Texas in July, I learned that I failed admission to Hopkins and Georgetown, but got into Fletcher. I spent much of August taking intensive Spanish language lessons at a local junior college, which did not make me fluent, but would add to my string bag of languages for the Foreign Service, I hoped.

In September 1963 I arrived in Medford, Massachusetts, with a loaded VW. The Fletcher School comprised two buildings on the Tufts University campus, one for classes and one a dormitory for most of the unmarried students. We were a mini United Nations of about seventy-five students, Americans from Occidental, Davidson, Bryn Mawr, Wellesley, Smith, Colby, Bowdoin, etc., along with students from a dozen foreign countries.

Big Gap Here Until Fletcher

Fletcher offered a PhD program, but most students went for a one-year master's or a two-year master of arts in Law and Diplomacy. I chose the one-year program. After all, Fletcher was supposed to be my professional "finishing school." The students were serious people, already beginning careers or in midcareer. One person was headed for the priesthood, another had flown B-52 bombers. The foreign students came from Liberia, Germany, France, Taiwan, and beyond, a monoculture of people in the "business of governing the world," as one of the students joked. We studied hard in this almost-monastic life. I took a range of courses in international economics, diplomatic history, and Latin American history and got straight B's. Kennedy's assassination that year put a pall over everyone's life. I was driving to Philadelphia that weekend and felt ashamed of my Texas license plates.

My personal disaster that academic year was the moment when the SS *Foreign Service* hit the iceberg and sank in minutes. Without trouble, I had passed the written test a second time. Then came my second oral exam. In a dim rented downtown Boston office, three unsmiling State Department examiners turned my lights out. There were no polite murmurings of "Get a little seasoning" or "Try again." After shooting questions at me about Egypt, the Soviet Union, US corn production, the marines, and Texas geography, they told me to "try another line of work." Oh, boy!

Even more mortifying, I was the only one of six classmates who flunked the exam. I had no Plan B. What was I to do now? Go back to Texas, but for what end? Go into the marines as an officer? For a few days I carried the stench of failure and embarrassment around Fletcher. But my roommate said, "Get over it! It's only a knockdown, not a knockout."

A number of the Fletcher graduates were headed for New York, to Chase Manhattan Bank and Citibank. Both banks had summer internships. Citibank had a burgeoning overseas presence. Why not apply? I did and got one of the slots. It was a great way to spend some time in New York City and incidentally learn something about banking. I crashed at two different friends' apartments, uptown and downtown.

I loved being in the Big Apple, wearing out a copy of *New York on $5 a Day* going to plays, concerts, the opera, and the World's Fair. I even joined a choral group, the Festival Singers, and visited Carnegie Hall for the first and last time—to sing a concert onstage!

But curiosity about banking was not the same as interest and dedication. Nevertheless, when they offered to keep me on, I agreed because nothing else burned in my professional fireplace. I did my work dutifully, took a basic course in accounting, and served in the European division, but began to feel like a sleepwalker wandering through the world of overdrafts, letters of credit, bills of lading, currency movements. Wearing a suit every day, too, lost its savor.

Other professions floated past my screen. Work for the government, but of course, not the State Department? Business school? Go back to Texas in the "awl" (oil) business? More academic study for a teaching career? And then there was law school. Could that be the charmed third time? Both Dad and Jan had law degrees. Law gave you a skill. It gave you command presence. It taught you how to think and search. As my law student roommate said, it also gave you the chance to put off for another three years what you really want to do. I didn't ache to be a lawyer, but I could use it anywhere as long as I passed the state bar exams. So, on a bleak March Saturday, I went down to a cavernous classroom at New York University to take the Law School Admission Test. I did well enough to get into the University of Texas, University of Michigan, and University of Chicago law schools. With my ego patched up, I chose Chicago because a cousin who was there said it was a good place, small and even friendly.

There is a Vermont parable that fits my first weeks at law school:

> With a yoke of oxen, a man was skidding logs out of the woods. In the snow, he lost the toggle bolt that held the loop of the chain that attached the oxen to the heavy, log-laden sled. In an absent-minded moment, he stuck his finger in to replace the bolt.
>
> "Those oxen hadn't more than begun to pull when I realized I'd made a big mistake."

I joke now, but law school provided the most miserable few months of my life. From my first days in the modern architecture of the Chicago Law School and the foreboding Gothic-style dorm with its cell-like rooms, I felt I was in the wrong place. The language was English, but the exegesis felt like reading Greek. I'd read passages three times, five times and retain nothing. Torts, criminals, corporations, procedure, and the basics were beyond me. Law school seemed to reward all the skills I didn't have—tough skin, brazen beliefs, intellectual fisticuffs, and sparring. I felt naked when called upon. I'd deliberately sit in the wrong seat or skip classes entirely. My brother flew out from New York to give me some comfort. My law-student cousin said everyone went through this. "The first year it's so bad, you can't believe it can get worse. Then the second year is just as bad, but then you are two-thirds through!" Little help. I was not comforted.

The law school dean listened sympathetically to my woes and lined me up with a counselor to whom I could pour out my fears and insecurities. I told him how after my brother's death I felt I had to live as two sons. I'd never allowed myself the freedom to choose my own path. I told him that Erik Erikson's study of Luther's identity crisis, which was almost an in-joke in college, now seemed desperately real. Luther's thunderbolt told him to become a monk. Mine only told me *not* to be a lawyer, and maybe not to try to please my parents. The law was a good profession . . . for someone else!

I went home to Texas for Christmas, where my parents were surprisingly sympathetic. I went to see some of my high school friends, who were comfortably on their way to careers in the law, medicine, architecture, and the navy. What did I have to offer? I found some tough love from Bill Wallace, my old track coach, who told me: "You've been trying to please your parents for too long. It's not their fault, it's yours. Every new thing you try has their stamp on it, not yours. They'll love you for anything you do. But you're the captain of your destiny; you can't sail in their crew. I don't know what you'll do now, but you have to do it for you."

~

When I returned to Chicago, salvation came in the person of a Harvard roommate's father. Levering Cartwright was a Chicago stockbroker who had once been an editorial writer for the *Chicago Tribune*, and he knew the world of Chicago journalism. "Why not apply for work at the City News Bureau," he said. "It's full of odd ducks and other social misfits. It's a great way to learn the ropes of reporting." (It had been made famous also through the play and then film *The Front Page*.) And so I did. With a letter of introduction from Mr. Cartwright, I went to see two editors, Larry Mulay and Walter Ryberg. In fifteen minutes, after a couple of desultory questions about college and past jobs, I was hired and my life would never be the same.

The City News Bureau turned out to be a journalistic Parris Island, and I loved it. It had been assembled seventy years before by the various newspapers in Chicago to blunt some of the competition between Chicago's boisterous baying hounds of journalism, and to provide some on-the-job training for aspiring reporters. Its cub reporters would provide basic coverage of cops, courts, and some politics for Chicago and its suburbs to all news outlets without crimping the ability of the big guys to cover any story they wished.

With all copy going to all news outlets there was almost no chance of scooping the competition, but that remote possibility added red meat to our young fangs. Under the drill-instructor-like tutelage of editors like Ryberg, Arnold Dornfeld, and Paul Zimbrakos, I learned to cover fires, murders, riots, basic cop reporting, and "coroner's cases," those deaths reported without a doctor's presence. My shift ran from 5 p.m. to 2 a.m. I was sent out to North, Central, or South Police headquarters and told to find news or be near a phone to get leads from the city desk. As in *The Front Page*, you learned to watch and listen to your fellow reporters, to follow their leads. The parallels with Parris Island extended to the tender mercies of editors. Once when I called in to start my shift, I reached night editor Arnold Dornfeld: "Hi, Mr. Dornfeld. This is Mares at South Police, what do you have for me?" "Infinite contempt, chum," he snarled, and proceeded to tell me about a robbery on the U. of Chicago campus. "Check it out!"

Before the City News Bureau, I had never done anything on deadline other than high school and college papers. I had no hidden skill for vivid descriptive prose that jumped off the page and horse-collared the reader. This was on-the-job training, plain and simple, telling real stories with real words, wrestling high crimes and misdemeanors to the ground with words, your words. And what a place to do it! Big-shouldered, meat-packing, a quilt of nationality-based neighborhoods, the domain of Mayor Richard J. Daley.

It was heady stuff, this basic police beat with its deadlines, the competition with the newspapers and television stations, writing that "first draft of history," and then hanging out in bars with fellow reporters. I covered fires, murders, robberies, muggings, even several open housing marches into white neighborhoods, led by Dr. Martin Luther King Jr. Unquestionably, the most dramatic story I covered was the mass murders committed by Richard Speck in the summer of 1966. At 4:30 a.m. on July 14, the night editor, Pericles Georges, called to say, "Get yourself down to East One Hundredth Street. Some guy has killed a bunch of nurses." Because I lived on the Chicago South Side, I was one of the first reporters on the scene. For the next two days I interviewed cops, neighbors, assistant coroners, and other reporters. About every two hours, I phoned updates of the breaking story to rewrite editors back at CNB headquarters. Journalists from across the country, including the famous Jimmy Breslin, flew in to cover "the crime of the century," in the words of the Cook County Coroner. Among the local reporters was one Kent Bernard of *The Chicago Daily News*, whom I had met on other assignments, who introduced me to John Tweedle, a staff photographer festooned with cameras and a voice that boomed along the somber street.

By this time, I saw that words were not museum pieces to be put on a shelf and worshipped, mute things to be strung together randomly. They had real utility. They were claws, brushes, nets, chains, and other tools for capturing the reality before me. More than anything they were mine, even as I turned them over to rewrite editors to transform into real prose. I thought of a quote from *The Atlantic* magazine: "The journalist's job is to describe the world in five minutes, and then get the public to take five minutes to read the description."

But then I saw, felt, that words were not enough, not enough to capture the world around me. Without conscious choice I slid laterally into photography. I bought a camera, a Pentax single-lens reflex, and began wandering around the city. (All my previous cameras had been family hand-me-downs.) At first, it was only a hobby. Since I couldn't sleep during the day, I had a lot of time to roam the city before my next shift. I would run a lot along Lake Michigan. I hung out at libraries. I played squash with an old friend from Texas. But there was still more time to kill.

Of course, I had taken snapshots on my various trips to Asia, the Soviet Union, and Europe and across the US. But this was different. Suddenly, I was a painter, equipped with his complete compact easel with paints and brushes, all entirely mobile. I liked the solitude and rhythm of composition. Or I was a sneak thief hiding behind my lens to pounce upon unsuspecting subjects. I played with design, textures, angles, all in black-and-white. I loved portraits, formal or secretive. Everything was grist for the lens: bus passengers, pigeons, skylarking kids, pickup sports, people in flea markets, high school sports teams, animals at the zoo, library patrons, sewer grates and fire escapes, the great Art Institute lions.

I pored over books by Henri Cartier-Bresson, W. Eugene Smith, Edward Steichen, Robert Frank, Danny Lyon, and David Douglas Duncan, to whom I wrote a fan letter. He wrote back: "Shoot close, then closer. If your pictures are not good, you're not close enough!"

I went to every photo exhibit mounted at the Art Institute. I fell for Henri Cartier-Bresson's pregnant phrase "the decisive moment" of maximum visual tension. I loved one quote from Eudora Welty: "A good photo stops a moment from running away." Best of all, I followed Dorothea Lange, the great photographer of the Great Depression, in adopting a line from the seventeenth-century scientist Francis Bacon: "The contemplation on things as they are, without error or confusion, without substitution or imposture, is in itself a nobler thing than a whole harvest of invention."

Here I realized that although I was getting good on-the-job instruction in writing at the City News Bureau, I had no comparable instruction in photography. Should I try another graduate school in photography? Night school somewhere in downtown Chicago? No. I was too impatient. Anything local? Well, nothing ventured, nothing gained. I walked into the office of the local weekly, the *Hyde Park Herald*, and asked the staff photographer, one Nancy Hays, if I could create my own unpaid internship.

Nancy had attended the School of Modern Photography in New York City and then moved to Hyde Park as a professional photographer, where she went to work for the *Herald* almost full-time. Besides the news, she did lots of public service photography, family portraits, and some advertising.

That Nancy didn't say no was a start. She warned me that she worked with a 2¼" square camera (not a 35 mm) and that most of her assignments were features, not breaking news. With those cautions, she volunteered to take me on if I would help her in her darkroom and take some of the assignments she could not manage. She was true to her word and gave me a basic education, showing me the value of patience, both in shooting and in darkroom work.

Her darkroom turned out to be a magic kingdom of total darkness at times, amber light at others, and white light at others. Time slowed. Music was optional. Water gurgled in print baths. In total blackness, I learned to take film from the camera, spool it onto screen reels, and put these into stainless steel canisters for development, fixing, washing, and drying. It was rather like assembling a rifle blindfolded at boot camp.

You took the snakelike strings of images to the light to choose which would be printed. In that process, the images would be magically reversed when the photosensitive paper slid into the development bath and the original snap emerged in the shimmering liquid-amber light. Then you, the artist, decided when the photo was ready to be fixed permanently, and on to the washing bath, where you became the obstetrician, plucking up these paper "babies" with tongs to see if they had all their fingers and toes.

For some training in covering hard or breaking news, I called John Tweedle, the *Daily News* photographer whom I had met at the Speck murders scene. Over beers at a bar in Hyde Park called Mr. Ups, I pitched my thin portfolio and thick enthusiasm. Would he become another mentor to me? I was happy to pay…

"Are you willing to work like a bastard? Can you take criticism?" I said *Yes* to both of his questions. "Good, we can talk about the money later, when we find out if you have any talent."

John was the first Black photographer hired by a major Chicago newspaper. He had grown up in Fort Smith, Arkansas. After high school he joined the air force. He had taught himself photography when he found on base that photography, and its darkroom, was the only extracurricular activity that wasn't segregated. He would disappear into the darkroom for twelve hours at a time. After the service, he moved to Chicago and built up a freelance wedding photography business. Then he began selling photos to *Jet* and *Ebony* magazines and the *Daily Defender* newspaper until 1964, when *The Chicago Daily News* hired him.

For over a year and a half, John was my teacher, uncle, and brother. I loved his boisterous diligence. He had a voice that rattled windows. His bear hug could crush ribs. He was big and jovial, smoked Kools, and drove the messiest car I ever saw. On top of all that, he played a wicked double bass in a pickup jazz band. He never stood on formality. When someone said something witty, or sharp, or stupid, he'd say, "That's a gotcha!" Ten "Gotchas" won an "Attaboy!" and ten "Attaboys" earned a "Distinguished Service," which no one had ever won.

John Tweedle, my Photography Mentor and Best Man

His advice mirrored that of David Duncan—"Shoot close, crop tight!" He told me to buy the best equipment I could afford, because then I couldn't blame bad pictures on the camera. So, I traded my Pentax in for the Nikon he preferred and several lenses. At first I felt presumptuous to have all this high-end gear. "No," he boomed, "those are the tools of the trade. Your job is to live up to them." He sent me out on assignments and then graded the results with a tough love that never granted an A. Once he even called me at 2 a.m. to go out and cover a four-alarm fire on the South Side. He also liked to send me to "dry-shoot" an assignment, that is, use no film, then come back and tell him what I had done.

In his prints (and mine), he always wanted the full spectrum. Yes, film is cheap, he said, but don't just press a button. "Make pictures, don't take pictures. Every time you push the shutter, it should be a deliberate capture. Get a light meter! Don't trust the one in the camera." He seconded advice from Nancy Hays: "It's all right to start with a cliché, as long as you don't end with one."

We built a darkroom together in an old coal cellar of a six-flat apartment building, one of whose tenants had fought in the Abraham Lincoln Brigade in the Spanish Civil War. And we drank lots of Pabst Blue Ribbon at local saloons. Through John, I met Chick Harrity, an *Associated Press* photographer who befriended me and took me to Chicago Bears, Bulls, and Blackhawks games to practice shooting next to the pros.

I began selling a few photos to the *Herald*. In a delicious irony, I received a commission, to take portraits of the professors at the law school. In the summer of 1967, I got a break when a distant cousin of my mother's who was an editor of *The Christian Science Monitor* in Boston put me in touch with Howard James, the Midwest *Monitor* bureau chief in Chicago. He had won a Pulitzer Prize for his series Crisis in the Courts and was then working on another large-scale book about children in trouble with the law.

Muhammad Ali in Chicago, 1967

Howard tried me out on a few photo assignments around the Midwest region, including illustrations for his forthcoming book. In the spring of 1968, needing extra coverage of the Wisconsin presidential primaries, he called me up from the minors to shoot some campaign events there. How exciting it was to be within three feet of Richard Nixon and Eugene McCarthy and then to see my photos on the front page of a national newspaper! Here was a graphic skill surpassing my verbal ability. Words needed friends and allies; photos acted alone. With the two of them I had a choice of weapons.

I began to wonder how I could get a full-time newspaper job as a photographer, not a writer. A few friends had gone directly from the City News Bureau to a major paper, but I had by now been out of the word game for a couple of years. For a photographer's slot, however, I would surely need an arresting portfolio of both features and breaking news. I could shorten the process by being on the scene at some dramatic event. But how do you plan that?

Maybe I could do a book of photographs. But of what? What did I know about? A travel book? Boring. Texas? Boring. People of Chicago? Boring. The political campaign? Too complex. The war in Vietnam? There was certainly plenty of good war photography out there. But the logistics and sponsorships and yes, the danger, were daunting.

Richard Nixon Campaign in Wisconsin

One evening I was reading John Sack's book *M*, in which he followed an army company through basic training to its first engagement in Vietnam. Suddenly, I saw my own training in quite a different light. When I had gone to Parris Island, it had been almost a lark. There was no war. It was get in and get out. Sack's book, on the other hand, showed a profound and desolate connection between training and potential death. It occurred to me—why not a photographic book doing the same thing for the marines? I waited a few weeks to be assured this was no penny arcade vision. Tweedle was skeptical that the Marine Corps would permit such an intrusion, but said, of course, try it.

Thus, as the Tet Offensive in Vietnam raged in February 1968, I wrote to Headquarters Marine Corps to ask if I, as a former recruit and now professional photographer, could follow a platoon through its ten-week training cycle. To my grateful shock, they wrote back in two weeks to say yes, with two conditions—I couldn't live in the barracks, and I'd need to show them all the photos I took. "Yes, of course," I wrote.

Thus, from early June to late August, I was with Platoon 360 at least twelve hours almost every day. The recruits were told nothing of my work, only that they should ignore me. At first in shock and later in familiarity, they did just that. My nonofficial status gave me a freedom of movement around the recruits that the drill instructors neither enjoyed nor sought. More importantly, my own experience gave me the signal gift of anticipation and preparation. For the first weeks, the recruits were so frightened, they probably thought I was part of their torment, having a civilian in quasi-military garb snapping hundreds of photos of their discomfort.

As the days passed, I became part of the furniture, accompanying them to class, to meals, to the rifle range, the obstacle course, interplatoon tournaments, the euphemistic "Strength Battalion," which was extra work for laggards. I never talked to the recruits, but I grew quite friendly with the three drill instructors. I was able to develop my film at the Depot's official darkroom each evening, which allowed me to reshoot scenes imperfectly captured the first time. In all, I produced some eight thousand negatives. My relaxation consisted of running in the early morning, reading, and occasional tennis with several of the base's officers.

In late August, after the platoon graduated, I returned to Chicago with my trove of images, one hundred pages of notes, and the formidable challenge of how to write this book. But first I got a chance to cover part of the tumultuous

Grant Park Demonstration, Chicago Convention, 1968

Democratic Convention for the *Monitor*, although not the epic night battle of Grant Park in front of the Hilton Hotel.

There was no end to the adventures of 1968. Even before I went off to Parris Island, I watched the Prague Spring of modest political liberalization unfold in Czechoslovakia. What a contrast to the repression I had found in the Soviet Union. Could the Czechs politely walk away from the Soviet grasp? What an interesting time to visit the land of my grandparents. I made a plane reservation for September after the Democratic Convention. *The Christian*

Prague Memorial, 1968

Milovan Djilas in Belgrade, Yugoslavia, 1968

Science Monitor invited me to send any photos I could.

Then came the three-pronged attack of the Warsaw Pact nations in August and the crushing of the Prague Spring. I thought my trip was off, but in September, I flew into Prague, Czechoslovakia, on the first civilian plane allowed to land. Prague was a city in shock. Russian troops were everywhere. Bullet holes dotted the National Museum at the head of Wenceslas Square. I stayed at a favorite journalists' hotel a block away. They were a disparate lot, although quite friendly and knowledgeable. I was lucky to be among them, although on one occasion it got dicey.

The second night I was there, the Russian tanks and troops pulled out of the city. About twenty tanks had been parked directly across from the hotel. As they clanked and rumbled off not twenty feet away, I got off six or seven good flash photos. But then I got greedy and continued to snap away. Suddenly, one of the tanks stopped, the turret opened, and one of the soldiers motioned me forward. Knowing they wanted at least the film, I was not about to argue, or run. I opened the camera, surrendered the roll, and they rolled on. When they were out of sight, I reloaded and snapped a few more photos of the end of the column—two trucks and a mobile soup kitchen.

"Gutsy move!" remarked one of the reporters nearby. "Not bright," I thought in retrospect.

Then it was on to Hungary, Bulgaria, and Yugoslavia, where with another introduction from *The Christian Science Monitor*, I was able to meet the famous Yugoslav dissident Milovan Djilas, author of *The New Class*, who had been placed under house arrest by the national leader, Josip Broz Tito. His English was excellent and we spent a delightful afternoon talking about the Czechoslovak situation, his meetings with Stalin, the future of Yugoslavia after Tito, and his own writing.

Through the fall, I worked on my book, which I titled *The Marine Machine*. For this writing task, I armed myself by rereading the Strunk and White classic *The Elements of Style* and George Orwell's rules for writing in his essay "Politics and the English Language:"

> i. Never use a metaphor, simile or other figure of speech which you are used to seeing in print.
>
> ii. Never use a long word where a short one will do.

iii. If it is possible to cut a word out, always cut it out.

iv. Never use the passive where you can use the active.

v. Never use a foreign phrase, a scientific word or a jargon word if you can think of an everyday English equivalent.

vi. Break any of these rules sooner than say anything outright barbarous.

I had originally planned to let the pictures tell the whole story, but at the urging of a girlfriend who was writing her first novel, I settled in to write a text. She was right. After I began, there seemed to be so many things that had to be described in print, that couldn't be captured with photos alone. Eventually, I added twelve thousand words of text to six chapters of photographs.

I wrote and rewrote until I lost all sense of quality. I did learn a lot about writing, and even a bit about the creative process. I made up a package and submitted it to Win Hodges, my platoon buddy from 1962, who now worked for Doubleday and Company. He passed the manuscript on to their chief military books editor. After six months, Doubleday bought the book with an advance of twenty-five hundred dollars. I felt like a lottery winner, a graduate student with a new PhD, and a new father all in one. With that imprimatur, I had the chutzpah to go downtown to approach Hugh Edwards, the curator of prints, drawings, and photography at Chicago's Art Institute. After I showed him eight or ten prints, he sat back, steepled his fingers, and said, "Let's do it. But please, get museum-quality prints."

My third book-related coup was to get former Marine Corps commandant and Medal of Honor winner David M. Shoup to write the foreword. I wanted someone with a lifetime in the corps for historical perspective. I only knew him by his current reputation, which was as a vocal opponent of the Vietnam War. A "vast waste of blood and treasure," he called it. He had elaborated on this critique in an article in *The Atlantic Monthly* magazine. Now, the *Atlantic* editor happened to be a Harvard classmate, Michael Janeway. Trading on the principle that it's not what you know, but who you know, I called him, got Shoup's address, and wrote to the general. Could I come to Washington and make my pitch in person? He said, "Sure," and he'd take me to lunch at the Army Navy Country Club.

We met in the foyer of the sprawling colonial-style club. It crawled with generals and admirals and spit-and-polish service. But when we walked into the dining room it felt a little like a sheriff and his deputy entering a hostile bar. The chatter became murmurs and the generals and admirals eyed us as we walked to a side table. Shoup ignored them. On the contrary, he was charming, and acute. He said none of his comrades in arms ever criticized the veracity of his statements, only that he had made them. "How could you write that about us!" they complained.

Over the meal, he talked about growing up a farm kid in Indiana, going to Purdue, then joining the marines, serving in China in the 1930s, then the bloody assault on Tarawa. He talked about why training troops at Parris Island in a humanitarian manner was the right thing to do.

Over dessert, he said yes, he would write the foreword. Anxious to make the meal last, I asked him when he had last seen President Kennedy.

He said in September 1963, he had a call at Marine Corps headquarters that the president wanted to see him. "When the president calls, you go!"

There, in the Oval Office, Kennedy sat him down, and after a bit of small talk, asked Shoup if he would agree to serve another four-year term as marine commandant. Shoup cleared his throat and said, "Well, Mr. President, I'd rather not." A surprised Kennedy rocked back in his chair and said, "General, would you mind telling me in a few words why not?"

"Loyalty, sir," said Shoup.

"OK, General, you have satisfied the requirement for brevity. Could you elaborate a bit?"

Chicago Sun Times Photographer

"Mr. President, my entire career has been the Marine Corps, and I've been privileged to rise to its top rank. Now there are a dozen or more marine officers who could do this job just as well. If I serve one more term, I will foreclose their chances ever to serve as commandant. I don't think that would be loyal to them."

Kennedy rocked a few more times then said, "General, I accept your reasoning." Shoup thanked the president and left.

He said, "I never saw him again." Two months later the president was dead.

Shortly thereafter, with a broader portfolio, which now included my book contract, I applied for a photographer's job at the *Chicago Sun-Times*, where some of my old City News Bureau buddies worked.

The editor, James Hoge, Jr., interviewed me briefly and said, "Join us!"

Chapter Five

Love and the *Sun-Times* (1969–71)

I joined the *Chicago Sun-Times* in mid-April 1969. They installed a two-way radio in my car and gave me a press card, a nickel-plated badge for the Chicago Press Photographers Association, and access to all the gear I wanted to supplement my own.

The first day's assignments were emblematic of the range of stories I would cover. First, I was sent to record the demonstration of a newly minted medical safety bracelet anyone could wear to alert emergency personnel of a preexisting condition. That meant taking close-ups with my macro lens of mens' and women's wrists wearing the bracelets. The second assignment sent me to a busy North Side street to take photos of foot-deep potholes that were causing havoc to traffic. I waited until the road crew had put up diversion markers and put a camera with a wide-angle lens into a hole with a time-release showing depth and cars whizzing by. Minutes later, the photo editor called to send me to the far South Side, where a distraught workman was barricaded in his house, shooting at people. One cop was already dead, and a siege was underway. I got there and took some photos of cops running for cover, while staying under cover myself. Then I raced back to the office, developed the film, and printed a selection, several of which ran the next day.

In a way, the photo department resembled the City News Bureau. There were some old-timers who had come up through the ranks using Speed Graphic 4x5 cameras where you got one, maybe two shots, and you had to make them count. They were dismissive (or envious) of the Nikon-clad new boys (all boys) with their motorized cameras and a forest of lenses. Most of them really knew the city because they had grown up there. Some of the over-the-hill photogs ended up on darkroom duty, whence came enigmatic shouts, such as "Don't raise the bridge; lower the water." This cohort was particularly disparaging of reporters. One loved to say, "The honorable reporter X, for whom I have the highest degree of low regard."

The majority of the photographers were in their thirties and forties, quiet and competent. Two of them would win Pulitzer Prizes. In ability, I was probably in the lower third. But I didn't mind. It was a yeasty experience, to be shoulder to shoulder with a squad of skilled, serious professionals. I tried to learn from them all. The photo editor was Ralph Frost, a reincarnation of a drill instructor, and the CNB editor Arnold Dornfeld, who sent out typed "Frostygrams" on yellow copy paper to praise or, mostly, criticize our images. It was like being around a dozen Tweedles every day. By this time, John had moved on to work for the educational TV station WTTW-TV to produce *Our People*, a weekly show about Black people.

I had a wide range of assignments, both alone and with reporters. The weather, teacher strikes, headshots of politicians, a Rolling Stones concert, society weddings, new births at the Lincoln Park Zoo, the Chicago Seven trial, political speeches, open housing marches. When I was sent to cover the aftermath of Black activist Fred Hampton's death in a police raid, I pointed out to the reporter that all the bullet holes in the house led inward; there was no return fire. On July 20, 1969, I went out to the Cook County jail with a reporter on the day of Armstrong's step on the moon and captured inmates with both lively interest and total disregard.

I liked going on stories with reporters, maybe because they were more interested in ideas, maybe because there wasn't much time to talk in the hurly-burly of the photo department. Some were remote giants, like Ron Powers and Mike Royko, both Pulitzer Prize winners, and cartoonists John Fischetti and Bill Mauldin, both of them Pulitzer Prize winners. Some became friends for life: Chuck Lewis in business, Dick Foster writing editorials, Tom Dolan on crime, Fritz Plous on general assignment, and Doug Woodlock doing courts. Doug (who would go on to become a federal judge in Boston) put me onto my second-favorite reference work companion. *Brewer's Dictionary of Phrase and Fable* is filled with wonderful, pre-Wikipedia definitions of phrases like "fata morgana," "omnium-gatherum," and "Quis custodiet ipsos custodes?" and then eight pages of nicknames of British army regiments and American army divisions.

The core group of Lewis, Foster, and Dolan often went out for early-morning tennis and after-work drinking at the watering holes of John

Barleycorn's on the North Side, the Billy Goat tavern downtown, and Jimmy's Woodlawn Tap in Hyde Park (a mere two blocks from my apartment). Over the bar at the latter was a famous sculpted hand with the middle finger extended and a small sign reading, YES, WE HAVE NO BUDWEISER! (It was a successful rejoinder to an Anheuser-Busch salesman who claimed, twenty years before, that the bar would be out of business in six months if it excluded the "king of beers.") Jimmy's was the only bar I've ever been in that had a full, if aged, set of the *Encyclopædia Britannica,* "for settling arguments," the wags claimed. Graffiti were plentiful, and cerebral, as in, "More people die in college than in old folks' homes." And "Milton Friedman is a classic asshole." Under which someone had replied, "Perfection of any sort is a virtue!" Our favorite beer was G. Heileman's Special Export, from one of the declining number of regional breweries in the country. For its lime-colored glass bottle, we dubbed it "green death."

One Sunday afternoon I went on an assignment that endured for a lifetime. The paper sent me and reporter Dick Foster to cover the opening of the First National Bank of Chicago building in the Loop. The photo editor said I should be sure to photograph the bank president's collection of Frederic Remington bronze sculptures, and separately, members of the bank's corps of "First Girls." These were attractive college graduates hired to decorate the lobby, show the visitors how to open a checking account, the location of the bathrooms, etc.

After we had dutifully seen and shot the Remingtons on the sixtieth floor, Foster and I headed for an elevator to search for First Girls in the lobby, when who should step out but the most beautiful, wholesome, confident blonde I'd ever seen?

"Gosh," I stammered, "would you mind coming downstairs with us so I may take your picture?" It happened that Foster had met her several months before. Quickly, he vouched for me. She agreed, but it took all my charm to replace her skepticism with a usable smile. I snapped away, and we headed back to the office. I was smitten. Back in the darkroom, I developed the film, made several prints for the editor, and then, my shift now over, drove back to the bank with a couple of extra prints.

I used my press sticker to lurk in a no-parking zone, hoping she would appear. I didn't even remember her name. But no matter, she emerged and I smartly asked if she wanted a ride home.

Since the alternative was the El, she gave me a cautious yes for a ride back to Evanston, where she had just graduated from Northwestern University in Russian studies, which she planned to continue at UC Berkeley in the fall. When I got to the office the next day, there was no picture of her in the paper. I asked Ralph Frost why. "Mares, you dummy," he yelled. "We weren't looking for headshots of the First Girls, but of them working! Were you falling in love?" I looked around the newsroom sheepishly.

I had been able to extract a phone number from her, and for a month I called every other night. No dates, thank you. She was adamant and wanted no entangling alliances before she headed west. Finally (with secret help from her roommate), I persuaded her to play some tennis. That was the beginning of more than fifty years of joyful companionship; Chris became, with my parents, the other bookend of my life.

We courted for the rest of the summer with weekend outings, concerts, tennis games, and visits to friends in the burbs. And I took hundreds of pictures of her.

At the end of that summer, Chris went off to Berkeley, and I finished and sent off *The Marine Machine* to Doubleday.

The next year, there was an opening for a staff photographer at the *Sun-Times* Sunday magazine, *Midwest*. Well, that looked interesting. I applied and got the slot. At first I was only illustrating longer feature stories by other reporters. Then gradually, the editor encouraged me to shoot and write my own stories, to "shoot with both hands," one editor said dryly.

But wearing two hats made me the subject of the next negotiations between the Newspaper Guild and the Field papers. (The photographers were afraid the paper would just give a camera to a reporter on an out-of-town assignment and save a second salary.) The parties agreed that beyond a certain distance from Chicago—I think it was fifty miles—a single reporter could carry a camera, or a photographer could write accompanying text. Thus I became the *Sun-Times*' first photographer-reporter. My friend Dick Foster joked about the "Mares Rule."

At *Midwest*, some stories were still photography only, but others became both. I did a story about being a passenger doing barrel rolls in a biplane. I hung out at a local boxing gymnasium for another spread. I went to Nebraska to travel with a crew of wheat harvesters. I joined reporter Bob Greene for two weekends of travel with the rock band Three Dog Night. I joined Fritz Plous to cover Bill Monroe's Beanblossom blue grass festival in Beanblossom, Indiana.

Inscription in our copy of Up Front by Bill Mauldin, staff cartoonist at the Sun Times

My most memorable and complex assignment was in April 1970, when SAS airlines offered the *Sun-Times* a promotional seat on an inaugural flight from Copenhagen to Tel Aviv. After majoring in Middle Eastern history, this was my first chance to go there. And ever since grade school I had wanted to see Lapland, so this trip was doubly attractive.

With help from the Israeli consulate in Chicago and the Norwegian Embassy in DC, we put together an itinerary. I would spend a week in Israel and then fly to Alta in northern Norway, to see some indigenous Sami peoples and then work my way back down the Norwegian coast to Bergen, Copenhagen, and home.

"You're more than a tourist, less than a political reporter," said Dick Takeuchi, the editor. "Think some sort of hybrid explorer. We have one contact in the occupied territories, in a story from *The Washington Post* about a poet. See if you can get her photograph. After that you're on your own."

From Tel Aviv, I went straight to Jerusalem. Like most visitors I felt dizzy treading its three-thousand-year-old stones of faith and torment. I did my own biblical walking tour of Mount of Olives, the Garden of Gethsemane, the Western (Wailing) Wall, the Via Dolorosa path, and Church of the Holy Sepulchre. I walked through the Arab quarter and the Orthodox quarter of Mea Shearim, sharing the streets with civilians and plenty of Israeli soldiers. The Israelis were in high spirits, three years after the Six-Day War. The Palestinians appeared grim, sullen, after this second Nakba, or catastrophe of losing their land.

With an Israeli army minder, I took a twelve-hour day trip down to the Dead Sea, then through Jericho to a nahal, or armed settlement, of young Israelis, one of dozens strung from Syria to Egypt in areas where Israel expected guerrillas to attack.

On another day I took a cab into the occupied territories to Nablus to photograph two Arab poets, one being Fadwa Tuqan, who had told the *Washington Post* writer of her pessimism for peace. "I think everyone is preparing for another war," she said. After one day in Tel Aviv to photograph Israeli Independence Day celebrations, I flew to Alta, Norway, one hundred miles north of the Arctic Circle, and met up with a tourist representative. He took me forty miles east to meet a Sámi family who lived in tents but managed their great reindeer herds with snowmobiles. From Alta, I flew to the fishing town of Stokmarnes, where I went out with a three-man fishing crew for the day. In the evening we had coffee and sandwiches in their dock office. I took my favorite photo of all time, a Vermeer-like shot of the three men having coffee and smoking.

I turned the rest of the trip into a travel adventure by different conveyances. I went thirty miles by bus toward the port of Svolvær, got out, and walked the last twenty miles. (I'd sent my bag on ahead.) On that six-hour hike, I saw only seven cars. Full of good pain, I found a simple hotel where I plunked my bone-tired body in front of the lounge TV. It was showing grainy images of the Kent State University shootings on that day, May 4, 1970. Shaken, I continued my journey the next day by ferry to Bodø, then by overnight train to Trondheim, whence I flew to Bergen, then Copenhagen, and home to Chicago.

I had three photo stories from each country. I had earned my pay!

I got back to Chicago in time for my exhibit of Parris Island photos at the Art Institute. There were good crowds and good press reviews. Chris was still in Chicago, and my parents flew up from Texas for the show and, incidentally, to meet her. On his return, my father wrote the following letter:

> Reflections of the eventful week-end you gave us linger on with undiminished pleasure. It was a rare occasion.
>
> To know that your work is holding your attention and providing a basis for your ambitions is comforting and assuring. To realize that you have gone so far, on your own, makes the achievement the more noteworthy. I congratulate you.
>
> But even more important, I congratulate you for having Chris to share your thoughts, your ambitions and your happiness. She was a joy to be with and held up beautifully under the glare of four curious, though well-wishing Mares'. Soon I hope there will be an opportunity to see you both in Texas.
>
> Dad

When curator Hugh Edwards asked to keep my prints in the museum's permanent collection, I was on cloud nine.

Shortly after Labor Day, before Chris went back to Berkeley, we took my vacation time and drove from Chicago to Vermont, a state she had never visited and where I had gone only once, to ski during college. Our only reference point was a restored red farmhouse owned by Dick and Nancy Hooker, just north of the town of St. Johnsbury in the state's so-called Northeast Kingdom. Dick was a retired American history professor at Roosevelt University in Chicago and a friend of Chris's parents. We hoped to use their house as a base to hike and camp through the three surrounding counties. But heavy rains washed out those excursions, and so we welcomed the Hookers' beds, meals, and conversation. Dick had written a well-received cookbook on chowder, and was then working on a more ambitious history of eating in America.

St. Johnsbury, a town of about eight thousand, we learned, was founded after the Revolution and remained the only town in the nation with that name. The town appeared on world maps after the 1830s, when three Fairbanks brothers invented the industrial platform scale, first to weigh hemp but then almost anything, from mail to iron ingots and sheep feed. Members of the Fairbanks family endowed the town with employment for over one hundred years and two magnificent public structures: the Fairbanks Museum & Planetarium, and the Athenaeum, a combined public library and art gallery. (Eventually, between Chris and me, we would serve on the two boards for almost thirty years.)

"You know," Dick said, "Vermont is becoming quite a destination for your generation. For fifty years, it's been summer people like us, academics, artists, poets, playwrights, retired State Department officers, and the like. Now that's changing. Younger people are coming and staying year-round. The politics are changing. We just had the first Democratic governor in a hundred years through the sixties. The legislature is both more progressive and more honest than in Illinois."

Dick kept going. "You could write here just as well as in Chicago. I don't know about the photographs. Go look around, see what you see. Maybe this life would appeal to you. It would surely be a contrast."

Crazy! Chris and I weren't even married. But the rain was unending, so we hooked up with a local real estate agent and drove around for several days looking at one dreary, sodden property after another. In the second week of our desultory search, Dick reported that an abandoned farm just two miles from their house might be for sale. He had never actually seen it, for the owner, Sadie Roberts, was known to ward off the uninvited with a shotgun.

Roberts was in a nursing home and her guardian, Fairbanks Museum director Fred Mold, had told Dick of her readiness to put the property on the market.

The next day we went to take a look. In more rain, it looked as forlorn as most of the other properties we explored. The house and two barns were barely intact. Weeds grew everywhere. Broken windows, peeling paint, a garage and barns full of junk, and abandoned farm equipment, all under a glowering sky, was disheartening. When we came back the next day with full sun, the flaws were even more visible, but the views, including of the White Mountains forty miles to the east, were spectacular. For two nights we camped out in the hayloft of one barn and woke each morning to find someone's cows down below. We never got inside the house.

The Hookers continued their recruitment/publicity campaign with a dinner party including Fred Mold and his wife, a local lawyer, John Downs, and a family doctor, Jim Russell. Mold said he would not put the property on the market for several months, which gave us time to mull such a momentous move. I went back to the *Sun-Times* and Chris went back to Berkeley to study Czech and Old Church Slavonic.

Deciding whether to move to Vermont would have to wait for a fourteen-thousand-mile detour.

Chapter Six

Appointment in Amman (1971)

Profile of Zamil

That fall, as if Vermont were not enough to think about, I had another life-changing encounter. I was walking through the main quadrangle at the University of Chicago, about three blocks from my apartment. Striding toward me was—really?—my Harvard junior tutor, Prof. William Polk. "Prof. Polk, what are you doing here?" He had become the president of the Adlai Stevenson Institute of International Affairs (ASIIA), a research center based at the iconic Frank Lloyd Wright House in Hyde Park, two blocks from my apartment.

"And you?" he said.

My Desert Garb

Barchan Sand Dunes

Feast in Buraydah

Rashid, One of Our Companions

Wilfred Thesiger, One of the Great Desert Travelers at Home in London, 1974

Drinking Coffee

Elders Hosting Our Visit at the Emir's Palace in Hail

Making a Camel Saddle

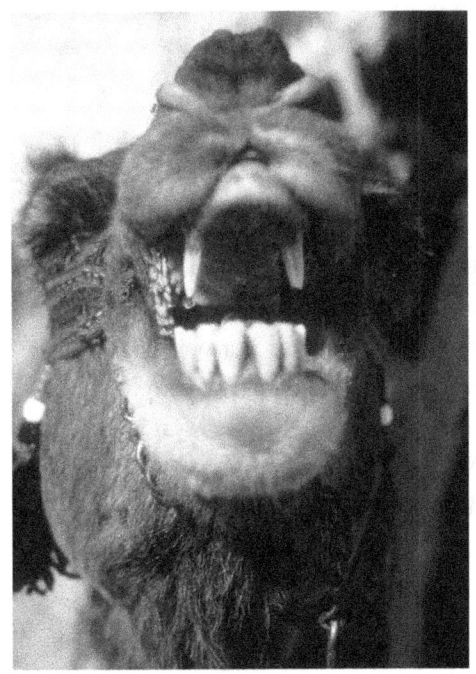
My Camel

Gathering Firewood

With Bill Polk and Members of the Badia

"Oh, I'm working as a photographer for the Sun-Times."

He did a double take. Then he asked, "How would you like to ride camels twelve hundred miles across Arabia?"

"Holy moly!" I said. "Sure! When?" The words poured out of him like a lecture:

> Since I began teaching Arabic, I have wanted to taste some desert travel like the explorers of the nineteenth and early twentieth centuries, St. John Philby, Richard Burton, and Wilfred Thesiger. I've obtained provisional permission from the Saudi government to ride across the northern Nafud desert from Riyadh to Amman, Jordan. I can only get away from the institute for about six weeks, not enough time for the much harder treks across the Empty Quarter in the south, but still 'deserted' enough.
>
> My winning proposal to King Faisal and his aides was to do a modern translation of a famous pre-Islamic poem, 'The Golden Ode,' and illustrate it with photographs. There are seventy-two verses. Thus, I need seventy-two photos and a cover. The University of Chicago Press will publish it. You already know something about the Middle East. You don't need to speak any Arabic, just take good pictures for every verse. What do you say?

I thought about it for about ten seconds and said, "Yes!" I floated home and called Chris with a "You're not going to believe this!" She was happy but cautioned, "Just don't get lost and miss our wedding!" (We'd become engaged earlier that year.)

I was able to get a leave from the *Sun-Times*, and over the next six months, I used my spare time to read accounts of previous travelers, study geography, buy two hundred rolls of black-and-white and color film, and assemble an array of cameras and lenses, including an underwater camera for possible sandstorms. Along with several very dated maps ("Terrain features incomplete" was one ominous inscription), we took two rifles, three compasses, and a sextant, good sleeping bags for chilly nights, dried food, pemmican. We would dress like Bedouins on a route no Westerner had traveled in a hundred years. (Remember: there was no GPS to guide us.)

In the then-dusty Saudi capital of Riyadh, we spent a week in further preparations and defending our trip from the polite yet insistent cautions of government officials. "We can certainly lend you the camels, but wouldn't you rather take a truck? It's safer." We certainly didn't want our bleached bones to embarrass them. Back and forth, back and forth we went. "A truck is no adventure," Polk kept saying. The Saudis finally relented and found us both camels and guides.

However, the camels were a pretty scrawny bunch, and the guides, all cousins, had not ridden or owned camels for years. Further, neither species had ever traveled this route before; it would be us and our compasses. The prince of Riyadh, perhaps to test us, said, "If you are going to travel the old way, you need some other companions," and he presented us with a saluki dog and a hunting falcon! (They became too burdensome, and we passed them on to the emir of Buraydah six days out.)

The point Prof. Polk kept making to the Saudis was that this trip was a bit of both history and literature, with adventure thrown in. We would be revisiting an oral tradition at the moment just before the rise of Islam when the Arabs would want and need a written language to carry the new globe-circling religion of Islam. As it were, we were "present at the creation." Prof. Polk intended the volume to be a coffee-table-style book with fine Arabic calligraphy done in Cairo, his English translation and exegesis, and my photos, one for each verse. How could they resist?

As we set off, we were intellectually aware of how little camel travel still existed, but between the guides' ignorance and the government's polite warnings, we wondered if the open road beckoned, or threatened.

The first few days was like a rocky marriage, getting used to the camels' temperament and gait. This was not like posing for a tourist photo atop one of the beasts in front of the Great Sphinx. The camels' legs seemed to move in an animal form of independent suspension. They weren't called ships of the desert for nothing. We were literally seasick for a day or two, and also sore, being tossed this way and that. But I discovered that if I could walk one-quarter or one-third of the time, I loosened my muscles. What's more, the walking gave a whole different visual perspective, where your gaze was horizontal rather than downward.

And my job was to take photos for all seventy-two verses of the poem, verses like:

> And so I stopped, asking them, but now can our questions [get answers]? Deaf things, rocks of the ages. Their speech is not intelligible.
>
> I bid up the price of the wine in every blackened aging skin or tar-smeared pot whose seal had been broached and deflowered.
>
> They do not follow [the lead of lesser men], nor will their deeds prove sterile.
>
> Their guarded reserve does not incline with mere caprice.
>
> A rough and rowdy crowd, as quick to spring in anger to vengeance as though they were Jinn of the desert, whose feet stride forth proudly.

Early in the trip, perhaps stunned into happy disbelief just to be on such a trip and momentarily bored by the landscape, I burst into song. I think it was "The Song of the Volga Boatmen."

The Bedouins looked at me and smiled. "Bulbul!" said one, and the others laughed; Polk too. "It means 'nightingale,'" he said. For the rest of the trip I was "Bulbul," and Polk became "Abu George," or "Father of George"(his son's name).

We intended to let the camels forage for themselves, hobbling them each night to prevent straying. Our camels kept their heads down, ever alert for what scraps of vegetation they could find. Seen from afoot, they looked like big, brown mine detectors, as they searched out any plant higher than a few inches. We named my camel Lunchbox because her eating habits were Darwinian. She would wait until she saw another camel inspecting a choice plant, then throw a wide body block on the unsuspecting sister and take for herself the bush, leaves, thorns, and all. She was the only one of our original camels to make it all the way to Amman.

As the trip progressed, Bill talked about how the poetry reflected the ritual and discipline of daily activities. Survival in the desert depended on the virtues of generosity, manliness, and one's loyalty to the clan. In these fixed patterns and routines, the Bedouin found variations on ancient themes and rituals, as in the pounding of the coffee beans and cardamom seeds in a brass mortar and pestle, the sound of which became our alarm clock, at 4:30 each morning.

Each night settled into a rough routine. First, a self-appointed saqi, or host, would pound coffee beans and cardamom in a brass mortar and pestle. He then brewed the coffee in a brass *dallah* and pour dozens of cups for his fellows, including Bill and me. Any time I wished, I could withdraw to my diary and just watch the ensuing conversations. Each evening I tried to read parts of the poem to seat its imagery in my head so that in the coming days I could fulfill Eudora Welty's happy observation: "A photograph keeps a moment from running away."

But watching the conversations was fun too. Each Bedouin told his stories differently, with different inflections, gestures, and emphasis. Over time their personalities emerged.

Zamil and Rachid, both about forty, were our favorites. We were drawn to their desert-weathered faces, their cheerful readiness to work, and their intelligence. Sultan, just released from prison, was the most elemental, the most primitive of the four (all of whom were related). Twig thin, and not too bright, he was the head guide's patsy, always stuck with the most distasteful jobs. His limited mind concealed a streak of gratuitous cruelty, which surfaced whenever he drove our lame camel.

Our bête noir was Huwaimil, the chief guide. Short and fat, definitely a settled Bedouin, he delegated tasks to everyone but himself. He could strut like a sergeant, but never shared the work. He also had the dismaying habit of preparing for every task by invoking Allah's mercy. "Allah karim!" ("God will provide!") He seemed far more interested in hunting bustards with the gift falcon than in getting us across the desert.

There was another private point of this journey. I wanted to explore the desert roots of my faith. If Christ could spend forty days in the desert, I could do thirty-five. I wanted to *feel* the desert, its privations, the reduction of every action and movement to its bare necessities. It was a private pilgrimage, full of solitude. I felt on the edge of a bowl, as finite as a grain of sand and simultaneously as infinite as the universe that domed over us. I never talked religion with Bill. He was at most a happy agnostic. Our own Bedouin companions were fitfully diligent in their prayers, and only upped the number when we got lost and ran out of water.

On this trip we were never in physical danger from other humans. Incompetence, yes, but no malice. Fortunately, this journey came before the rise of Palestinian Islamic Jihad, even before the Sunni-Shia war between Iraq and Iran.

On the fifteenth day, we limped into Ha'il, capital of the Nejd district of the kingdom. Immediately to the north lay the first sand stretch of the great Nafud. The route ahead lay through genuine desert, i.e., wasteland, inhabited only by nomads whose whereabouts could not be predicted. There would be no more occasional settlements or marked trails. For nine days we would have to maintain a course of 330 degrees north-northwest or risk missing the only wells on the whole desert.

Like the officials in Riyadh, the emir of Ha'il also tried to dissuade us from what he deemed a fool's errand. But we declined. We did accept his offer of a local guide, several new camels, water bags, and five kilos of his best dates. That guide, however, had only crossed the Nafud once, and that had been by truck ten years before, traveling in the opposite direction. Would the blind lead the blind?

In preparation for this most arduous stretch, we reduced our equipment to what we considered bare essentials. We focused on the details because by now we realized our Bedouin companions relied more on faith than on foresight. Their repeated mutters of "Allah karim" ("God is merciful; God will provide") placed too much reliance upon the Almighty for our faith and safety.

Our first day in the Nafud put us quickly into a region of craggy and forbidding hills. The area had been the favorite haunt of the famed eighteenth-century land pirate Ibn Rachid, and we fantasized about raiding parties lurking in the rocky fastnesses on either side of the trail. But none of his descendants appeared.

We made camp that night in sight of the famed red sands that marked the true beginning of the Nafud. Finding no firewood for our cooking, we were dispatched to hunt for shirtfuls of camel dung. To the great amusement of the Bedouins, I proudly delivered my share of nonflammable sheep dung. We baked some bread in the coals and that, along with dates, coffee, and tea, was our dinner. Polk was tired and went straight for his sleeping bag, but I allowed myself the pleasure of the campfire.

On these evenings, before sleep came, we would muse about the stars, the clouds scudding past, the journey, the exquisite pain of camel riding, and each other's lives. We were companions yet individuals, possessors and possessed.

Around those campfires, I learned more of Prof. Polk's Texas roots in Fort Worth, that his ancestors included President James K Polk. He told me about his brother George, a CBS news correspondent who was murdered in Greece during the Greek Civil War, and how he then took a year off from Harvard to learn what happened and how he was warned by CIA director William Donovan to desist. I observed the striking coincidence that at about the same time (1948) that he was butting heads with Donovan, my mother had solicited him to write a foreword to her book about Communism, *Know Your Enemy*. Prof. Polk talked more about his service in the government as a Middle East specialist on the Policy Planning Staff of the State Department.

"Did you ever dream of being secretary of state?"

There was just a short pause. "No, I don't think I'm much of a team player. I like being a critic from the outside of both Republican and Democratic administrations. And I've got more books to write. And you, Bulbul, what are your plans?"

"Gosh," I said, "they are evolving as I speak. It's getting hard to think of going back to the same job at the *Sun-Times*, fun as it is. The purity and isolation of this place doesn't make for balanced decisions. Another book, maybe. The isolation of this trip has me thinking about one I might write. I'd call it *Solitary Men*, about men in jobs where they work alone. For example, fisherman, fire tower warden, sheep herder, truck driver, etcetera. But first I have to get married! I hope you'll come." As the embers crackled their last, we drifted off to sleep.

After a hard day in which the local guide kept deferring to the imperious Huwaimil, we spent the night in a Bedouin sheep sty in Jubbah, the last tiny settlement before the central Nafud. We awoke to the noise of bleating sheep and a new misfortune. One of our camels had pulled up lame. While the rest of us filled water bags and saddled the camels, two men removed a cluster of stones from the injured hoof and sewed a thick leather patch over the entire foot. Only after this flat tire was repaired did we load that camel and get underway.

Other disturbing events followed. The local guide admitted that he was lost. Meanwhile, the sky took on a dull reddish-brown-tan cast, like the sand itself, and the light became so flat and diffuse that we could not distinguish even nearby terrain features. Every depression seemed to shelter the ominous white bones of a sheep or camel.

Suddenly, I noticed a trail of what appeared to be water drops behind three camels. I played all sorts of mind games as I tried to avoid the obvious implication. "Don't worry!" said Huwaimil, with regal unconcern. "We overfilled the skins; they will seal themselves." His explanation seemed as lame as the injured camel. Those drops did continue, and each morning the water bags looked slacker.

That evening, a sudden rainstorm and wind ripped at our garments and soaked our heavy farwas (sheepskin coats). The next morning our spirits soared when the morning sun revealed a desert blooming. This was the first rain in three years, the guide said. I grabbed a camera to frame the glorious scene. Awakened by the rain, the valleys had bloomed overnight with millions of tiny yellow, violet, and white flowers. Then, by noon the sun departed this lovely stage, and by midafternoon the flowers were gone.

That night we followed a Bedouin custom and sat on a ridge to watch the lightning flashes in the distance. In the old days, the Bedouin had a highly practical reason for this: The lightning showed them where rains were falling and hence, where to take their flocks for grazing the next day.

We were deep in the Nafud now, in an area filled with the region's most characteristic feature, the fulges. These were cavernous depressions, often two hundred feet deep, with a seventy-degree slope on the southwest, or windward side. This base is flat and then slopes gradually to the northeast. Nobody knows exactly how they were formed. From above they look like the hoofprints of a running horse, or lumbering camel.

On the edge of one of these fulges, we came upon a Bedouin camp, the first people we had seen since Jubbah—three men, four women, and a slew of children from a family of the Ruwallah tribe. Polite and gentle, they invited us to share their food. We, in turn, shared what we had—medicine. When one woman complained of a stomach ailment and her husband showed us a nasty cut on his leg, "Dr. Polk" dispensed nostrums from his kit, along with advice.

Next morning found us on a featureless plain so barren the Arabs speak of it as "the back of a shield." Heat waves rippling on the horizon reminded me of the opening scene in *Lawrence of Arabia*, but no Omar Sharif or any other figure appeared on the horizon. The ground was so hard, animal tracks did not register.

A critical moment was approaching. We had enough flour for one more day's bread and some doughballs for the camels, three liters of bottled water, and maybe three more liters in one water bag. The camels' shrinking humps signaled their increasing thirst. We needed to reach the wells at Ash-Shaqiq by tomorrow, or . . .

All day we plodded northwest in the hot sun. The six of us spread out across a front of three hundred to four hundred yards to cover as much area as possible. In the absence of landmarks and animal signs, we began to doubt even the compasses. Where were those wells? And would they appear as some verdant, leafy oasis? About 4:30 in the afternoon, we heard a shout from the far-right flank. It was Huwaimil, signaling that he had found the wells. He was sitting at the edge of a bone-dry watering trough. There were no trees or any other sign of human activity, just the same arid territory we had traversed for eight days.

"Where's the water?" we asked. Huwaimil pointed to a tiled hole in the ground about a foot across. We dismounted and peered into the opening. No water was visible. I took a stone of about half a pound and dropped it. Distantly, there came a faint splash. We tried another stone, and counted, "One thousand one, one thousand two, one thousand three—" *Splash*.

"OK, Huwaimil, where's the rope and bucket?" asked an annoyed Prof. Polk.

"I have none."

Polk was livid. "Do you mean you brought us out here knowing we'd go this distance without water and these would be the only wells in the area and you brought neither bucket nor rope?" When Prof. Polk translated, I felt homicidal. After the first wave of rage passed, he hissed, "In our country we don't say 'God will provide,' we say 'God helps those who help themselves.' Just get out of our goddamn way, and we'll go on by ourselves." Among the gear the foresighted Prof. Polk had packed was about 170 feet of parachute cord and a small collapsible canvas bucket.

Carefully securing one end of the rope around my waist and the other to the bucket, we weighed down the bucket with a pound of stones and lowered it until it touched water, and sank. There was seven feet of cord left aboveground. Then, for an hour we hauled up bucket after bucket of water for the camels until they were sated and we refilled our saddle bags. Huwaimil had the gall to pipe up, "Allah karim!" My shoulders ached and Polk wrenched his back, but we didn't notice the pain until that evening. Happily, we were now pretty sure we had enough water to get to the real settlement of Sakākā, two days' travel. That gave us the confidence to tell our trusty native "guides" to get lost. We spent the night by ourselves, one hundred yards from the guides. I missed the regular evening coffee, but sending Huwaimil to Coventry was more satisfying.

Of course, we knew we could not really abandon them. The next morning, we made peace with all the guides except Huwaimil. Bill made him ride at the rear of our little caravan. We rode hard that day and the next, hunting vegetation that never appeared, fighting a fierce wind that blew for two days straight. Sand penetrated everywhere—bedding, clothing, the medicine kit, the cameras, and, crunchiest, our meals of bread, dates, rice, onions, and spices.

As we approached Sakākā, we came upon a Bedouin shepherd, with a truck and a transistor radio. He offered us coffee. As we sat in the shade of his vehicle, his curiosity bested his traditional polite suspicion. "Where have you come from?"

"From Riyadh," we said, rather proudly. (About a thousand miles by then.)

"Oh, how marvelous! You are riding in the old way. Stay for lunch. I'll slaughter a sheep." We demurred, saying we had to get to Sakākā, to which he replied with (to him) unassailable logic, "If you eat with me, I'll take you there in my truck." Again we declined.

Our host was more modern than we wanted to be. So were most of his fellow Bedouins. We were fortunate to have sampled a slice of his nearly extinct culture, and we were elated to have completed the trek in the face of so much contrary advice. One of the joys was that, like the glee club trip to the Far East, we were giving something in return for the magic of the adventure—a book about the culture of our hosts, the Bedouin. We were not just taking.

Although it would be eight more days to Amman through different terrain and country and among different people, our spiritual odyssey ended the day we emerged from the desolate intimacy of the great sandy desert called Nafud.

Little did we realize that in less than three years, the empty, ominous Nafud would begin to be crisscrossed by some roads, more settlements, the hum of oil-seeking crews. There would be fewer camels there than wild mustangs in the American West, and no traveler would be dependent upon finding obscure water wells for survival.

We didn't have jihadists to worry about. Our rifles were good only for target practice, not defense. We learned to shed comforts for the purity of the experience, to taste the unknown in very small cupfuls. And I had to document it all with lens and film.

Two days later we reached the Jordanian border, unsure how we would cross and then get to Amman. We knew the government was still fighting against Palestinian Black September fighters. Maybe we would be turned away.

Instead, we were met by four members of the Badia, or Desert Legion, who introduced themselves as our escorts into Amman. In their splendid khaki-and-scarlet uniforms, they were as impressive as Buckingham Palace guards. Astride our worn and scrawny beasts, filthy and shaggy ourselves, we felt like poor relations as we moved into the Hashemite kingdom. Under their protection, we rode on in our northwesterly course through areas of increasing vegetation and population density.

On our final night, we rode until past midnight and finally made camp along a tiny stream. The moon was half full, just light enough to outline the Badia police ghosting along on their huge beasts, the only sound the padding of the camel hooves. For a moment, we felt immortal.

Late the next day, we rode into Muagre, an Amman suburb.

There we left our redoubtable camels and Badia companions. Two enlisted Jordanian army men took over and packed us and our gear into a jeep. Between the soldiers was a box of hand grenades and two submachine guns. There was fighting in the city, they said.

But we arrived at the American embassy without incident to meet Hume Horan, a political officer and former student of Prof. Polk's, for a shower and a beer. After a few days' rest, during which I got to play squash with Peter Jennings of ABC News, we flew back to Riyadh to thank King Faisal, who, in an unsmiling manner, seemed impressed.

Then it was on to Beirut, Lebanon, where we had lunch with a journalist friend of Polk's, John Cooley, the Middle East correspondent for *The Christian*

Science Monitor. He was fascinated by our trip and scribbled away as we gushed about our adventure. Two days after we got home, there appeared on the *Monitor*'s front page an article titled "Vanishing Camels." That was cool! I'd had my photos appear in the *Monitor*, and Polk and I were fodder for a news story (and a later full-page spread of my photos).

More dramatically, a week later came a letter from the prestigious publishing house of Alfred A. Knopf. A senior editor wrote to ask if we would like to do a book about our trip (separate from "The Golden Ode"). Quick thinkers we were. Yes, of course! I selected photos and Prof. Polk spun out three to four thousand words of vivid prose, and we sent off the package. In two weeks, Knopf came back with a contract, and just like that, we were to write two books about one trip. Oh, our ego garments were gaudy, indeed!

Adding to the excitement, my book on Parris Island, *The Marine Machine*, arrived in bookstores the same month, to good reviews across the country. I remember going into a big downtown bookstore where the clerks had placed a stock of the books on a front table. I began signing each one modestly, but with a certain flourish, when a clerk rushed up to say, "You can't do that!"

"Why not?" I said. "They are mine!" Sheepishly, he began affixing "Signed by the author" stickers.

How different Chicago looked, and the States felt, after the privations and purity of the desert! The traffic, the noise, the clothing, the buildings, the cars, the food, the infinitude of Lake Michigan's water, the plenitude of stuff. Polk was aghast at a closet full of suits, when he'd been in one thoub (Arab dress) for forty days.

Gradually, I adjusted to the paper again, feeling like an exotic zoo animal for several days, then was accepted back into the fold of bipeds. But being so far away from the Midwest in body and spirit had broken the mystic bonds to the city and its people. It wasn't Chicago's fault. I had lots of good friends there; I'd begun a dual career in journalism there. But I was still restless. The desert's slow pace had lured me toward more adventures, to do something else.

Now came a flurry of decisions. Chris and I confirmed our marriage plans. We decided I would leave the *Sun-Times* and Chicago to buy the farm in Vermont and set up as a freelance writer-photographer with an agent suggested by Ash Green of Knopf. Becoming a Vermont writer did not seem so far-fetched with one book out and three more in the works, not to mention the elusive "next one." And maybe I could take Polk up on his Stevenson Institute fellowship offer.

In May, Chris (now with her newly minted master's degree in Slavonic Languages) and I packed up and headed for Vermont, leaving some great experiences at the paper and abroad but also taking a gift from cartoonist Bill Mauldin, a signed copy of his recent cartoon showing a parson blessing newlyweds: "I Now Pronounce You Man and Mrs."

Chapter Seven

Vermont; Chicago; West Virginia; East Africa; and Back to Vermont (1971–74)

In early June 1971, Chris and I pulled a small U-Haul across Michigan, Ontario, and New York to the farm in St. Johnsbury. I was still in the middle of working on the three desert books. For a week we lived in the hayloft of one barn while carpenters and plumbers made the house livable. Although Sadie Roberts's son had taken whatever he thought he could sell, a lot of detritus remained—enough to fill twelve U-Hauls of garbage, broken furniture, newspapers, appliances, and several wheels of cheese left in the derelict refrigerator. In the debris, however, there were some treasures—sixty copies of *Life* magazine from the 1930s, a couple of handsome wooden chests, two rocking chairs, two beds, a straw beehive skep. Also, we found three leather-bound account books from the 1840s onto whose pages generations of Roberts children and wives had pasted newspaper and magazine articles and schoolwork from the 1860s and 1870s.

I created enough space for a desk and chair for writing in a back room, away from the distracting fifty-mile view of the White Mountains to the east. We assured ourselves there was no skeleton in the attic as our neighbor Joe Bedor had suggested, with a twinkle in his eye, because there was no attic, only a tin roof over two upstairs rooms. Fred Mold, the museum director, let me use the quite serviceable darkroom in the museum basement. Through the summer we entertained a parade of guests, whom we, Tom Sawyer–like, put to work scraping, painting, and hauling.

Our wedding at the end of August included some thirty-five people. It was not lavish, and cost maybe a thousand dollars, including the food and our lost wax wedding rings that Chris had bought in Berkeley, but it did have unusual charm. First, we postponed it for a day, when a hurricane blew through the Kingdom. On that day, all the young people fled downtown to Caplan's Army Store to buy a variety of nonmatching hats. On the following day, one couple flew over from New York in a seaplane. Another guest was a friend of my parents, the astronaut Rusty Schweickart from Apollo 9. He had checked out a T-33 in Houston and flew into Burlington. Three friends from the *Sun-Times* made their way to the event, and all four parents and four siblings came. John Tweedle came as both best man and wedding photographer. We added a dozen or so local friends we had met. We all climbed up a hill above the house where there was a 360-degree view from the Green Mountains in the west to the White Mountains in the east.

Chris read some folk advice from one of Sadie's account books. At Rusty's last-minute suggestion, I read e. e. cummings: "i thank You God for most this amazing day . . ." My father read a selection of his favorite aphorisms, such as "The harder I work, the luckier I get," and "The steam that toots the whistle never turned a wheel." My mother's cousin, Jim Nichols, a Presbyterian minister, married us. His daughter, Sue Nichols Miller, who had married one of my Harvard roommates, brought her son, Ben. The wedding feast consisted of homemade bread, bowls of wild blackberries gathered by some of the guests, great blocks of Vermont cheddar cheese, and two cases of two-dollar champagne. The star of the show was bagpiper David Grieve of Beebe, Quebec, who piped the procession up

Chris and My Wedding on St. Johnsbury Hilltop, 1971

the hill and gave impromptu (and hilarious) lessons on his pipes.

Two days later, Mrs. John Gray, who wrote the socials for the Stark District in the *Caledonian-Record* (for a dollar an inch of copy), made sure just about all the guests were named, and added flourishes, such as "Rusty Schweickart, who had walked in space."

Low-Grade Homesteading

After a post-wedding victory lap to Washington, DC, to see many of Chris's family friends from the Foreign Service, we returned to the farm for work on the sills, painting the roof, and everything in between.

While I worked on my Arabian book projects, we waded into the country life, and made all kinds of rookie mistakes. To heat the house with wood, we bought an underpowered chain saw and cut down the wrong kinds of trees. A neighbor gave us a quick tutorial in ash, maple, and birch and advised us to buy a short-bladed, heavy-duty Jonsered chain saw, which made all the difference for the next thirty years. We tried making maple syrup that turned out as black, thick, and tasty as engine oil. We tempted fate with a leaky central chimney. We bought a snowblower we didn't really need since the town snowplow came practically to the doorstep.

On the good side of the homesteading ledger, Chris's father turned out to be an excellent dowser when he took a metal coat hanger up the hill above the house to find the waterline from the spring to the house. We had to replace the old wooden pipes with new plastic ones. We put in a big garden with a tall fence to keep the deer out. We got chickens, geese, and two sheep named Howard and James, for my old journalist friend, Howard James.

Weather was not just a silly space filler for conversation, but something we learned to prepare for. When we went out on winter nights at below zero degrees, we learned to take along extra boots and sticks in case we had to walk the last half mile home. We debated the relative merits of tire chains, which worked but were hell to put on, or simply putting 150–200 pounds of concrete blocks in the trunk of the car. We were lucky that the town snowplow came to the doorstep, but sometimes even it failed to make the grade.

Our friendships were few but deep. They included the town manager,

American Gothic

Dave Clark, who tapped our maple trees and paid us back with syrup and hard cider. There was John Downs, our lawyer, Jim Russell, our doctor, and Fred Mold, the museum director. Chris got to know Harold Penniman, a retired postman who had delivered mail for fifty years, by horse, wagon, and Model T, all the way up the hill to Sadie's house. Harold collected furniture and duck decoys, four of which I bought from him. Our neighbors the Bedors were happy to cut our hayfields for their cows and sell us fresh milk. We became friends with Nat and Pat Tripp, fugitives from New York City, who helped us put in some new fencing, and in return, we helped them hay their fields. There was also Dudley Bell, the coach of the local college tennis team, who invited us to join late-afternoon doubles games, with half a dozen academics and writers.

Without advertising, we became a destination resort for friends from New York, Boston, and further climes. They were bemused by our decidedly non-suburban digs, staying for a few days of hiking or skiing, cold sheets, and lots of root vegetables. One of them was John Kifner of the *New York Times*, whom I had met in Chicago when he was covering the Democratic

Work on the Farmhouse. Not Much Left of the Dining room

Our First Sheep

Convention. Kifner was now the *Times'* New England bureau chief and would go on to hold the so-called Homer Bigart Chair, named for a 1960s *Times* reporter who kept a bag always packed like a paratrooper to head out for stories here and abroad. John would build up weeks of compensatory time from covering extended distant and sometimes dangerous stories, then visit us on extended hiking or skilling vacations of up to six or seven weeks.

Bees and Beers

Two of our best new friends were Arnold and Betty Waters. Arnold was a geologist who had traveled the world in search of gold and diamonds. His family originally came from Vermont, and now he and Betty had retired to the nearby village of Lower Waterford. Coincidentally, Betty had known my mother at Bryn Mawr, and when Mom visited they had an instant bond.

A beekeeper in his youth, Arnold soon set up an apiary of fifteen to twenty beehives behind his house. Once he had his own hives under control, he became a benevolent pied piper of beekeeping, by counseling aspiring beekeepers across the county. I became one of those pupils. With a missionary's passion, he told me what equipment to order and then showed me how to assemble the pieces. "Don't buy just one hive," he counseled. "If they are healthy, the bees will naturally increase. If one hive swarms, you can split the remaining hive into two. Always work with the bees, not against them. That means tending them on sunny days when they are working. When the weather's bad, they don't fly and when they're stuck in their hive, they get peppery."

I would learn that "peppery" covered a range of apicultural truculence. Arnold usually worked barehanded, but always with a smoker and veil. Getting stung came with the territory. Once I saw him take six stings on an arm in a matter of seconds. All he did was grunt, and calmly scrape off the stingers and poison sacs with his hive tool as if they were pieces of lint. Arnold taught me how to collect swarms of bees. He usually carried a spare hive body, complete with interior frames and top and bottom board, and an old sheet in the back of his car in case he was called to "come over and get these damn bees out of here!"

Arnold also comforted me one fall when a bear tornadoed through my two hives. He looked at the devastation scattered like sticks among the goldenrod stalks and said, "It's too bad, but you just have to start over." Arnold's specialty was honey in the comb, that is, four-and-a-half-inch square frames of basswood with wax foundation onto which the bees built their comb and filled the cells with honey. These boxes were taken straight from the hive and packaged in cellophane and individual cardboard boxes. This was honey straight from the bee to you, and the wax was as much a part of the product as rinds were in orange marmalade.

From the first day I tasted Arnold's comb honey, I vowed to produce my own. Sure, to produce this style of honey, one had to crowd the bees and invite swarming. But this kind of honey was, as Arnold put it, "one of nature's masterworks." Arnold urged me to subscribe to at least one beekeeping magazine. He bought me the first of what would be scores of beekeeping books, *The ABC & XYZ of Bee Culture*.

"But don't get pulled from pillar to post by too much conflicting advice," he told me. "Work out your own system. Remember, beekeepers are like lawyers—six beekeepers, seven opinions."

My second enduring homesteading adventure was to brew my own beer. The mid-1970s were the nadir of American brewing, with fewer than sixty breweries in business across the land. Except for a declining number of regional breweries, America was the land of bland "hop pop." Imports from Europe and Latin America gave some relief, but many people longed for more and began to make their own.

I was among that cohort. Unfortunately, unlike in beekeeping, I had no mentor. Moreover, equipment and ingredients, even recipes, were almost nonexistent. When my first two batches exploded from too much carbon dioxide pressure, I had to make a choice. Do I continue with my sometimes dangerous do-it-yourself experiment, or go back to American beers that tasted as if they had been brewed through a horse?

Fortunately, I kept at the craft and, as Paul Harvey would say, "the rest of the story" would become a lifetime of brewing and drinking home brew and craft beers. Between 1973 and 2023, the US brewery count went from fifty in 1973 to over nine thousand in 2023. And I would help to document that brewing revolution.

The Adlai Stevenson Institute

As I was finishing my parts of the two desert books, I also worked on a children's book about the desert trip. I packed it with some adventures from our trip and then went to the well of imagination. *Footprints in the Sand*, and its twelve-year-old protagonist, Abdul, appealed to my agent, Joan Raines, who promised to look for an illustrator and a publisher.

But then Polk asked me what was next for adults. "If you come up with a good idea," he said, "I'll give you a fellowship at the institute." Boy, that sounded cool.

The Adlai Stevenson Institute of International Affairs was established in 1965 as a memorial to the recently deceased former governor, presidential candidate, and UN ambassador. As its first president, Polk had collected a number of academics, journalists, and researchers from many disciplines to do work that varied in intensity and subject matter. He had turned it into a sort of private think tank. In the years 1970 to 73, some of the fellows were former UN secretary general U Thant, ecologist Barbara Ward, journalists David Halberstam and Neil Sheehan, columnist Murray Kempton, political radical Eqbal Ahmad, Egyptian architect Hassan Fathy, and others. The fellows gathered monthly to present their works in progress. How exciting it would be to spend time among such distinguished figures. Could I think of something up to their level?

Credit: University of Chicago *Maroon*

With New York Times Reporter, David Halberstam, at the Stevenson Institute, Chicago, 1973

I thought. While still at the *Sun-Times* I had begun discussing a book about an Appalachian coal mining town with a sociologist at the University of Chicago, Tony Platt. The idea was to use the model of Ronald Blythe's *Akenfield: Portrait of an English Village*, where Tony would do the interviews and I would do the photographs. Then Tony had gone off to teach at the University of California, and I had gone east. The collaboration withered. Now, the idea snuck back into my consciousness to do it solo.

A clutch of books now helped refine the idea. I was reading psychiatrist-writer Robert Coles's volume *Migrants, Sharecroppers and Mountaineers*, especially focused on Appalachian coal-mining families. That got me to look again at the James Agee–Walker Evans classic *Let Us Now Praise Famous Men*, with its combination of words and photographs about Alabama sharecroppers in the 1930s. Another compelling book about that region was by Kentucky lawyer Harry Caudill, whose work *Night Comes to the Cumberlands* detailed the struggles of miners in Eastern Kentucky.

There was plenty of current news about the coalfields: the turmoil of intraunion corruption and rebellion, the battle over strip-mining vs. traditional underground mining, the recognition of a new miners' illness, black lung disease, which was more insidious than silicosis, which had long plagued miners. One insurgent leader and his wife were murdered in Pennsylvania. Now there was a group of insurgents trying again to topple members of the union leadership.

The year before, reporter Brit Hume had written a book about the bloody struggle in *Death and the Mines: Rebellion and Murder in the United Mine Workers*.

Maybe I could go spend time in one community and examine all these forces through the eyes of a small number of miners and their families. It would be something like my book on Parris Island, although there I was an observer to a fixed narrative, beginning middle and end. aHere, unlike Agee and Evans, I would do this mixture of journalism, art, and sociology alone.

Polk was hospitable to the idea and told me to write it up for submission. When I told Chris's father about the miners idea, he said that if West Virginia was in the search, I should contact his old friend Rep. Ken Hechler a Democratic congressman representing western and southern West Virginia. He and Fred Hadsel had been combat historians together during World War II. For five terms he had been a liberal thorn in the side of Republicans and the coal companies.

I wrote to Hechler with my idea. He immediately wrote back and invited us to come work on his reelection campaign in southern West Virginia to get a lay of the land.

The Hechler connection sealed the deal for Polk. Now, all I had to do was complete it.

Faces of Coal

Me After a Shift at the Stotesbury Mine

Miner

Miner

Miner

Miner

Miner

In May 1972, Chris and I drove down to West Virginia and joined the volunteers at Hechler's regional office in Beckley, the Raleigh county seat in southern West Virginia. The campaign office was based atop a bakery whose sweet, greasy, and none-too-fresh miasma filled the office day and night. For three weeks we ran errands, made copies, passed out fliers, went to rallies, and once or twice drove Ken between rallies. Mainly, however, we met dozens of people.

Hechler introduced us to members of the rebel Miners for Democracy and some of their civilian supporters, including Dr. Don Rasmussen, a local pulmonologist, who was crusading to establish the depredations of black lung disease.

From Beckley, we moved to Stotesbury, a village of two hundred people in a valley known as Winding Gulf, which early in the century had over fifty mines along a twenty-five-mile stretch. Only one remained, that of Eastern Gas and Fuel Associates. Its entrance was two hundred yards from the lodging we found: a very modest apartment in a very modest rooming house.

By living in the middle of the coalfields, I hoped that a story would emerge from all the intersecting forces of geography, politics, danger, economics, sociology, and personalities, all in a landscape so deep and dark the sun hardly penetrated.

Like a bucket brigade, the miners I met on the Hechler campaign passed me on to others, who passed me on to still more. All but two of the miners I interviewed lived away from the mine, requiring commutes of up to an hour. I can still see their faces. Junior Gilbert, who took me down into the mine, had broken bones too numerous to count and served up great squirrel stew. There was Harry Barnhardt, who had lost three fingers in mining accidents and who by July 1972 had figured out what Watergate was all about—"Nixon!" There was old man Ziegler, with a biblical beard, who had worked in mines for forty years and now needed five minutes to climb a set of stairs. When the Virginian Railrway set track down the valley, Ziegler had sung songs to set the rhythm for tie-laying crews. There was Major William Tams, the bachelor retired owner of another defunct mine, living in a house with eight thousand books and doing the daily *New York Times* crossword puzzle. There was Tracy Hylton, an unapologetic strip miner who sneeringly compared miner fatality rates above and below ground.

With equal measures of curiosity and caution, I went down into the eastern coal mine half a dozen times, claustrophobic, and jumpy at the sounds of blasting and the cracking timbers. I paid for those trips with pneumonia and coughed for three weeks. By that time, I had hundreds of black-and-white photographs from above and below ground.

It was lonely living among strangers, especially for Chris. We decided to get a dog, but no purebreds were for us. At the Raleigh County Humane society, an ill-kempt place with a lot of noise and strays, we found a loveable black-and-white-mutt puppy with big paws. "Gonna be a Saint Bernard," said the attendant. His price: two dollars with tax. Back at the apartment, the puppy pooped and piddled and howled and howled. But we overcame our annoyance when we realized that his wail sounded uncannily like the voice of a nocturnal marsupial in West Africa that howled the same way as it descended a tree, supposedly warning off predators. Its common name was a tree bear, and our puppy, soon a recognizable border collie cross, became probably the only Tree Bear in America. He lived with us through fourteen years and the birth of our two sons.

As I moved around the county interviewing miners, I was pleased with the photos. The personal stories were compelling as they talked about the miners' insurgency, the economy, strip-mining, and the black lung danger in the mines. But the more I got into the lives of the individual miners, the harder it was to weave in the larger issues of politics, medicine, and changing mining technology. The miners and their families treated me with invariable politeness and good humor, sharing their meals of game and fish and beer. I kept hoping a thesis would rise from the faces and lives and pages of notes. I was caught in a literary no-man's-land. I could aspire to Walker Evans's photo skills, but I didn't have any of Agee's literary ones.

One problem was that the heyday of underground mining was past. And my physical community was a skeleton. Stotesbury was not even a coherent municipality, certainly not a company town with a company store and scrip.

The "us" vs. "them" battles were within the union, between underground and strip-mining on the surface. Those battles were industry-wide, not in this one community. Finally, very few miners in Stotesbury's mine actually lived there. The rest commuted, up to an hour each way.

When I came to give my fellows report, "Faces of Coal," as I called it, I was able to cover all the major problems the miners and their families faced, with a selection of good photos above and below ground. But my lack of a strong message haunted me.

Among the Stevenson Fellows, the journalist Murray Kempton had become my closest friend. His writing style had been described as baroque, piling clause upon clause like Bach fugues. He read Proust in the original French. In temperament, he was gentle, and mean only to scoundrels. He would win a Pulitzer Prize in 1985 for his newspaper commentary. It was Murray who gently tolled the death knell for the book when he said:

"You probably know this and by now are sick of the topic. But you can't do this kind of a book with just one source, that is, twenty people saying roughly the same thing. The photos are powerful, but they aren't enough.

You've got their voices, but not your own."

Back in Vermont, I went ahead and finished the book. My agent, Joan Raines, wasn't as pessimistic as Murray. She thought it good enough to send it out to a succession of publishers, which she did. The manuscript would come back rejected one day by one publisher, and off it would go to another publisher on the next. Like most agents, her ego was not at stake.

But after eight submissions, even she gave up. It would be the first and last book I would do without some visceral desire or comfortable knowledge. I had been too ready to believe the photos would tell most of the story; I needed more context, and I needed a narrative, something that got readers to turn the page.

However, there was good news that year, for the two desert books came out and were received well by both public and academia. What's more, just as I wondered what was next, Polk stepped in.

Shift to Liberty and Africa

Another Fellow, Liberty Mhlanga of Rhodesia (now Zimbabwe), was developing a regional training seminar/conference to add an environmental perspective to development in the new sub-Saharan nations. Liberty had a degree in ecology from Clark University and a PhD from Colombia University. He had worked for Lady Barbara Ward and Maurice Strong at the first great United Nations Conference on the Human Environment in Stockholm. Liberty had already visited thirteen countries, sounding out their interest in such a gathering. His premise was the old environmental slogan "You can't do just one thing." His plan was to apply to a fictional country such skills and ideas as wildlife management, soil science, industrial and agricultural pollution remediation, renewable resources, etc. In this work the Stevenson Institute would pair up with the Nairobi think tank the Institute for Development Studies.

Bill Polk had realized that the project was simply too big for one person. He called to ask me to help Liberty with the logistics, perhaps some of the writing. He would extend my fellowship for another year. After a few days' thought, I said yes. If the miners' book never got published, I wanted something tangible to show for my work at the Stevenson Institute

(ASIIA).

In the winter of 1973–74, I spent two to three months in Chicago helping Liberty to assemble the conference, at a distance. For background reading, he assigned me a thousand-page collection of papers on ecology and the environment entitled *The Careless Technology*. (The term "climate" earns a two-page reference, with the aid "*See also* temperature and rainfall.")

From the day I arrived in Nairobi in January 1974, I knew the job would be more than arranging hotel rooms and sharpening pencils. In no uncertain terms, Maurice Strong, the head of the UN Environment Programme, which was now based in Nairobi, told us that this would be one of their first public projects. "We are now in the wide realm of international relations. We can't afford to have anything but a smashing success."

I signed up with the St. Johnsbury newspaper the *Caledonian-Record* to write biweekly dispatches about our work there as well as occasional touristy outings.

I immersed myself in the logistics: rent, meals, secretarial help, translators, fitful electricity, and small and large egos.

Even in a new building, there were character flaws, like the elevator. Not infrequently, the lift zipped skyward toward our offices on the seventeenth floor, slowed down as it approached the floor, then, with what sounded like a squeak of delight, descended to the fourteenth floor or squirted to the thirteenth. If I made it within two four floors away, I didn't push my luck—I got off and walked. Once we posted a notice on the inside control panel: "Press and pray!"

The conference itself was almost flawless. The sixty-four-dollar question, of course, was what would happen next. How soon would politics take over? We ended with a dozen questions, not answers. For example, "How can land capability estimates be included in national development plans?" "Should a developing country be allowed to become a 'pollution haven'?" "Should a developing nation go hell-bent on exploiting its nonrenewable resources now in hopes of developing renewable ones in the future?" "What should be the balance between rural and urban development?"

Now it was up to those people, nations, the UN Environment Programme, and the institute to follow up. How soon would politics take over? As one wag has said, "Technology says what can be done; economics says what should be done; and politics says what will be done."

Farewell to Polk

In the fall of 1974, after Liberty and I had presented our report, I said farewell to Bill Polk, who had also decided to leave the institute. He would move to Southern France, where he lived until he died in 2020. I visited him twice there, once with our son Tim in 1997 and once with Chris in 2018.

He was an intellectual polymath who supercharged my curiosity. He read voraciously. He wrote without stop, over twenty serious books on history, politics, and policy, from the founding of Israel to guerrilla war, from the history of diplomacy to a survey of the entire Middle East. He was a one-man university, minus the arts and sports, although he was a passable tennis player. He loved the good things of life, a lush garden, good food, good wine, a houseful of friends, and Old English sheepdogs. (He once had six at one time.)

He took me on the greatest adventure of my life, a sharing of the desert, its surprises, joys, and privations. The Texas and Harvard connections probably helped. We had both lost brothers. It wasn't just meeting the king of Saudi Arabia, or working in the same building with David Halberstam and Murray Kempton.

Polk had a tire-size Rolodex of friends. He dropped names like someone broadcasting seeds, but most of them did germinate. I did josh him that the difference between one of his friends and one of his old friends was about five minutes. We both loved true history and tall tales. One of Polk's favorite remarks was "The truth is a precious commodity, and you must use it sparingly." This admitted paraphrase of Mark Twain became one of my own favorites.

"Brilliant, but also courtly," is how I have described Polk to my friends. To me, he was always Abu George (father of George) and I was Bulbul (the nightingale).

Cooking a Literary Stew

With the miners and Abdul making the rounds of publishers, I thought maybe this was the time to try writing some fiction. We were surrounded by legions of literary talent. Maybe I could pick up ideas and talent through osmosis?

Just as we lived on the outskirts of the town of St. Johnsbury, we lived on the fringes of a diverse collection of artists and writers: poets Rachel Hadas, Galway Kinnell, and David Budbill; artists Claire Van Vliet and Val Hird, and the cartoonist Jeff Danziger; writers Ward Just, Geoffrey Wolff, Ted Hoagland, Don Bredes, Bill Lederer, and Howard Mosher.

I also toyed with the idea of graduate school or taking writers' workshops. But what portfolio did I have? Why should they take me on a handful of newspaper clips? Moreover, I was terrified at the thought of public criticism. I hated the idea of being in the mosh pit of other aspiring writers, being picked apart by niggling if honest comment, by the torture of a thousand literary cuts. It was silly and sophomoric, but there it was.

Was it Balzac who once said, "I invent my characters and then write the stories to see what happens to them"? "Write what you know!" spoke louder. Well, I'd done it with the nonfiction *Marine Machine*. But fiction asked me to create, to tap into my imagination, a heretofore unheard-of request. I gave myself three months, not enough to finish anything, of course, but to see if a story and characters had legs.

My first novel idea was to build a story around a country newspaper editor, à la Sinclair Lewis's *It Can't Happen Here*. The politics would be adjusted, but with Watergate reaching its climax, local political high crimes and misdemeanors might sell. I would bring the main action back to the village and town. To get some flavor, I hung out with a couple of weekly newspaper editors and read avidly of their products, especially the police blotters.

But I found it hard to build independent, believable characters and a compelling narrative. I couldn't decide whether to write it in the first or third person. The characters were all two-dimensional. The exercise gave me only one good image—describing a farm's milking barn lights at night as like a Halloween pumpkin's teeth.

In the previous summer, the visit of a Marine Corps buddy who had gone off o join the Peace Corps gave me a more plausible narrative. Conflating my own academic experience in Africa with imaginary ones in the field, I sketched out a narrative of a couple of returning Peace Corps volunteers, now married and moving to Vermont after a shattering (and depressing) experience in the midst of Africa's environmental ills, wildlife destruction, pollution, overpopulation, and tribal wars. They come home to American excess and Watergate's corruption. They joined the pilgrimage to Vermont, not to live in a commune with others, but to live alone in an abandoned farmhouse, vocally child-free and determined to cause the minimum impact on the land and people around them. Their guidebook for this back-to-the-land quest was *Living the Good Life*, by Scott and Helen Nearing. I made him a schoolteacher and her an hourly worker in a local health food store. I piled on them the physical and meteorological human disasters, like neighbor shoots dog, floods, a chimney fire, rebellious students, etc. Just as I had their literal well go dry, my own literary well did so as well. The story didn't pass the giggle test.

While I worked on fiction, Chris worked on reality. Out of her volunteer work for the Caledonia County Democrats, presto, she was chosen, pushed, or nudged to take on a local Republican incumbent, State Representative Ed Crane, who just happened to be married to Ruth Crane, an assistant at the Fairbanks Museum. Chris put in her time driving through the hills around St. Johnsbury, for this was the town district, not the village district, and all the campaigning was by car over its thirty-nine square miles.

She lost but did respectably well. Her moment of glory came when the Republican candidate for governor, Walter "Peanut" Kennedy, came to town to support his "good friend Ed Crane, who is running against a woman who is afraid to use her own name." The next day appeared a letter in the local daily *Caledonian-Record* that read: "Chris Hadsel is not afraid to use her own name; nor is her husband Bill Mares afraid to use his!"

For me, I missed daily journalism, humans in action, not in my thin imagination. It was time now to find another newspaper job.

Chapter Eight

Finding a Place; Finding My Voice (1974–1979)

> "Writing is easy. All you have to do is sit down at the typewriter, cut open a vein, and bleed."
> —Red Smith, *To Absent Friends*

Amid soaring inflation, rising gas prices, and a nascent recession, I went looking for another newspaper job. Easier said than done. I applied for jobs all over New England, including at the *Caledonian-Record*, to which I had sent my African reports. With each rejection from them and others, my résumé felt more threadbare. I recalled those years of losing high school football seasons, when we were told we were "building character." A number of papers used the tiresome falsehood "You're overtrained for this job."

Finally, I found a slot across the Connecticut River in New Hampshire at the weekly *Northland News*, now owned by my old friend the ex–*Christian Science Monitor* reporter Howard James. In Chicago, he had given me my first photographic break with freelance assignments. Now, he was willing to take me as one of two reporters at a weekly he and his wife Judy ran in New Hampshire's northernmost county. The *News* was a three-year-old start-up determined to compete with three existing weeklies and one daily along fifty miles of the upper Connecticut River in the towns of Littleton, Lancaster, Colebrook, Groveton, and Franconia. Even more generously, Howard gave Chris a part-time job selling ads and delivering the paper to all the small towns we served.

It was a big chore, covering that immense territory. With another reporter, I shared government reporting, features, even a little sports. Like any new reporter in a new region, I had to learn the landscape, its people, economy, and politics. I had to schmooze people to find sources. Howard was a wonderful teacher-boss. I felt like an undergraduate assigned to work with a tenured professor. He urged us to compete "in the quality of our writing. Learn to prioritize the stories." He pointed out the peculiar hybrid nature of stories in a weekly newspaper, caught between the immediacy of a daily or the leisurely pace of a magazine while still holding the advertisers' attention.

This was broader than the crime-and-fire reporting at the City News Bureau, and there was no "rewrite" or "desk" to edit our stories. I had to keep three, four, five stories in my head for days, until Chris and I drove them east across the state to the parent paper, the *Berlin Reporter*, in the paper mill town of Berlin. We tried never to stay overnight in the town, for the noxious rotten-egg smell of the kraft paper process blanketed everything.

How I envied the reporters for the daily paper who got the overnight gratification of getting a story done and then on to the next day's hunt. Hanging over all public affairs in New Hampshire was the malign influence of the single statewide newspaper, the *Manchester Union Leader*, a precursor of Fox News whose archconservative owner, William Loeb, campaigned relentlessly against any statewide sales and income taxes. Locally, a prominent target was the small progressive school named Franconia College. Leon Botstein, its twenty-eight-year-old president, told me that Loeb's paper's reporting and editorials reminded him of the *Völkischer Beobachter*, the German Nazi Party newspaper.

Gradually I got a handle on basic stories, some features, and even some high school sports. Howard urged me to try a weekly feature we dubbed Of Cabbages and Kings, with personal reflections on local events and larger affairs such as the drinking age, the preservation of open space, running a local ten-mile race in one-hundred-degree weather, even book reviews. I worked hard at Orwell's impossible dictum to "efface my own personality" even as I wrote in the first person singular.

In the winter of 1975-76, alas, the national recession made it to northern New Hampshire. As I had been reporting, I had noticed a number of business closings, just as Chris saw declining ad revenues. Howard and Judy decided to concentrate on the home paper, the *Berlin Reporter*. They gave us as soft a landing as they could. I went right back into an even bleaker job market. But now at least I felt like a high school student applying to college, instead of a high school freshman. I had some modest skills and more confidence in my ability.

As I began my search, my father suffered two strokes. In retrospect, my jobless status allowed me to go back to Texas twice in two months before he died on his seventy-third birthday, on April 13. I was able to get to his bedside just at the moment of his passing. When his minister at the First Unitarian Church in Houston asked me for material for his eulogy, I wrote the following.

> Dad was a careful, deliberate man, who seldom expressed himself without the listener feeling he had chewed over the subject material for a long time. He had his blind spots. His discomfiture with the Church when it got into more active social concerns is an example. He was a deeply conservative Republican closer to Goldwater than to Rockefeller, but he also said that Nixon and the Watergate gang should be drawn and quartered.
>
> He never seemed to question the fundamental egocentricity of people. He practiced great philanthropy with his money, but his time went into his profession. He always believed he could make a greater contribution to society by being a first-rate chemical engineer than by serving on a school board. His principal charities were educational.
>
> Popular culture largely passed him by. Once, at dinner, we were talking about movies, and the name Marilyn Monroe came up. "Who's she?" said Dad. We boys hooted, and my mother said, "Oh, she's one of those chesty blond actresses!"
>
> His lifestyle was modest. He hardly bought new clothes. He bought books and records and with Mom traveled widely to enlarge his knowledge of other cultures. He was fascinated with how things worked, the mechanics of daily life in the many countries they visited.
>
> Of course, he had a darker side. He and Mom fought like cats and dogs over our entering St. John's School. Actually, they fought over a lot of things. As a father of the old school, he

brooked little criticism and believed that children should be seen and not heard, unless spoken to, at least until we were 10 or 12.

According to his partner, when he was plant manager at Monsanto, he ate in the general lunchroom, but some engineers and foremen would flee with unfinished plates, rather than be grilled by him. At the same time, he loved to take Eastern chemical executives down a peg, leading them into the forests of their ignorance about certain chemical processes, and letting them find their own way home.

Dad had one of the most practical turns of mind of anyone I ever knew. He was always searching for the Why of a process, the What of a geologic formation, the How of a particular invention. He was fascinated with how scientists' minds worked. Theory he could handle, but he was most at home with practical, plodding answers to practical questions. He loved the laboratory he built behind our house and dreamed of finding ways to use ethanol as a substitute for gasoline.

His youth in Montana gave him a love of open spaces, some of the same purity and solitude that I experienced in the Arabian desert. Time and again, I remember his delight on hunting trips to the Hill Country, just sitting in a blind, listening for turkey calls and waiting for deer.

"Take a hundred years of this to kill you," he would muse.

A few weeks after Dad's death I again checked the traps of New England newspaper jobs. Nothing. Then I remembered that Tim White, an old friend from Texas, was now an executive with the Booth newspaper chain, with eight papers across Michigan. I sent my résumé to him with a glowing recommendation from Howard James. When Tim sent my résumé around, mirabile dictu, the *Grand Rapids Press* offered me a general assignment job in the Bicentennial year of 1976. I knew this was the hometown of then-president Gerald Ford, and the center of the Dutch reform movement in the United States, but little else.

Loyally, but not gleefully, Chris agreed to come along. Having worked for a Vermont large-animal veterinarian, she was able to find another vet assistant's job working with pets in a Grand Rapids suburb. We rented a house across the street from a Reformed church, which had English services at 10 a.m. and Dutch services at 2 p.m. Our landlord reminded us that car washing on Sunday was frowned upon.

~

My Father's Favorite Boots

As at the City News Bureau, I worked mostly nights, covering mostly police and fire. But there was also quite a variety of day work, including a few book and movie reviews. I loved the variety. Every story, however imperfect, was a world of information, and someone else's experience. I was packaging the human condition, and putting it daily on peoples' doorsteps.

I did stories about cops trying to calm domestic disputes, a judge who packed a pistol in court. I got my first smell of burnt human flesh at a highway head-on. I wrote about Sargent Shriver's visit to Grand Rapids on a quixotic presidential campaign as "down the up political staircase." I spent a weekend with a National Guard unit on maneuvers. I covered a battle between a liberal and a conservative court judge over how severely to punish juvenile offenders.

My writing did improve, but it was a slow slog. I wrote a story about a police officer trying, unsuccessfully, to talk a man out of suicide. As the man crouched behind the car in his garage, I wrote that sweat "dappled" the cop's forehead. I was proud enough to send the clipping to my *New York Times* friend John Kifner. He gave it some friendly praise, but his criticism lasted forever. "Re: dappled," he wrote back, "other words would have been better—peppered, spotted, mottled, dotted, etc. Remember Mark Twain: 'The difference between the right word and the almost right word is the difference between lightning and a lightning bug.'"

After six months of grunt, or general assignment work, the editors asked if I wanted to take over the religion beat. While I took my own religion seriously, I wasn't that interested in covering a region dominated by one particularly conservative brand of Christianity. Then another opportunity sailed into port—the creation of a work beat that would combine the traditional labor and business portfolios into one. I was excited about this one. As a trial run, the editors sent me to a weekend conference in Chicago of "Alternatives in the Workplace," an exploration of how to change the (largely factory) work environment for more humane production. It was fascinating, and I got fired up for the new job. But then the editors bagged that slot and put me on general assignment days.

With me working mostly nights and Chris working days, we saw little of each other. We shared the dog and a stray cat we named Tigger that loved to climb up the cold chimney. I found a well-stocked home brewing store with an energetic proprietor who helped me begin to make beer that friends even liked. We socialized with a few work colleagues, a juvenile court judge, and an environmental activist, but they were not seeds enough to plant a crop of community for us. I felt Chris's growing disenchantment. In February, she went back to Vermont to help nurse Betty Waters, who was dying of cancer. At the end of that stay, she said she was fed up with the "barren intellectual and social landscape of southwest Michigan. Where you live is half of life itself," she wrote. Well, the domestic fat was in the fire! What was it going to be? The marriage or the job?

Rather than lose Chris, I applied to all my New England news outlets for the third time. Luck struck. The *Burlington Free Press*, on the other side of the state from St. Johnsbury, had a job. After I sent my résumé and a now-bolstered set of clippings, they said yes. So did I!

The *Free Press* job got us back to Vermont, not to the deep country of the Northeast Kingdom but to a vibrant small city on the shore of Lake Champlain. Never again would we leave the state, except for vacations and various work projects. Burlington was the perfect size for almost limitless public engagement. You could walk up Church Street and almost always meet someone you knew. Within a year, Chris was on three nonprofit boards and I had three different hobbies. Some of our friends in St. Johnsbury joshed us and said, "How nice it is to have you back in Chittenden County;

it's so close to Vermont."

We rented a small Victorian house two blocks from the university. Within months I joined both a choral society and a running club. I brought my bees over from St. Johnsbury and placed them at the home of another beekeeper in the suburb of Williston. I added home brewing to the mix of hobbies and within a few years helped found the Vermont Homebrewers Association, a very, very loose organization of which I became the first president. We picked up friends like flowers in a garden—singers, runners, brewers, and beekeepers, as well as my colleagues at the paper.

We put down roots to last forever.

The *Free Press* gave me a variety of assignments and the freedom to find more on my own. I interviewed Lewis Thomas, author of *The Lives of the Cell*, Edward Hoagland, an essayist in the Northeast Kingdom, and other authors, such as Helen and Scott Nearing, George Seldes, and Noel Perrin. I interviewed a University of Vermont chemistry professor who warned that the beloved folk food of fiddlehead ferns was possibly carcinogenic. I became friends with the outdoor editor Bish Bishop, who took me duck hunting several times. I even persuaded my editor to let me write a story about playing in a bagpipe band in a Fourth of July parade.

The next year I became the first business editor of the paper, covering local and state business affairs. I followed the stock and housing markets with local brokers and bankers. I found the irate owner of a train museum who complained that the state anti-billboard law was cutting into his business. "You can drive all the way from Massachusetts to the Quebec border and never see any advertising!" he moaned. I wrote about plastic maple syrup containers made of supposedly carcinogenic plastic. I did a series about alternative energy projects, including one family who built their own high-head hydro project to provide all the energy they needed. Another series I wrote on six local business leaders won a New England Press Association award for business reporting in papers of less than seventy-five thousand circulation.

I tiptoed into personal columns again, such as riding a shift with a garbage-collection crew and another about whether the Audubon Society would frown on my love of duck hunting, and speculating upon development proposals for Burlington's aesthetic gem, its waterfront. I wrote a piece about training for and running my first marathon in a respectable 3:14. This led to a whole new circle of friends.

My friends came, first of all, from the *Free Press*, especially editors John Read and Jim Welch. Then came running buddies Ralph Swenson and Norm Stebbins. Then gold and silversmiths Marty and Doug French. And Geoffrey Burnham, another singer of whom we joked that he was born seven hundred years too late. He was an adjunct teacher of art at Saint Michael's College, but as a passionate and professional calligrapher, he should have been making illuminated manuscripts in a twelfth-century monastery. A bachelor who owned neither a car, a television, nor a computer, he collected twenty-five used tweed jackets and six road bikes and a Michelin-three-star array of cooking pots. Geoffrey helped edit several of my books and calligraphed some of my favorite quotes, such as "The union of the mathematician and the poet, fervor with measure, passion with correctness, this surely is the ideal," from philosopher William James.

Also singing in our choral group, Musica Propria, was a true Renaissance man—Bill Gray. Born in Vermont, he had gone to Harvard, captained the ski team, and become a lawyer, a prosecutor, and then US attorney in Burlington before moving into private practice. He was an avid cross-country skier and bicyclist and had run several sub-three-hour "Bostons," and sang solos in another small local chorus. He raised sheep and apples, kept bees, and had a huge garden. He loved opera, and when he was a prosecutor in New York City, would get standing-room-only tickets to the Met. In Burlington he carved out a niche as a newspaper reviewer of new productions in Montreal. While a friend drove him back to Vermont, he perched in the station wagon's rear and wrote his copy, to be delivered to the *Burlington Free Press* for its 2 a.m. deadline. When he was chair of the Vermont Bicentennial Commission, I was the vice chair. In the early nineties he was headed for a federal judgeship, when he contracted leukemia and died in 1994 at the age of fifty-two.

Chris threw herself into a job as assistant to the director of the Vermont Mozart Festival and served on various nonprofit boards, such as Planned Parenthood, the Fletcher Free Library, and the Vermont Symphony Orchestra, of which she became president. We remained loyal to St. Johnsbury, however, and both served on the board of the Fairbanks Museum. We sold the farmhouse but retained enough land to build on the property a small cabin without water or electricity.

Soon after I started at the Free Press, a foreign journalistic thunderbolt struck, in the form of a query for regional story ideas from the Washington bureau of the *Economist* magazine of London. Nancy Balfour, a friend of Chris' parents, had just retired as American news editor and she had passed my name to her successor. In fact, I did have a story idea: Burlington, and the state, were in the middle of the environmental story of the decade. The Pyramid Companies of New York wanted to build a giant suburban shopping mall that would change the county's character and devastate downtown Burlington, seven miles away. The approval process would be the greatest test yet for the state's landmark development-control law, Act 250. I scoured news stories, picked the brains of other reporters, attended hearings, and wrote what became four successive drafts for the Washington bureau. Each came back with questions and suggestions for more brevity. When it finally appeared in the magazine, I was, of course, ecstatic. I got no byline, as was the *Economist* custom, but a nice check and an invitation to submit other story ideas. Ultimately, I wrote about twenty pieces on such topics as judicial malfeasance, a secret gun factory astride the Vermont-Quebec border, clothespins manufacture in Maine, paintball in New York, and skiing in New Hampshire. Jokingly, I described myself as the *Economist*'s Northern New England correspondent.

In the fall of 1979, I went hiking in the Green Mountains with two old friends, John Kifner of the *New York Times* and John Simmons, a fellow Bill Polk tutee from Harvard. Kifner regaled us with stories of covering Kent State, Wounded Knee, Boston school integration, and beyond. He was about to be sent to cover the Iranian Revolution never having been on the foreign desk before. Not to be outdone in the accomplishment field, Simmons began telling us about his work as a professor of labor-management relations at UMass Amherst. The economics department there was a hotbed of leftist theory and practice, involving workplace power.

For these academics, the evil had begun with the nineteenth-century engineer and inventor Frederick Taylor and his theory of scientific management to get the maximum out of workers, a tactic he dubbed "the plum and the lash." That model led to time and motion study, which spawned a reaction with the rise of stronger labor unions in the 1930s. But by the sixties and seventies, labor-management relations had again deteriorated. Salary differentials rose, workplace discontent rose, quality and productivity suffered. Meanwhile, foreign competition was also rising. Companies responded with a variety of quality of work life experiments, labor-management committees, employee stock ownership, and, even, in desperate circumstances, employees buying the factory or company.

Lights went on. I recalled that conference I had attended in Chicago dealing with how to improve labor-management relations. I had written an article for the *Economist* the previous year entitled "Asbestos Farm." Desperate to save their company from closing, employees at Vermont Asbestos Group bought the mine and buoyed by higher prices and ran it profitably until the market soured and the workers couldn't adjust to their new roles of owner-worker-managers. They ended up selling it to a local businessman.

I got chills of excitement. "Are you going to write this up, John? Sounds like a book to me!"

John demurred. "I don't know . . ."

"Come on," I said. "I'll help you. You're a C-plus academic; I'm a C-plus reporter. Together we could write a B-minus book. Kifner, what do you say?"

"Try it," he said dryly. "But have a plan. Don't try to cover everything. This is not another Watergate. You're looking for information, not mousetrap moments. Test yourselves. Don't lead the witnesses. Interview both sides. The follow-up questions are often the more fruitful."

Kifner's cautious approval gave me the confidence to strike out on a new book. I did an inventory of what I'd learned in the past decade. At each of the four papers where I had worked, I had learned more techniques of basic journalism. The six interrogatories were now in my bloodstream. I knew the wag's comment that "the only way a reporter should look at a politician is down," but I never had the arrogance to practice it. I was better at establishing some rapport on a subject or source. And this was not a "Gotcha!" story or breaking news. We were breaking ground to explore a changing workplace.

To follow up, Simmons gave me a reading list of the relevant literature. Later in the fall I drove down to Amherst to talk further. I told him I believed there was a book to be done. I was ready to help with the research. I knew an editor at Knopf publishing company, which had done the desert trip book *Passing Brave*. Maybe we could try them? John was game.

Chapter Nine

Three Books and a Son (1979–1984)

"Ale, man, ale's the stuff to drink for fellows whom it hurts to think."

—A. E. Houseman

"Real Vermonters don't milk goats."

—Frank Bryan

Working Together

In our ten-page précis to Ash Green, my editor at Knopf, we proposed to combine John's academic perspective and my journalistic one to explore a spectrum of responses to the current economic tumult and workplace disaffection, from traditional top-down management to full employee ownership. We would look at participatory experiments and practices in companies as large as General Motors and Hewlett-Packard and as small as the Vermont Asbestos Group. We would tie case studies to the larger theoretical work of Peter Drucker, Michael Maccoby, William Whyte, and others. We would even include Swedish and German models. Workplace democracy, we contended, was not political democracy, but there was a continuum of worker control that we wanted to explore. At this bright beginning, we believed that greater worker participation brought both high production and more satisfied employees.

Then, mirabile dictu, Knopf accepted our proposal, with the caveat that we write a trade book for the general public, not just a collection of case studies for the specialists and business schools.

Now we had to write it. For this full-time commitment, I had to leave the

Free Press—that was OK, I was ready for another book project, especially one for which I had some skill and interest. John's life was more complex. He had three kids under ten and his wife Adele was president of Hampshire College. But she said, "Go ahead!"

The book, titled *Working Together*, began with a chapter about Frederick Taylor, the first person to study the work process deliberately and who coined the term "scientific management." This was the systematic study of the work process and how to seize all information and skill ("de-skilling" was the Marxist term) from workers, on the premise that workers were purely economic creatures who responded only to financial rewards. The title of Taylor's study and our chapter was "The Plum and the Lash."

After a week's trip to the Cornell University School of Industrial and Labor Relations, the academic center for this field, John and I drove on to Jamestown, in Western New York, a whole city working on improving the labor climate in public and private employment. Then we split up. John took on the big industrial cases, like General Motors, Hewlett-Packard, the Dana Corporation, and the academic studies. I went out to the Midwest, to interview at the *Star Tribune* newspaper in Minneapolis, and Kawasaki Motorcycles in Lincoln, Nebraska, to see how Japanese management methods translated to the US. I went on to Denver, Colorado, to interview a cooperative cab company. By phone and mail we studied garbage collectors in San Francisco, and Scandinavian-based lumber cooperatives in Washington State.

Together we went to Sweden and Germany to look at their industrial models. Then I went on to Yugoslavia to look at their model of worker participation under the authoritarian rule of Marshal Josip Tito.

By splitting up our duties and case studies, John Simmons and I surely covered a lot more ground. At the same time, such disparity in our experiences, professional training, and, dare I say, temperaments found us drifting toward different impressions and conclusions. For example, while John thought that Japan Inc. was a model of high impact and low discontent, the manager of the Kawasaki plant in Nebraska said the Japanese saying for obtaining unanimity on the shop floor was quite un-American: "The nail that stands up gets hammered down." We found large differences between companies trying to convert to worker ownership while they were still successful and those who came to worker ownership in distress, like Vermont Asbestos. The calls to "flatten the management structure" were fine, except for the middle managers, who could lose their jobs.

From the beginning, John wanted to produce an elaborate road map showing the sure way from workplace acrimony and alienation to full participation. I was more pessimistic about how far such participation could go. I was happy to lay out the case studies as vividly as possible, showing some connective tissue, but not as an apostolic succession. My caution was crystallized in talking to Robert Oakeshott, an English author of a book called *The Case for Workers' Co-ops*, who said the only truly successful cooperatives in the world were in the Basque region of Mondragon, Spain.

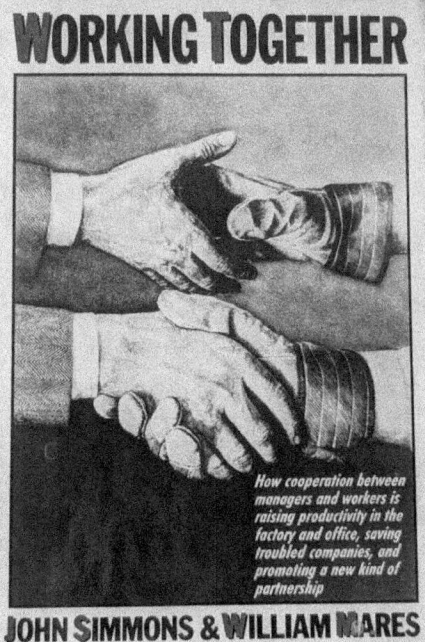

Working Together Cover

As we wrote the conclusion to our book, some of John's and my exchanges got heated. John was devoted to the continuum model of workplace organization, from the plum and the lash to full ownership and cooperation.

Working Together Co-Authors

I just thought that Americans were more individualistic than the Japanese or the Germans, or Yugoslavs. Successful co-ops usually had ethnic factors reinforcing them. Further, I found no assured formula for developing a successful "uniform culture."

It took eight or ten drafts, but we finally found enough common ground to finish the book. Knopf was pleased. The public was pleased. And we basked in blurbs like that of Studs Terkel, author of *Working*, who wrote, "If ever a book were stunningly contemporary, this is the one. Industrial democracy has been a dream of American working men and women for more than a century. This book shows how it's done."

As for our own collaboration, Chris needled me with the irony of our authorial disagreements over a book titled *Working Together*. More bluntly still, Joan Raines, my agent, dryly advised that one should never cowrite a book—"It's worse than a bad marriage."

Making Beer

In the middle of working on *Working Together*, I picked up another book contract with Knopf, this one involving beer and home brewing. After my initial home brewing failures, I improved. I received a qualitative boost when President Jimmy Carter signed the law in 1978 legalizing home brewing. A wave of good ingredients and techniques began to flow into the States from England. Home-brewing clubs sprang up across the country, including in Vermont, where I named myself president of the seven-member Vermont Homebrewers Association. Across the state, another Vermonter, Stephen Morris, published an odyssey of visiting every extant brewery in the country, *The Great Beer Trek*.

With better equipment and better ingredients, I could make, taste, and share better and better beer. I learned about all-grain brewing and mashing. I even tried lagers, but I didn't have the refrigeration for proper fermentation. I also realized that since most American beers were light lagers, mine would inevitably be compared to them, invidiously. And why would you want to make a beer like Miller or Pabst or, God forbid, Bud? And if it was off the slightest degree, it would be the skunk at the picnic.

My beer gradually improved, so much so that on several occasions, going to New York to talk to Ash Green at Knopf, I brought a couple of bottles. I gushed about how this hobby's popularity was being matched by a nascent professional microbrewing movement, primarily on the West Coast, a few "Jacks" out to slay the "giants" of Bud, Miller, and Schlitz. I showed him the Morris book. Not given to small talk, Ash asked, "Do you think you could do a tour like this *and* a how-to? We think the latter element would be the draw. There are a lot more people who will read this book for its home-brewing advice than for tips to start their own professional breweries."

"By all means!" I fairly shouted.

So there I was, writing yet another book for the best publishing house in New York. Holy moly!

Ultimately, the beer book traced the evolution of this hobby but with some jovial religious hyperbole, and how it first tempted, then seduced, and finally abducted me. When Ash asked how I proposed to illustrate it, Chris had a brilliant idea. Instead of using boring photos of brewing equipment and bottles, I should find a local cartoonist, "I know just who!" Jeff Danziger. Jeff had left high school English teaching to be a freelance political cartoonist and was now the staff cartoonist for the *Christian Science Monitor*.

Born in New York City and educated at the University of Denver, Jeff had been drafted during the Vietnam War, where he became a Vietnamese linguist and intelligence officer and was awarded the Bronze Star and the Air Medal. He was a real polymath, an artist, writer, mechanic, cook. He had drawn and self-published some hilarious cartoon stories about the fictitious Teed family in rural Vermont. He did cartoons for two family-owned daily papers in Vermont. Rather than call, we drove to his home far in the woods and found him splitting logs with a twenty-pound maul, which, he said, was easy once you got the triangular head over your head. To my query, he simply said, "Yes. Send me the manuscript," and went back to work.

I spent three or four months nailing down the how-to elements of home brewing, culling the modest but growing literature and commercial sources for ingredients, education, information, and equipment. By then, in Boulder, Colorado, Charlie Papazian, trained as a nuclear engineer and employed in a day care center, had penned *The Complete Joy of Homebrewing* and founded the American Homebrewers Association. Through those two endeavors, he became the most influential home-brewing guru in the world. His book would sell over a million copies and make his motto "Relax, don't worry.

Have a home brew!" as well known (among home brewers) as "E pluribus unum" was among schoolkids.

Charlie's book was a blessing for me. I was able to persuade Knopf that his *Complete Joy of Homebrewing* was definitive in the how-to realm. I could not compete in that arena. My goal was to demonstrate and describe the normal ambition of a home brewer who gets to a point of such confidence that they begin to dream of making a business out of that love of beer. This was not idle fancy. Indeed, a handful of microbreweries in California, Oregon, and Colorado had been launched; not just home brewers but nonbrewers and investors saw a market for import-style beers made in the US.

So I went on the road to visit some of these new breweries on both coasts. Brazenly, I called upon some of the pioneers and gurus: Fritz Maytag of Anchor Steam, Ken Grossman of Sierra Nevada, Jim Koch of Samuel Adams, Prof. Michael Lewis of UC Davis, Jack McAuliffe of New Albion, and beer writers like Charlie Papazian, Fred Eckhardt, and Bill Owens.

Not content to cover the US, Chris and I went to England, where I did a few PR interviews for the newly released *Working Together*, but the broader goal was to tour breweries—ten of them in Oxfordshire and London. They included such gems as Donnington Brewery, in Stow-on-Wold, the classic tower brewery of Hook Norton, and David Bruce's Firkin chain in London.

I recounted my visits to these revolutionaries, and some of their choices, e.g., freestanding brewery or brewpub, ales vs. lagers, etc. A few had already failed. A few would become world-famous. In this first-person odyssey, as I took my readers into the saloons, breweries, and basements, I got more and more excited. Maybe I could do this.

Then reality brewed a bitter batch. I invited Jim Hinkel, a friend who sold dairy equipment, to speak to a small group of home brewers about the prospective costs and challenges of launching even a small brewery. The numbers tolled like a death knell. He got to three to four hundred thousand dollars very quickly, and "that's not counting permits, wages, salaries, rent, advertising, etc." Yikes. I didn't have that kind of money, and I didn't want to raise it. I wanted to do other things with my life, like finish this book and go on to other things. Which I did.

The editors at Knopf found a suitably cautioning subtitle for the book *Making Beer: How to produce excellent home-brewed lagers, ales, and stouts, with notes and comments on the pleasures and pitfalls of this venturesome art.*

And how to avoid the temptation of starting your own brewery. When I wrote the first edition in 1984, there were fewer than ten microbreweries in the country. Ten years later, when the second edition came out, over six hundred breweries were up and running. I was proud to have been present at the creation of this new industry, even as I went home to home brew.

Birth of Timothy

In the middle of *Working Together* and *Making Beer*, our first son was born.

Making Beer Illustration by Jeff Danziger

Gushing with quiet parental pride at age forty-one, I wrote a letter to him every day for 365 days, and then my blustery ego sent a selection to Ash Green at Knopf. He had the grace to say, "It's not for us. Oh, and don't let it take you away from the other books." Five years later, unwilling to give up on our son as a subject (and how could he object?), I wrote a short essay for the then magazine of Vermont Public Radio, *North by Northeast*, titled "Parenting on the Lee Side of 40." This is the essay:

> This summer [1987] I will go to my college's twenty-fifth reunion. I will have the same graying hair, the same disquiet about the future, the same anticipation of seeing classmates. While most will have children in high school or college, however, I will be carrying my second son, Nicholas, on my back. My other son, Timothy, will be only five.
>
> I didn't get married until I was thirty, much later than my contemporaries. I had grown up to believe you didn't get married until you had been educated and accomplished something worthwhile—in my case, my first book. My wife Chris was 23. Neither of us wanted to have children. We didn't want to be tied down, and with the Vietnam War, pollution,

resource depletion, and the nuclear threat, we wondered why anyone would want to bring children into this world.

But by the time I turned thirty-five, Chris and I had changed our minds. Part of the reason was the birth of my brother's and Chris's sister's children. Their parental delight was manifest and infectious. Several million years of human evolution helped. But willingness and desire did not bring fulfillment. We tried for five years, joking about wasted precautions when we hadn't wanted to have children, and riding the monthly roller coaster of hope and disappointment, until the last available drug worked.

We elderly parents are more patient with our children, I think, but more impatient for them to grow up. We tire more easily. I may still run five miles under forty minutes, but getting up twice or thrice at night makes havoc of the next day. I can carry twenty-five pounds of baby and backpack up and down Camel's Hump but my legs feel it for days afterwards.

Gone, too, are the times when I sat down to read the newspaper or a book without interruption. Now, I cram those free minutes with "sixty seconds of distance run." It's striking what you can do during the six-minute cycle of a wind-up baby swing.

Time, already one of the most precious commodities, has even greater value for older parents. We hear the march of time like the tramp of hobnailed boots. Some extra slogging is necessary as we glimpse the empty pedestal of our own mortality. Three months before Nicholas was born, I had a heart attack. During those first hours, I was scared witless. When Chris came to see me in the hospital I wondered if I would ever see the child she was carrying.

I recovered fully, but it will be harder to do the things with my son that my father did with me: camping, baseball, fishing, and more. I wonder if I will have the equanimity to deal with adolescent rage and outrage that will inevitably come. I hope that awareness of my shorter fuse will keep the matches away. And while some of my classmates are now grandparents, I wonder if I will live to see grandchildren.

At the same time, being well past forty, I feel more at peace with my failures, more forgiving of my failings, and, I hope, less taken with my accomplishments. Moreover, twenty years ago, before men took on a greater share of parental duties, I might have felt my manhood imperiled if I had carried a child in a backpack. Today, I don't mind at all. I've even used Nicholas to shameless political advantage. For too long politicians have made hay by kissing constituents' babies. Last fall I reversed the roles and took Nicholas on the campaign trail. It worked so well that one woman looked at his cheery face and exclaimed, "That's not fair to your opponents!"

If age confers anything it is experience, and experience corrals our opinions with the barbed wire of facts, choices, and trade-offs. We older parents have seen more, tried more, failed at more than our younger brethren parents. We have watched friends' marriages collapse and their children crash. We have seen parents, against all kinds of adversity, raise superb children.

Children are our eternity. I don't know that I am more optimistic about the future of the world, but having children means believing there will be a future.

"Are you a better parent starting so late?" asked a forty-year-old friend two months away from having his first child. Gosh, I don't know. I think I know myself better than a decade ago. While I have no lack of ambition for the boys, I am also worried about smothering them with late-arriving love. I know I am more grateful to have them than I would have been at thirty.

Having children late has rejuvenated me, just when I might have become set in my ways. With kids, every day is novel, tending a bloody nose or building a space station or watching birds at the feeder. Late parenting has also given me a new cohort of friends, the parents of our kids' friends. Thus I've kept my own generation of friends and added a new battalion ten or fifteen years younger.

Now it's the kids themselves who do the most to keep me from being a middle-aged stodge. When Timothy was about six months old, I cooed to him that I wanted him to do only three things when he grew up: play the cello, learn Chinese, and play rugby. First, he spewed tapioca at me. And then he laughed and laughed and laughed.

Real Vermonters Don't Milk Goats

In the spring of 1983, Book Stacks, a bookstore in Burlington, had a signing party for the newly published *Working Together*. I invited a host of friends, including Frank Bryan, a buddy who taught political science and public administration at the University of Vermont. His earthy humor and libertarian streak made him one of UVM's most popular teachers. He had been a serious amateur boxer. He taught in short-sleeve shirts. He logged his property with two oxen. He collected old Chevettes for parts. He became the world's expert on town meeting and annually sent students to cover his beloved institution.

Liberals thought he was a conservative, and conservatives thought him a traitor, and many, like me, thought he was right, some of the time. He was a Vermont Eric Hoffer. I'd gone to a few of his lectures and we would have periodic breakfasts at the famous Oasis Diner in downtown Burlington. We got along because I was a moderate, dutiful "Dimmocrat," and he called himself a "conservative, period."

At the book signing, Frank burst out in full lecture voice, "Mares, forget all this workplace democracy and changing society BS! Someone has to do a book about how Vermont's human landscape is changing. You know this new book called *Real Men Don't Eat Quiche*? Well, with the flatlanders taking the state, the title will be *Real Vermonters Don't Milk Goats*!"

On the spot, my agent's warnings about coauthoring went out the window.

Real Vermonters Illustration by Howard Johnson

Best Selling Vermont Book in 1983

Me and Four-Time Co-Author Frank Bryan

"Frank, that's a great idea," I said. "Now, you go home and think of twenty-five one-liners on that theme. And I'll do the same thing. And we'll meet at the Oasis Diner on Monday and see what we've got."

He did and I did, and off we went. For about eight weeks we met every

Monday at the Oasis and tested our jokes and chapter ideas on each other and the clouds of witnesses who passed by. It was almost like holding court. The kibitzers sometimes offered their own jokes, names, ideas.

The synergy between us didn't just bubble; it boiled! I could do the flatlander, high-stepping cultural stuff, and Frank handled the barn and country store. Cars and clothes became two of the countless throwaway lines of what Real Vermonters *don't* do and flatlanders *do*. I drove a Volvo, for God's sake! Frank drove a Chevette and collected others for parts, and ticked off the neighbors in the process. I wore L.L. Bean boots! The multipronged cultural shift was the perfect trope for that era, when the balance of Vermont's ethnicity was tipping toward the newcomers.

Brimming with confidence, we approached two UVM English professors, Al Rosa and Paul Eschholz, who owned a small regional publishing house, the New England Press. They loved our idea and added more suggestions and angles of their own. Chris and Frank's wife, Lee, also got into the act, batting ideas back and forth like ping-pong balls. By the end, we had a genuine fifty-fifty collaboration. Only rarely did I remind Frank that he *was* born in New Hampshire.

Our timing was impeccable. A big demographic shift was underway that would change the tone, texture, and character of the state. What was essentially a one-joke book about the differences between the real article and the new arrivals included lists, names, quizzes, social comments, pokes at religion, style, autos, schooling, and social habits. Our shaky but plausible premise was that just about all virtue resided in the natives, and all pretense, hollowness, striving, and ignorance came from away. We poked fun at real politicians, like Pat Leahy and Madeleine Kunin and Jim Douglas. We listed real people, like Iva Lack, Norm Sleeper, Royal Cutts, Cola Hudson, Hazen Wood. We had a Real Belief System, a section on Real Vermont Women, Real Vermont Politics, the Real Vermont All-Time Enemies List. On and on it went, including a double-page spread that showed how "A Real Vermonter is someone who gets up in town meeting, identifies himself as a farmer, and nobody laughs."

Howard Johnson, the cartoonist of the *Burlington Free Press*, added graphic brilliance to our work. Coming out at the beginning of leaf-peeper season of the fall of 1983, the ninety-six-page book would sell forty-five thousand copies by Christmas. We had written a true bestseller, indeed, a cultural sensation.

I realized that some of my sense of humor probably came from my father, who was given to aphorisms like "The steam that toots the whistle never turned a wheel." And "I notice that the harder I work, the luckier I get."

After the *Goats'* striking success, Frank and I went on to write three more Vermont volumes in six years. The first of these, *OUT! The Vermont Secession Book*, was a full-blown satire about Vermont leaving the Union.

On the discovery of the fictional Moscow (Vermont) Covenant—signed by George Washington and Ethan Allen—to the bloodless (and also fictional) Strafford Massacre, we contended that Vermont had never joined the Union, the Union joined Vermont, and that after two hundred years of intrusive bureaucracy, federal mismanagement, and other un-Vermont-like actions, Vermont wanted *out*. With maple syrup as the national currency, and town meeting rules universal, Vermont took on President Alexander Haig (remember, it was 1991) and some of his misguided minions, Lt. Col. Bentley, USMC, Adm. John Poinsettia, and Col. Robert McNearland, who were determined to put down the rebellion.

In the third collaboration, Frank and I decided that it was not so important who was born here and who wasn't. What mattered was keeping Vermont unique and, well, Vermont. It was not easy. We were constantly told that bigger, faster, and more convenient is better. But that's just not the way Vermont is meant to be. So what to do? Frank and I, intrepid defenders of democracy and the Vermont way of life, had an answer. Don't just appreciate Vermont—*own* it. Learn about it, maintain it, and drive it with skill, attention, and pride. *The Vermont Owner's Manual* would show readers how to:

- Celebrate the best day of the year in Vermont, January 4.

- Recognize the symptoms of the dreaded malady, Flatlander Syndrome, and how to cure it.

- Survive deer season and town meeting—not necessarily in that order.

- Understand and love (OK, at least tolerate) your neighbors.

- Accept that this land belongs to you and me!

Both *OUT* and the *Owner's Manual* were illustrated by Jeff Danziger. I confess that I contributed relatively little to these middle two books. It wasn't intellectual disagreement, as with Simmons. My first excuse was that I was working on other books and teaching. But more than that, Frank's narratives sprang almost fully formed from his lifelong study of Vermont. Most of my ideas just seemed to get in his way.

I redeemed myself—partially—by doing the bulk of the work on a collection of political humor, *Out of Order!* Here, we collected stories and anecdotes from what we saw and what we extracted from the 180 members of the Vermont house and senate. I created a narrative of two statehouse custodians who collected these tales and hid them in the basement men's room. For illustrations, we gave Danziger a rest. I found a local artist to do the illustrations, namely fellow legislator Don Hooper. His wacky style was just right.

After the *Goats* success, I was in a daze with all the publicity. I'd never thought of myself as a comedian or humorist. I'd never been famous before. Could I use these fifteen minutes of fame for some other purpose? Another book? Social service? Politics? Now, there was an option. As a reporter, I'd always been on the outside of the political process. Here was a chance to get inside. Notoriety was a terrible thing to waste.

Chapter Ten

Of Legislation and Pork Sausage (1984–1990)

"It is better to be silent and thought a fool than to speak and remove all doubt."
—Abraham Lincoln

"Politician's logic: Something must be done. This is something, therefore we must do this."
—BBC TV sitcom *Yes, Prime Minister*

As the applause over the three books subsided, the political bee stung me. I'd been a reporter-photographer- writer for almost twenty years, on the outside looking in. Why not take this brief moment of fame and try to ride it into some political arena? Chris was already on the Burlington school board. I didn't fancy the city council, with its year-round meetings or being the target of everyone's immediate civic complaints. What about the state legislature? It met for four to five months every year, in a block. I'd get a chance to wrestle with statewide problems in a serious, not a humorous, manner. I'd often said everyone should run for some kind of political office—here was my chance to follow that ex cathedra statement. In a way, it was easy. I just needed to introduce myself the old-fashioned way of ringing doorbells. When Chris ran for office, she had to drive everywhere. I did my campaigning all on foot. This two-person district, covering Burlington's South End, was heavily Democratic. Madeleine Kunin, who was for governor, had held one of its seats from 1972-1978. Now one seat was held by Mary Evelti, grandmother who had been in five terms and was unbeatable. The other was occupied by a member of an old local family, but he was a bit lazy, and dismissive of my candidacy.

In a word, I out-hustled him and shamelessly used my secret weapon of campaigning with our one-year-old son Timothy in a backpack. I learned that the average doorstep exchange lasts twenty to thirty seconds. No one asked a question that wasn't the preface to a statement about the subject most on their mind. There were no candidate forums, no advertising. I just assembled two brochures with a good photo and a short bio, not failing to mention my coauthorship of the *Goats* book. I came in second in the primary and then, when the loser ran as an independent in the general election, I beat him again, by a larger margin.

Now what do I do?

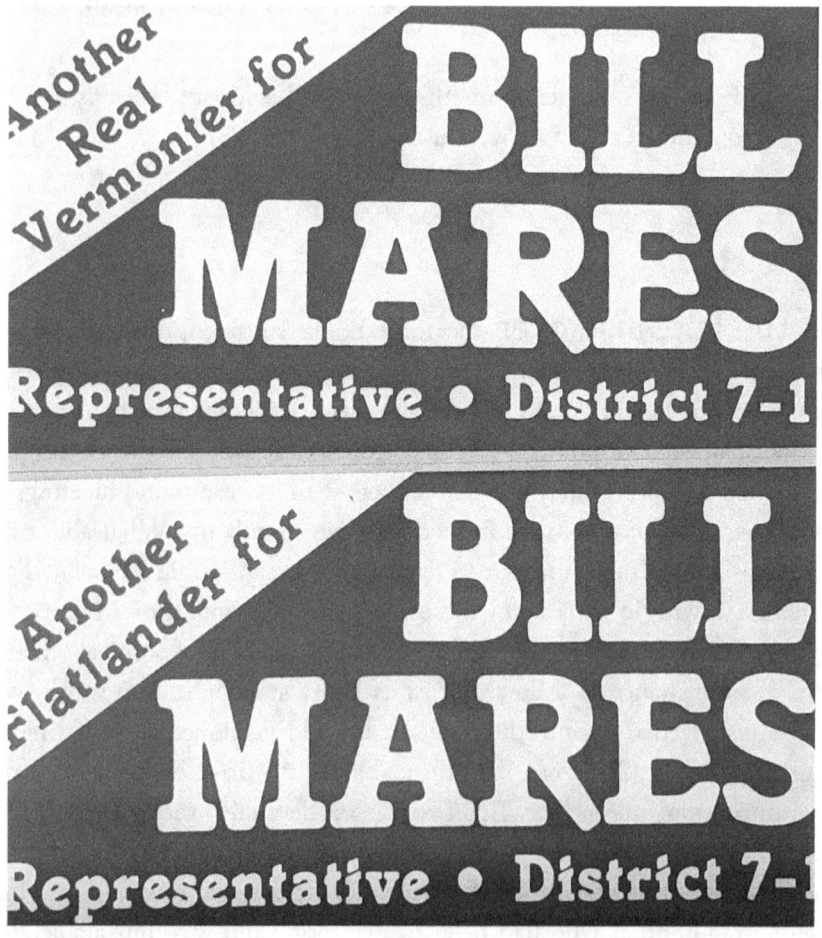

Looking for Votes from both Real Vermonters and Flatlanders

An Outsider's Inside View of the Legislature

Campaigning in 1984

When I joined the convening Vermont legislature in January 1985, the atmosphere was a heady mix of coronation, wedding, reunion, fish market, freshman orientation, and prizefight.

We freshmen had had one day in November for orientation, but that was hardly enough time to savor our victory or to admire the statehouse's marble floors, soaring columns, Civil War banners, and gubernatorial portraits. While the public focused upon the historic inauguration of Madeleine Kunin as the first woman governor of Vermont, we freshmen struggled through more mundane tasks of learning procedures, getting bills drafted, locating rooms, and meeting some of our 179 colleagues.

Second in importance to Kunin's elevation was the race for Speaker of the House between Democrat Ralph Wrght of Bennington and Republican Robert Kinsey of Craftsbury. I didn't know either of them. Ralph had the reputation for taking no prisoners, and some Republicans talked darkly of what his reign would portend. Conversely, the Democrats dismissed Kinsey as out of step with the changing nature of the legislature. Much legislative gossip centered on what promises each candidate had made to members of the opposite party. Despite a four-seat Republican edge, Wright emerged victorious, giving Democrats only their second Speaker in the twentieth century.

Once that battle was over, the House clerk administered our oath of office, which read in part, "I do solemnly swear that as a member of this Assembly, I will not propose or assent to any bill, vote or resolution which shall appear to me injurious to the people, nor consent to any act or thing which shall have a tendency to lessen or abridge their rights or privileges."

Another small ritual followed. After returning legislators took their seats, we freshmen drew lots and entered the chamber to claim the seats that were still free. Randomly, I chose number eighty-two and found myself between Betty Nuovo, a lawyer from Middlebury, and Republican Roger Kayhart, a Waltham dairy farmer. On my maple flip-up desktop, as on everyone's, were six plastic-covered documents for sets of covers, house calendars, house journals, and house bills, and an identical set for the Senate, with accompanying proletarian black shoelaces, for adding new pages every day, our daily diary of past and future work.

Sixty-three house bills greeted us that first day. As I read through them, my eyes and mind began to glaze over. I didn't know whether to smile or frown. They were all serious moves to change the law, I had to assume. How was I to decide whether to increase the veterans' tax exemption, accept DWI samples taken out of state, require all drivers to carry liability insurance, or how the state should regulate underground oil storage tanks?

In the hours and days that followed, we heard the governor speak twice, accepted first readings of bills, and were assigned (with little choice on our part) to committees. Around the halls and chamber, through the cafeteria, moved other legislators with roll call lists hawking would-be cosponsors for their draft legislation. One member advised me to sign up for all the bills I could—that would help my reelection campaign. I was nonplussed. The reality of my first election had barely sunk in, and now I was supposed to be thinking about reelection!

I got my chosen committee, Commerce, and began to meet its members and learn its routines. As I entered the world of utilities, banks, insurance companies, energy regulation, and unemployment compensation, I was dazed by how much there was to know. I struggled to learn the names and faces of all the committee members of the two bodies. I tried to read every bill that was submitted. I volunteered to be the clerk because veteran legislators told me that lining up witnesses and keeping committee notes was a quick way to learn the system. "By managing the assembly of witnesses, you have a first small taste of power and influence," one member told me.

In the committee, I was relieved to discover that the bills as introduced were only the raw materials for our deliberations. They looked fancy, clean, and finished when they arrived on our desks, but in fact, they were often the very imperfect translations of legislative draftpersons' understanding of a lawmaker's dream, annoyance, or crusade. It was our job as a committee to decide on the bills' merits, hear testimony, shape them into forms the majority could agree on, and finally take them to the floor of the House to try and convince the entire body of our wisdom and rectitude.

As the weeks went by, I took the measure of my fellow committee members. Only one did I know beforehand, another Burlington representative, a civic activist named Barbara Hockert. The rest were as random a collection as a lifeboat's survivors—Jack Candon, a witty lawyer from Norwich, a hospital administrator from Newport, a retired banker from Derby, a credit union manager from East Montpelier, a retired electrical equipment salesman from Hartford, a political consultant from South Burlington, a small businessman from Chester, and an office-equipment-company sales manager from Proctor. The chair, Mike ("Obie") Obuchowski, was only thirty-two, but already a seven-term veteran and former chair of two other committees. Our home for the next two years was a corner second-floor room, ten by fifteen, with a blackboard, a clock, two calendars, and two filing cabinets. Our "offices" were our desks in the House chamber, one filing cabinet drawer each, and the table space in front of our seats. I had to share mine with the tape recorder for taking witnesses' testimony. We sat around an oval table that eventually disappeared under accumulated newspapers, legislative drafts, and special interest reports. Obuchowski's pile grew so much that by the end of the session we dubbed it Mount Obie.

The first bill that came to us was H.5, "relating to unemployment compensation." It was sponsored by Rep. George Crosby of St. Johnsbury, at the behest of the *Caledonian-Record*. The bill sought to exclude news stringers, or freelance writers, from coverage under the unemployment compensation laws. Several newspaper publishers, including one good friend Chris Braithwaite of the *Barton Chronicle*, argued that stringers were independent contractors, and the unemployment claims of stringers elsewhere should not be charged against the papers' rating. The Department of Employment and Training—which administered the unemployment compensation system—however, argued for coverage. I was torn between the department's legal interpretation and my respect for Braithwaite. With the majority, however, I finally voted to table (kill) the bill. (Making it moot, six months later, the state Labor Relations Board ruled that stringers were not employees, and thus the publishers were vindicated in their complaint.)

In that small debate over newspaper stringers, I saw a similarity to and a difference from my career in journalism. As a reporter, I was trained to look at both sides of an issue, then lay them out and let the reader decide. Here in politics, I listened to both sides, but then had to choose one side, even if I agreed with only fifty-one percent. To paraphrase Samuel Johnson, When a politician has to vote in the morning, it concentrates the mind wonderfully. As I learned later, so wonderfully does a roll call vote concentrate the mind that some people are inclined to "take a walk" when they can't square conscience with constituency.

From the debate on stringers and many more to follow, I gathered a feel for the philosophy of each member around the oval table. Obviously, we didn't all think alike. Nor, and this was the important part, were we always consistent in our own voting. That made for fascinating coalitions and alliances, both in the committee and on the House floor. On the big issues, partisanship burnished off some independent edges, but as one leader said with only a modicum of hyperbole, "On all but the half-dozen issues of pure party, you're free to vote your own way." That didn't mean the leaders wouldn't try to persuade you if they needed the votes, but that was the fascination, the thuggery, and the art of politics.

My first roll call vote was on the hardly earthshaking question of whether to eliminate the six-inch minimum length of trout taken in Caledonia and Lamoille counties. All the rest of the counties had gone along with the biologists of the Fish and Wildlife Department, who said there was no harm in anglers taking these smaller trout. Fish and wildlife bills, I understood quickly, strike some primordial chord in certain legislators and almost never fail to arouse even the drowsiest members to fiery parry and thrust.

As a rule, I tended to support the biologists in the department. For example, I felt that they, not the legislature, should manage the deer herd. But in this case, I thought it was simply not sporting to take trout under six inches, no matter what the biologists said about a high mortality of fish thrown back anyway. After a few questions of the bill's reporter, the speaker rapped everyone to silence and the clerk read the names: "Allendorf of Underhill, Amidon of Bennington, Auld of Middlesex . . ." As his voice approached the M's, I saw that the bill would pass. But, what the hell, I still thought it was wrong, so when the clerk got to "Mares of Burlington," I said "No!" I was both bemused and exhilarated. This was democracy in action, more exciting than when I first voted for president. I had voted my conscience, and, I had to admit, it had cost me nothing in my trout-free district.

A more substantive baptism of fire came on the vote to raise the drinking age to twenty-one. I was torn. How could we allow our young people to vote, make contracts, and serve in combat, but not let them drink? On the other hand, I saw merit to the argument that if Vermont was an oasis of eighteen-year-olds drinking legally, we could have on our hands the blood of kids from neighboring states with higher drinking ages. To take the pulse of my district, I spent two evenings calling about forty constituents for their opinions. They were little help; they were split down the middle. Since one of the most vociferous opponents owned a bar, I didn't want to appear to be in his pocket, so I finally voted with some unease to raise the age. My disquiet didn't end with the vote. My gut warred with my head. These kids were going to drink anyway and probably under more dangerous circumstances than if they did it legally. We were practicing a neo-prohibitionism that felt more uncomfortable. So, the next day at third (final) reading, on another roll call I reversed my vote. It made no difference in the final outcome but I felt better nonetheless. One of my constituents, however, was so outraged that he vowed to do all he could to unseat me. I heard later that his daughter had been killed by the car of a drunken teenager. From that vote, I learned that in deciding how to vote, it is helpful to project myself forward and imagine how to defend or explain that vote. After a month or so, I realized that I didn't have to read all the bills. When I saw how we gnawed at some bills and never considered others, I learned to be more discriminating in which bills I studied. However, the time I saved by not reading all the draft bills now went into the complexities of the bills we did consider.

The most exhausting experience of that first session was the constant activity and the inextricable interweaving of people and issues. As committee clerk, I had to scramble around the building lining up sponsors, witnesses, and bureaucrats. But even as an ordinary representative, I had to exchange greetings, or information, or gossip, or jokes with well over a hundred individuals a day. A mixture of curiosity and obligation made me feel I should know what everyone else was doing, when of course that was impossible. To all I had to be polite, and by the end of the day, my face was frozen into a tired, ironic smile.

A key lesson I learned was to learn from others. To the public and your constituents, you were supposed to be all-seeing, all-knowing, with an answer for every topic. In the legislature, you couldn't possibly keep up with the hundreds of bills, dozens of issues, all by yourself, especially with no staff. You learned to evaluate the probity and knowledge and instincts of other legislators. Whom could you trust for good information and advice? So you were evaluating not just issues, but people.

Representing Burlington in Montpelier had its special tensions. A hundred years of envy of the Queen City infused the votes of some legislators on any bill that seemed to benefit Burlington. And whenever former Burlington mayor Bernie Sanders excoriated the legislature, as he loved to do, there were plenty of legislators who delighted in making the long-standing animus personal.

As the session progressed, I found the going harder, not easier. The more I learned, the more I felt I had to learn. I was running faster and faster to stay in the same place. When I added to my House duties the necessary consultations with constituents, I felt almost as tightly bound as Gulliver. I got one warning. When the Vermont Nurses Association came to the statehouse to "show the flag," they gave free health checks. My blood pressure was over the danger point. By the end of the session in early May, I had lost ten pounds and I was exhausted.

Two months later I had a heart attack. The damage was minor, requiring no surgery, and I was out of the hospital in a week. But it scared me. The doctors were loath to ascribe it to the pressures of political service, but in retrospect, my headlong pace and personality were factors. Then the doctors decided that the attack was relatively mild and put me on a morphine drip. On this drug, I soared into an altered state, where I had a flashback to that camp song of yesteryear. Surrounded by half a dozen docs and nurses, I sang:

> Morphine Bill and Cocaine Sue, walking down the avenue
> Turned up Fourth and walked down Maine
> Looking for a place to buy cocaine.
> So, honey, have a sniff, have a sniff on me
> Better hava hava sniff on me.

Surprise hardly captured the medicos' reactions.

I didn't want another heart attack, but I didn't want to quit. I loved the mixture of issues and personalities. I wanted to get back and serve my constituents, my flock, not just those in my district, but all the people in the state. If I did go back, I knew I would have to slow down and follow Reinhold Niebuhr's prayer to know the difference between what I could change and what I could not.

I went back the next year determined to pace myself. I took short naps at noon instead of gossiping over lunch. With more time to myself, I think I came to understand the system better. I could see how people counted chits to be traded at an appropriate time. As I learned more of the rules, I could see how people used them to delay, obfuscate, or kill. I understood that warning lights should greet a bill described as "just a little housekeeping," such as when a proponent argued for changing "may" to "shall" in a particular law. I learned that with some lawmakers, there was an inverse relationship between the number of times they spoke on the floor and their influence. I began to learn whom I could trust, who went about their business with silent effectiveness, who were the sycophants, who were the windbags, wafting on clouds of self-importance.

Shaping bills made me think of a short-order cook serving a café with fifty seats. You try to keep all the dishes straight, but of course, they don't cook for the same length of time, or go to the same customers, all of whom want their orders first. Meanwhile, you're not alone in the kitchen. You have 179 other cooks (not counting the governor and all the lobbyists) who want to season dishes a different way, want them baked, want them grilled, some longer, some shorter. Some of them don't even like the dish. And some of them, even if they like it, don't know how to cook.

I never stopped being awed by the sheer number of issues we dealt with: criminal sentencing guidelines, universal health care, bridge financing, the length of trout, putting the state into the electric power business, certifying psychotherapists, and evaluating the true cost of a child's education, to name only a few.

Of course, such mangling and revisions were inevitable considering the dozens of perspectives, egos, philosophies, constituencies, and competing legislation affecting a particular bill. In few other fields is ambition so naked, yet politicians love to wrap their actions in the purple raiment of public good. In few other jobs ought skins to be so thick, yet are so thin. In few other activities is there so much artlessness on the surface and so much calculation underneath. We politicians sail along on innocent-looking pleasure craft, but few lack torpedo tubes beneath the waterline. I didn't think anyone in the statehouse was a megalomaniac. Nor was any legislator a complete wimp. Between those extremes, we all found our respective points, according to temperament and ambition.

Raw power did not often rule the day; civil behavior and good humor helped. Schmoozing was integral to good politicking. Most of the legislators I worked with liked people. They were interested in their fellow legislators even when they disagreed with them. There were a few misanthropes who were, in turn, roundly disliked. But in the tight, tense quarters of the legislature, people needed some extrovert genes. If you didn't like people invading your space, being solicited as boldly as by a streetwalker, if you didn't like being interrupted fifty to one hundred times a day, you were probably in the wrong game. Also, I think my outsider streak kept me at arm's length from many legislators. It was through the legislative card games at lunch, the communal newspaper reading over breakfast, the random socializing in the corridor, on the floor, over coffee or beers that legislators got to know and trust each other, trading stories, information, and ultimately votes. In retrospect, I didn't socialize enough, partly because I commuted almost every day, and evenings I wanted to be home with my family.

In the legislature, gossip was the coin of the realm. It reminded me of high school and the endless fascination of who was going with whom. In a debate over whether legislators would get a thirty percent pay raise, one member stridently argued, "We have no benefits!" I rose to disagree. "Of course, we have benefits," I said. "This is the only job I've ever had, aside from journalism, where I was paid to gossip!"

Another advantage of schmoozing was the cultivation of friends who could tell you what was going on.

Another Bryan-Mares Humor Book about Legislative and Political Hijinks

Since you couldn't be on every committee, you needed someone on each whom you could trust. So when you had only five or six minutes to learn about a proposed piece of legislation, you were not totally in the dark when the vote came.

Votes on complex issues were hard enough by themselves. When we added partisanship for its own sake, they became tougher still. I had taken an oath to the state of Vermont, not to the Democratic Party or its leadership. I wanted to be free to decide when I was right and my party was wrong. Yet, I knew intellectually that unless you had some discipline, a party program would be nigh impossible to pass.

Someone once told me: Even if you agree with the leadership on every bill, you ought to be contrary every once in a while, just to keep them from taking you for granted.

One year the governor pushed a so-called homestead bill that was supposed to solve the property tax dilemma. I thought the bill was mostly words, and I told the Democratic whip I would vote against it. Successively, I was lobbied by the governor, majority leader Paul Poirier, Speaker Ralph Wright, and Senator (and former governor) Phil Hoff. By the time Hoff got to me, I was bemused by the attention, yet unmoved to change my vote.

"Why all this pressure?" I asked Hoff.

"This is not a lot," he said. "If you were known as a waverer, you would have gotten real heat!"

The session of 1987-88, following my un-opposed re-election, marked another transition for me. I became vice chair of the Commerce Committee, and the leadership hinted I might move up the next term. In that year, we had three major (and controversial) bills before us—control of interstate banking, deregulation of the telephone industry, and a move to put the state into the retail electric power business.

For me, the most bitter was the power bill. On its face, the issue was the protection of a historical anomaly, a block of cheap power from the New York Power Authority. The Federal Energy Regulatory Commission had been asked to rule whether Vermont qualified as a public body, and therefore deserved the power. In 1985, we had changed the law to make the state the purchaser of the power. But the principal proponents of this bill were hunting bigger game. They wanted to make the state the direct competitor of the private and municipal power companies.

I saw no reason for the state to sell electric power at retail, especially when it was regulating the companies with whom it would compete. That seemed both hypocritical and bad public policy. As a Democrat, I was supposed to believe that public power was automatically better, more humane than private power. But if that were the case, why were the municipally owned and cooperative utilities united against this bill? I finally held my nose and went along with the bill because I couldn't answer the charge that Vermont might lose that block of cheap power. If ever there was a fifty-one-percent vote, it was mine on this bill.

On a happier note, I helped to make state and regional history through my home-brewing background. One day during the 1987 session, I got a call from one Greg Noonan of Massachusetts. I recognized the name, for he had written a fine technical manual on brewing lager beer. He wanted to build a brewpub in Burlington, but needed the law changed to permit it. Could I help?

The existing law, passed after Prohibition was repealed, proscribed "tied-houses," or brewery-owned bars, the general practice in England. That practice allowed manufacturers, i.e., brewers, to sell retail. US laws required a three-tiered system that separated brewery, distributor, and retailer. The Vermont law said that no second-class licensee—that is, someone who sells beer for off-premises consumption—could also make the beer. Knowing

Cutting the Ribbon to open the Pub and Brewery, 1988

that there were several ways to skin the legislative cat, Greg and I turned the challenge upside down. What if a brewery (manufacturer) could obtain a retail license to sell beer on its premises? After a certain amount of drafting acrobatics, the idea found favor with the state Liquor Control Board. We then marched the bill through four legislative committees and both chambers and finally to the governor's desk. In November 1988, the Vermont Pub and Brewery opened its taps as the first brewery in Burlington in ninety-four years. I cut the ribbon.

In my third term, given a choice between staying on the Commerce Committee and being the probable chair and moving to another committee, I moved over to Education. That our first son, Timothy, was entering the first grade made the abstractions of education suddenly flesh and blood—mine. Rather than having a big role in utilities, banking, and insurance regulation, I preferred a small part in shaping state educational policy, especially in a time of ferment and reform.

Being a grunt on the Education Committee also gave me more time to serve as vice chair for the Statehood Bicentennial Commission.

I wanted the celebration to spawn as much interest as possible for Vermont, the first new state to join the original thirteen. I loved serving under my good friend Bill Gray, the commission chair. I poured myself into a variety of activities, from speaking engagements to developing a bicentennial license plate to lobbying my fellow legislators for a larger appropriation.

Special Plate that helped fund Bicentennial Activities

By the middle of this third legislative term, I wondered if I had had enough. Oh, yes, I enjoyed the heady feeling of being in the know and debating some of the big (and small) issues of the day. I liked the "clubbiness" of the place, some of the pomp and circumstance, special license plates and being addressed as "the honorable Bill Mares" (who wouldn't?). I liked doing small favors for my constituents and colleagues.

I felt that I was probably too thin-skinned for part of this work. I could not separate my private from my public personality, the public one expected to be the lightning rod for lobbyists' guile, constituents' ire, and opponents' fire. One result was that at floor debate I was, at best, inept. I could give a prepared speech, but in debate, I was miserable.

At the same time, some parts of the job were increasingly noisome and wearying. The sessions grew longer and longer. There were often summer committees. Maybe the day would come when I would write on my tax form "Politician-Writer," not the reverse. I felt more alienated from the jingoistic brand of partisanship—Republicans who voted occasionally with the Democrats were "statesmen" and Democrats who voted occasionally with Republicans were "traitors."

Besides the extra-curricular work with the Bicentennial Commission, I got bit again by the humor bug. With Frank Bryan's encouragement, I began collecting political stories and anecdotes from House and Senate. I created a narrative of two State House custodians who collected these tales and hid them in the basement men's restroom. For illustrations, we gave Jeff Danziger a rest. I found a more local artist to do the illustrations, namely fellow legislator Don Hooper, from Brookfield. His whacky style was just right for the book, *Out of Order: the Unofficial Statehouse Archives*. It sold modestly well, but not nearly as well as the *Goats* book.

~

On balance, I would give myself a C-plus for my accomplishments and service. To the experience, I would give an A. Since I never expected to win in the first place, I had six years of fascinating work, gratis.

In March 1990, my mother died. Her death joined an unusual number of deaths in legislative families that spring. On March 27, 1990, I stood in the well of the House on a point of personal privilege and spoke the following words:

> I thank you all for this card of sympathy.
>
> Yes, the end comes for us all. Sometimes it arrives in tragedy, often it comes in fear, and almost never does it come when we are ready.
>
> My mother was an exception. Few have ever prepared for their own passing with more deliberateness or more consideration for others. Since my father died 15 years ago, she has told us, her family, that she had lived a full life and if she became seriously ill, she would refuse any heroic measures to keep her alive and imprisoned in technology's web, the law's shackles, or her family's guilt.
>
> Three weeks ago she did become quite ill. And true to her vow, she went out her own way, asleep in her own bed, refusing medicine that last day.
>
> Next to her bed we found two quotations. The first is from Pericles's funeral oration to the Athenian dead:
>
> So they gave their bodies to the commonwealth and received, each for his own memory, praise that will never die, and with it the grandest of all sepulchres, not that in which their mortal bones are laid, but a home in the minds of men, where their glory remains fresh to stir to speech or action as the occasion comes.

The second is from Boris Pasternak, the Russian author of *Doctor Zhivago*:

> For life, too, is only an instant,
> Only the dissolving of ourselves
> In the selves of all others
> As if bestowing a gift—

Her death had a curiously liberating effect on me. Suddenly, being a teacher was fascinating, not a fool's errand like law school. Maybe the teaching genes of generations of Smiths, Nichols, and Hastings flowed through me after all. I tested the idea on a couple of normally skeptical friends. "Go for it!" they said, without polite hesitation. The ever-steady Chris agreed. The whole notion of teaching didn't feel like another book odyssey; it could be a new profession. But I wouldn't know unless I tried it. It was time to enroll in graduate school.

Chapter Eleven

Gladly Teach (1990–2007)

"Gladly would he learn, and gladly teach."
—Geoffrey Chaucer

"Maturity is learning to live with ambiguity."
—Bill Mares

In the summer of 1990, my political life ended. I enrolled in the education department of Saint Michael's College, a small Catholic liberal arts college about ten minutes' drive away. A state certificate would take fifteen months and include a stint of student teaching. A full master's degree with a thesis took two years, but I already had a master's degree from Fletcher. I would take the shorter path.

My most influential teacher was Prof. Susan Kuntz, whose course Teacher as Decision-Maker consisted of watching real teachers at work and then writing about what we saw. Because I had the time, I visited twice as many classes as other students because I could, and I wanted to see the maximum number of styles. In one sentence, Sue Kuntz summed up our professional duty: "Your job is to raise each kid at least one intellectual notch. If you can say that at the end of each year, you have fulfilled your mission."

I did my student teaching at South Burlington High School with Bob Walsh, a retired Marine Corps colonel with whom I had served in the Vermont House, and Bill Price, who taught American foreign policy and PIWA, Public Issues and World Affairs. I had my share of stumbles and bloopers, but I got a hint of satisfaction and praise when the AFP class gave me a book inscribed with notes like, "Your classes were like eating dense chocolate!" And "You are the first teacher I know who actually asked his students whether they thought something would work. It did work!"

The next fall, four weeks into the school year, I got a job at a high school in the blue-collar suburb of Milton, teaching three US history classes and two Vermont history classes. Milton was my real baptism by fire. The students had been sharpening their knives *on a monthlong substitute. I was fresh meat. I made all kinds of rookie mistakes. I felt so exposed, so ignorant, so inept, and so nervous. I once used a big felt-tip pen with permanent ink on a blank wall. Boy did the students hoot!

But things gradually improved. I gained confidence by the week. I came to class prepared. I learned command presence. I returned homework the next day without fail. Student faces changed from slabs of hostile or indifferent flesh to living, breathing individuals. I developed some lasting techniques, such as posing a new quotation each day.

I also ran my first Boston Marathon that year, with student signatures adorning my singlet.

By June, I was happy, confident, and then, RIF'd ("reduction in force"). When the town cut the school budget, the last two hired were the first two dismissed me and a middle-school teacher.

On my last day, I told the students how much they had taught me and that I had concluded that there was less adolescent behavior in high school than in Montpelier.

I called my old track coach Bill Wallace in Houston to report on my first year and how much I had grown to love teaching, though it was terrifying at first. "Maybe that's why some teachers never seem to change their lesson plans again," I opined. "That's why I burn mine every year," said Wallace. "Keeps me fresh."

There were no high school jobs available the next fall within driving distance of Burlington. While I worked on the last of the Bryan-Mares books, I went back to school to get a middle school certification, although I was pretty sure I didn't want to teach kids at that level. As a class project, I persuaded my cartoonist friend Jeff Danziger, himself a former English teacher, to work on an illustrated booklet teaching middle school students critical thinking skills, such as awareness of stereotyping and circular reasoning. Alas, though Danziger's cartoons were good, I realized that middle schoolers were not yet in Piaget's stage of conceptual thinking. I put the manuscript on the shelf.

In the fall of 1993, Champlain Valley Union High School, in suburban Hinesburg, had a social studies slot open. I applied and made it to the interview round, where one teacher asked suspiciously, "I've read your books on Vermont. Would you take this job just to write another book about the experience?" No, I hastened to say. "I really want to teach history. Three generations of my family have taught it. I majored in it." And I pointed out how much I liked the CVU mission statement to help all students become "contributing members of a democratic society." I even proclaimed that my license plate was THINK. They hired me.

~

In the first class, I would assign seats and then walk around and shake every kid's hand and make them look me in the eye. I wanted that tactile and visual contact from the very beginning. My second trick was to begin the year with twelve to thirteen different hats from my life, some easy to identify, others impossible. "This is your first of many thinking activities in this class."

> Two questions:
> A. Where is the hat from?
> B. What does it say about Mr. Mares?

In the preamble to my syllabus I wrote:

> One of the long-standing complaints about history is that it is a mass of unrelated dates and events. I won't apologize for giving you certain dates and making you study trends over time. You can't understand history without learning lots of facts. However, my philosophy is *ONLY CONNECT*, which means making sense of those facts by seeing patterns, and interrelations. We will work on the critical thinking skills of analysis and interpretation. As trained historians you will come to understand chronology, the interaction of cultures, multiple perspectives, the relationship of historical events to current events, cause and effect, and the evaluation of various source materials.

> We'll use cooperative groups and different learning styles, mix in some art and music, use a variety of technological tools, such as the Internet, study the geographical context, and WRITE. I believe passionately that we learn best when we write, when we try to shape and organize our thoughts on paper. I promise many assignments in writing, often through the 5-paragraph essay form.

I wrote up eight mega-questions to guide the entire sophomore Western Civilization classes.

1. What is democracy and how did it evolve?
2. Why would one people or nation conquer others?
3. Why do nations and peoples revolt against their masters?
4. How should a society be organized and how should its wealth be distributed?
5. How has technology helped and hurt society over the last 500 years?
6. Where does art fit into society?
7. Why has religion been a huge force for both good and ill?
8. How has human history been influenced by geography?

One of the joys of teaching high school history was watching kids learn to do their own kind of sorting out as their minds matured. That's the way we all develop—to go from concrete to abstract thinking at those midteen years. Nevertheless, I enjoyed telling them that my small contribution to their learning would be to turn them all into "intellectuals."

When they looked at me suspiciously, I said all it means is that you be able to handle concepts, not just facts. The key to being an intellectual, I said, is learning how to think critically. It was Prof. Arthur Schlesinger, Jr., who defined an intellectual as a person "at home with ideas."

And I launched into the only sermon of the year.

I was raised to believe ideas are important, that what you do with your mind was at least as important as what you do. I was also taught that maturity does not bring certitude but the ability to live with ambiguity and complexity. While many questions might be clear, most answers are murky. Not for nothing does my license plate read THINK!

Thinking IS hard work. It means being curious about and tolerant of others' ideas. It requires patience to follow or develop arguments. It means acknowledging, probably privately, that we can be wrong. In a nation with a streak of anti-intellectualism going back to frontier populism and religious fundamentalism, it's well to remember that ideas are not tablets of stone, carved once and forever, by some divine hand. Our history of preaching and building democracy gave us each a mental hammer and chisel, to improve our political system . . . or destroy it.

I enjoyed teaching reflective thinking. Not only did I get to watch mental flowers bloom, I got to do a little fertilizing. Students came to us high school teachers believing in the steadfast absolutes of good and bad, fair and unfair. We tried to show them the shades of gray. In debates, we pushed them to see the other side. We taught about the tricks of dishonest argument, such as attacks on the person, not the idea, guilt by association, stereotyping, and sloganeering.

Finally, we tried to discuss a quotation each day. My favorite aphorism of wisdom and ambiguity was from the theologian Reinhold Niebuhr: "Man's capacity for justice makes democracy possible; but man's inclination to injustice makes democracy necessary."

I was also happy to learn from other teachers, either in formal exchanges or by the by, as when running after school with chemistry and shop teachers. From a physics teacher, I picked up something of the multiple-intelligences theory of Howard Gardner. To broaden the notion of intelligence, Gardner introduced eight different types of intelligences consisting of: linguistic, logical-mathematical, spatial, bodily-kinesthetic, musical, interpersonal, intrapersonal, and naturalist. This new version of learning styles helped me shape lesson plans that aroused, evoked, and played to those various temperaments and skills.

One art teacher at another high school gave me a simple and powerful exercise in art appreciation: Have individuals and groups look at a work of art, preferably one they can hold or touch, and answer four questions.

- A. What do you think this is, or represents?
- B. What materials is it made of?
- C. What was the artist's vision or purpose in making this? "
- D. Do you like/dislike the work? And why?

The key to this exercise was learning to defer judgment.

In European history, we held two historical trials each year. In one we put Christopher Columbus on trial for "crimes against humanity." And in the other, we reenacted the Versailles Treaty negotiations of 1919. I picked the four smartest kids as lawyers on each side and then let the others choose their characters, complete with costumes if they wished. To let me manage the whole affair, and avoid the ire of half the class if I were the judge, I invited friends to school to serve as judges and then write opinions. Several were retired lawyers and one was the mother of a former student. It was the activity the students remembered most.

To help me with electronics, the nascent world-wide web, and organizing lesson plans, I "hired" a computer whiz among my students every year to help me. It was a good education for me, and fine responsibility for the students. (One of them later invited me to officiate at his wedding!)

I even liked parent conferences—because they gave me a chance to see whence these kids came. Of course, some of the kids with the biggest problems at school had very complicated lives at home.

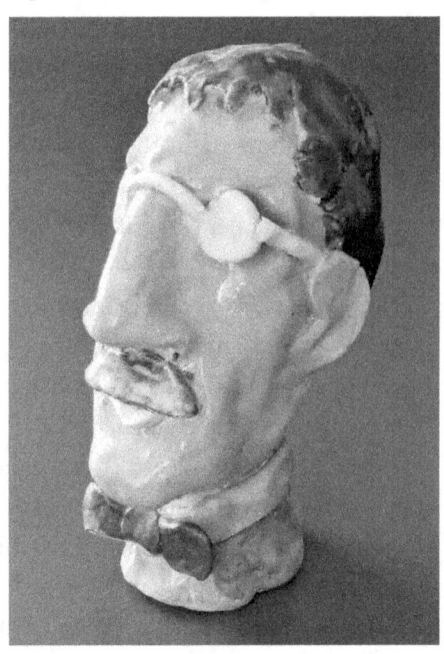

Sculpture of Me by Aaron Wisniewski at CVU Highschool. From a 10th Grade Class on the Renaissance, when we made clay sculptures.

Based upon the American foreign policy course I taught in my practice-teaching phase, I designed one of my own, got it approved, and entered it into the elective sweepstakes. Our motto was an aphorism from the book *The Bar Kockhba Syndrome: Risk and Realism in International Relations*, by retired Israeli general Yehoshafat Harkabi: "Policy is not a choice between good and bad, but between bad and worse." The first year it was oversubscribed. I was flattered to see that some of my best Western civ students signed up for it and brought their friends. It had no AP imprimatur, but it was probably on that level. Indeed, I had one parent tell me that the course was excellent but so hard it was scaring off students worried about their GPAs. I said nothing and waited to see if either of his sons took the class. Neither did.

Shamelessly, I invited friends with international experience to speak. They included two former CIA operatives; my father-in-law, who was a former ambassador; economists; newspaper editors; and Peace Corps volunteers. I made students write "Johnny Deadline" stories about the visits, and then we'd gather them up and send them to the speakers as thank-yous.

Looking back to those years of teaching, I would give myself a B for my performance, and after I was voted teacher of the year, perhaps a B+.

In 2009, I was invited to give the graduation speech at CVU. Of course, I was flattered. Now, I thought, how to avoid making it the most clichéd event since the first baby's birth? Such speeches are usually filled with puffery about how the graduates have the world by the tail, and how they are commencing a grand journey of success upon success. But that message was boring; I decided to ruminate on *failure*.

I talked about the obvious kinds of failure, like flunking an exam or losing a game or forgetting a line in a school play. But also, I spoke of the inability to achieve one's own aspirations.

I told them:

> You are going out into a world that is changing by the minute, where events far from your doorstep will affect your lives. It will be like one of those space shuttle simulators, spinning, shaking, rattling, in perpetual, hair-raising motion, a world moving even as we walk on it. Anyone who promises that you will be masters of your destiny is either smoking or snorting something!
>
> So, what does all this mean?
>
> First of all, don't be afraid to fail. A story, attributed to Mark Twain, that a Mississippi boat pilot applying for a job said he deserved the post because he knew where all the sandbars were. The captain asked, "How?"
>
> "I hit 'em," the man replied, and was hired.

I pointed out Thomas Edison, who, by his estimate, tried over seven hundred substances and combinations of substances to get the right material for the light bulb. On this labor, his reflection was not "I have failed seven hundred times." Instead, he wrote: "I have succeeded in proving that those seven hundred ways don't work."

One of my sons lives and works in Thailand. When I told him I was to deliver this speech on this subject, he wrote back to say, "Don't be dull, Dad!" and attached a YouTube clip of an ad Michael Jordan did for a small, struggling shoe company:

> Jordan arrives for a game. As he walks slowly toward the players' entrance, out of the darkness you can hear him say: "I have missed more than nine thousand shots in my career. I've lost almost three hundred games. Twenty-six times I've been trusted to take the winning shot . . . and missed. I have failed over and over and over again in my life. That's why I succeed."

I closed my speech by wishing the graduates: "Good failure!"

Looking back to those years in the classroom, I realized I was the beneficiary of my mother's and grandfather's lives of teaching. Overall, I give myself a B or B+ for my performance. And for the experience? An A.

Chapter Twelve

Selection, Infection, Reflection (1982–2012)

"Hobby: 'an individual pursuit to which a person (in the eyes of an observer) is unduly devoted.'"
—*Oxford Universal Dictionary*

"The secret of leisure is to find work that is play."
—Barry Strauss

"If Bach's not in Heaven, I'm not going!"
—William F. Buckley, Jr.

Autographs and Bagpipes

In 1999, Barry Strauss, a professor of classics at Cornell, published a small book called *Rowing Against the Current: On Learning to Scull at Forty*. The book captured his passion to learn the tricky, physically demanding craft of rowing a single scull, or a narrow boat with two oars. He writes of its mystique, solitude, ritual, detail, history, and "redemption." One sentence summed up the why of his obsession: "Because the secret of leisure is to find work that is play." That aphorism describes the seven hobbies I have had in my life, although the first two were test kitchens for grander intellectual dishes.

When I was ten years old, my mother gave me an autographed copy of a biography of Abraham Lincoln by Benjamin Thomas, who had been one of her students. "To Billy Mares, with best wishes," he wrote on the flyleaf. It joined a copy of an encyclopedia of the First World War, volumes of which my father had sold as a summer job in Idaho. That volume had the real signature of Canadian flying ace and Victoria Cross–winning captain Billy Bishop. I began my own collection of autographs in college and graduate school when I bought books of some favorite professors to have them sign, scholars like John Fairbank, Oscar Handlin, Edwin Reischauer, and Bill Polk. I found other signed volumes on scouting trips through the many used bookstores in Cambridge and Hyde Park, Chicago.

Over the years I posted letters (care of their publishers) to authors such as John le Carré, John Hersey, Peter Drucker, C. P. Snow, and John Updike to ask for their signatures. Or I'd send them my copy of their books with return postage. Over three-quarters of them wrote back. Another group of autographed books came from my brother Jan, who lived in Washington, DC. On his walks home from work, he would buy newly released and signed books at bookstores and send them to me.

My collection grew to over five hundred volumes. I liked the feeling of possessing such concentrated packets of wisdom, exploration, and curiosity, made more exciting with their inky links to history. But eventually, my literary avarice cooled. It felt more appropriate to follow the Quaker injunction to "Pass it on." I kept about fifty prizes. I gave a few to the library at the school where I taught, and the bulk went to Saint Michaels College, where I had earned my teacher's certificate.

A second, shorter-lived hobby was to become a novice bagpiper In college, I had been envious of a classmate, Jamie Pusey, who played them. My parents loved to travel and once, returning from a trip to Jordan and Egypt, my father brought back a set of bagpipes he purchased from some Jordanian soldiers. The pipes remained in Texas until my marriage, when we brought them to Vermont. I bought a beginner's manual and practiced fitfully until I realized that, of course, I needed a tutor.

Asking around, I found that one Scott Hastings, in the town of Taftsville, was one of the best players in Vermont. When I went to see him, he was polite but dismissive of Pakistani-made pipes. They were not even tuned correctly, he said. "If you really want to play, get yourself a proper set."

Two years later, when I went to Nairobi for the Adlai Stevenson Institute, I happened upon two Scots who agreed to give me a few lessons. One of them even lent me an extra set. Over four months, we met once a week to practice. By the time I left, I felt I was good enough to buy a real set. On the trip home, during a stopover in London, Chris and I took the train to

Glasgow, Scotland, and bought a middle-tier set of standard pipes along with a practice chanter, some extra reeds, and an elementary primer with basic tunes.

For a couple of years, I practiced diligently in St. Johnsbury, then Grand Rapids, and then in Burlington, where one happy day, I was admitted to the St. Andrews Pipeband of Vermont. I was able to march with them in a few parades, wearing kilt, cap, and sporran. But I was never good enough to relax and enjoy the experience. I didn't spend the thirty to sixty minutes a day that the other pipe band members said I needed. Moreover, I doubted I could ever develop the manual dexterity other pipers had learned early in life. It was more work than play. On the premise that the best place to perform before a crowd was where there was no competition, my last public appearance was to play "Scotland the Brave" in the well of the state House of Representatives during the end-of-the-session high jinks.

One of Several Hobbies

Fishing with the Presidents

The origin of this book was an incident on the last day of another legislative session, in May 1989. As a lower-tier representative, I was not part of the negotiations between Senate and House versions of individual bills. Thus, I didn't need to be in the building. What could be more fun than to walk down to the meandering Winooski River two hundred meters away, suit up, and cast a line at some of the trout lurking below a pedestrian bridge? As the golden mote of the statehouse dome caught my eye, I got to wondering if there was anything other than lying and tall tales that politicians and fishermen shared. Then the fish started biting and I forgot about exaggeration and deceit.

As a kid growing up on the Texas Gulf Coast, and then on trips west with my family, I had been a desultory fisherman. But when we moved to Vermont, I found friends who were avid fly-fishers. I tagged along. Despite my diligence, I never mastered the finer points of technique, and never even tried to tie my own flies. But I loved the pace, the silence, the solitude, and the occasional trout. Three men in particular labored to make me a better fisherman. The first was Dwight Dickinson, like Chris's father, a retired US ambassador, whom we had met in West Africa. The second was Syl Stempel, an auditor in the Vermont tax department, and third, Jake Wheeler, our lawyer. All of them were excellent at the craft and sport, and acerbically generous in tutoring me.

Once I shared my fishy-political musing with Chris. At the time, she was the executive director of the nonprofit Vermont Museum and Gallery Alliance. Without missing a beat, she said, "Why not go down to the American Museum of Fly Fishing in Manchester and see what they have?" I knew that Jimmy Carter and Herbert Hoover were avid fishermen. OK. It was only a two-hour drive. It turned out the museum had quite a bit of presidential fishing memorabilia. Museum curator Jon Mathewson was happy to show me John Quincy Adams's fly wallet with flies from the 1830s, a fly box owned by Herbert Hoover, and reels donated by George H.W. Bush and Jimmy Carter. Two books caught my eye, one by Grover Cleveland and one by Herbert Hoover. Sitting at Mathewson's pin-neat desk, I slowly turned the age-stained pages of an autographed copy of Cleveland's hundred-year-old *Fishing and Shooting Sketches*. In gothic prose, he described the joys of fishing and defended his chosen recreation against the philistines:

Salmon Fishing on the St. Paul River, Quebec

The narrow and ill-conditioned people who snarlingly count all fishermen as belonging to a lazy and good-for-nothing class, and who take satisfaction in describing an angler's outfit as a contrivance with a hook at one end and a fool at the other, have been so thoroughly discredited that no one could wish their more irredeemable submersion.

In his book *Fishing for Fun*, Hoover laid out all the reasons why angling is good for individuals—"to wash your soul"—and good for society, by quoting a four-thousand-year-old Assyrian tablet: "The gods do not subtract from men's lives the hours spent fishing."

Gosh, I thought, maybe there was a book here that could knot my loves of history and fishing. As boys, all the presidents probably would have fished, and a few had carried that pastime into their presidencies. When I gushed to Mathewson about this trove, he said I should visit the Franklin D. Roosevelt Presidential Library in Hyde Park, New York. "I'm sure there is meat for your stew there," he said. And, boy, was he right! In one day at Hyde Park, I changed the entire format of the prospective book from a straight chronology to themes, three of which arose from the Roosevelt archives.

My fascination with presidential fishing became scores of expeditions, with their variety, excitements, disappointments, and ultimate rewards. The nibbles and strikes were not just how presidents fished, or with whom, or what they wrote about their experiences. Just as interesting were the ways in which the public, press, and friends responded to presidential anglers. I found dozens of editorial cartoons about presidential fishing per se and hundreds more that used fishing as a metaphor for the issues of the day. Various presidential archives held thousands of letters and some gifts sent by ordinary citizens who offered advice, fellow feelings, or even invitations to fish on a favorite pond or stream. I wrote another chapter just about presidential fishing companions. Ultimately, I focused on the most prominent fishing presidents, at least in the records I found—Washington, Chester Arthur, Grover Cleveland, Calvin Coolidge, Herbert Hoover, F. D. Roosevelt, Dwight Eisenhower, Jimmy Carter, and G. H. W. Bush (whom I interviewed in person).

Presidents, I found, had fished everywhere—in Georgia sloughs, on Pennsylvania streams, Adirondack lakes, Kentucky creeks, and Wisconsin, Oregon, and California rivers, off the coasts of Maine, Florida, and Texas, in Alaska, down the Potomac, and up the Amazon. They had lodged in luxury and tented in simplicity. They had pursued the lordly salmon and the lowly perch. They had caught bluefish and trout, tarpon and bass, pickerel and cod, shad and herring, catfish and pike.

In many ways, presidents fished like the rest of us. They fished with cronies and they fished alone, the Secret Service notwithstanding.

Fishing with the Presidents

They brought home their limit, and they got skunked. They killed fish and they released others to fight again. They told the truth and they lied, when they could get away with it. They swung between contemplation and competition.

Yet, Presidents also had fishing experiences that were uniquely presidential. Calvin Coolidge had Secret Service agents scare off anglers who dared to fish waters reserved for him. Dwight Eisenhower failed to catch any of the hatchery trout dumped into a Vermont stream the night before his arrival. And only a former president like Jimmy Carter could compare the theft of two prized fly rods to defeat in a national election.

The book was about presidential recreation, not statecraft, although the inescapable backdrops of war and peace, boom and bust, promise and deceit, and the aching, lonely responsibility of the office, gave many of their fishing stories luster and life. When presidents themselves equate angling with democracy, as Hoover did—"[Fishing] is great discipline in the equality of men—for all men are equal before fish"—what better excuse could there be for me, and the reader, to go fishing?

The book took five years and a lot of permissions to complete. As with the beer book, I avoided the researcher's curse of always looking for one more source, one more anecdote. I went where no one else had gone and came back to tell the tale. It was perhaps my favorite book for style, originality, and illustrations. It was fun to visit various presidential libraries and the National Archives. The blurbs from people like historians Stephen Ambrose and James MacGregor Burns were icing on the cake. Capping it off, I got my cartoonist friend Jeff Danziger to do the cover, which showed the "big seven" presidential fishers standing in a circle, all facing outward to fish in different directions.

Bees Besieged

In 1996 I lost all my five beehives. As a hobby beekeeper for twenty years, I was devastated and embarrassed. The state inspector, Steve Parise, gave cold comfort. "You are not alone. Varroa mites are the cause and they're a problem across the entire country. All beekeepers will have to up their game to deal with them."

And so I did. With improved management techniques and the well-established agricultural practice of IPM—integrated pest management—including an insecticide called Apistan, I recovered. Three years later, I won best in show for my comb honey at the Vermont Farm Show. I began selling some of my combs to local markets and a specialty foods wholesaler. But I had not dodged the bullet—varroa mites would bedevil my beekeeping and everyone else's for the rest of my life.

My baby steps into honey commerce got me thinking not just about bee health but the honey market. I subscribed to the two leading bee magazines, *American Bee Journal* and *Bee Culture*, which were full of articles for amateur and backyard beekeepers. Then, on the Internet one day, I stumbled upon an electronic fraternity of beekeepers from around the world. This listserv, BEE-L, whose editors were in the US, Canada, Ireland, and Australia, described itself as the "oldest continuously running forum dealing with the informed discussion of beekeeping issues and bee biology." The seven to eight hundred members of BEE-L chatted and argued about hive construction, cell size, honey prices, diseases, chemicals, feeding regimens, and much more. George Imirie, an inveterate poster from Maryland, used almost every one of his posts to crusade for turning neglectful "BeeHAVERS" into responsible "BeeKEEPERS."

After lurking for several months, I waded in with a question to the collective: "What are the biggest problems facing beekeepers?" Within a day there were twelve replies from across the country. One person named varroa mites as the chief culprit. Another condemned the improper use of pesticides. Another blamed cheap honey imports. Still another condemned the United States Department of Agriculture. One writer echoed Pogo's famous aphorism: "Let's not forget the bees' worst enemy; we are it."

Among the frequent writers on BEE-L was one Mike Palmer of St. Albans, Vermont. I knew him from Vermont Beekeepers Association meetings. I called him and we met in his workshop, surrounded by barrels of honey and scores of hive boxes under construction. Gangly, intense, wearing steel-rimmed glasses and a ponytail, he wasted no time. After attending the University of Vermont in the early 1970s, he started a maple sugaring business, but then switched to bees and in ten years built up a business of nine hundred hives spread across northern Vermont and New York. In machine-gun fashion, he raced through a list of pressures that put beekeeping "at a crossroads" including:

> Farming practices are changing every year. Much of the clover is now cut before it blooms. The price of corn went up a few

years ago. Farmers began planting more of it. Now, many of my Champlain Valley yards are surrounded by nothing but corn with no forage for bees.

Pests, parasites, and diseases are also a major problem. First, the tracheal mite, *Acar woodii*, invaded our bees. Lots of beekeepers lost fifty percent or more of their colonies. Then came the second mite, varroa. It was much more severe. There was no resistance among our bees. The chemical Apistan worked for a while, but it was pricey. We had no choice, though. Now the varroa mite is becoming resistant to the chemical, as mites always do.

Then there's the development all over Vermont. There used to be lots of places to locate bees. Now it's fewer and fewer. And the biggest problem of all, low prices. When I started in 1974, bulk honey, in the fifty-five-gallon barrel, sold for fifty-five to sixty cents per pound. The cost of supplies didn't go down though, and neither did the price of honey at the retail level. Who is making all the money? Not us!

He caught his breath. "Don't take my word for it. Go see Drutchas!" Rick Drutchas was a former state bee inspector and good friend of my early mentor, Arnold Waters. He had about six hundred hives around the state and sold the honey in several dozen outlets. Rick indeed echoed what Mike had said about pests, loss of forage, development, and generic honey promotion. "If you don't stress *American* honey, it just brings in more from Argentina." He was also worried about the growing power of the honey packers and distributors. "It's an age-old problem in agriculture," Rick said. "The middlemen always make more money than the producers."

I began to feel that familiar triple itch of journalistic curiosity, ego, and the urge to travel that usually heralded the onset of my periodic "book flu." Here was a perfect storm of bee troubles: the cumulative effect of the various biological, economic, environmental, and political forces acting on bees and beekeepers. The bees couldn't stay alive without the beekeepers, and the beekeepers couldn't stay in business without the bees. I saw that my own future as a hobbyist with five or ten hives was inextricably bound to that of professional beekeepers with five thousand to ten thousand hives. If the industry collapsed, I wouldn't be able to get equipment or replacement bees. All beekeepers were imperiled.

My Home Apiary

Bees Besieged

Catching a Swarm in Downtown

Why not write a book covering all these problems facing the beekeeping industry? Maybe I could use the techniques I'd learned with *Working Together* and *Making Beer* to take on this adventure. Yes, it would be a long slog across the country, to visit individual beekeepers, importers, packers, competing beekeeping organizations, USDA laboratories, pollinators' operations, and equipment suppliers. But wasn't that the point? What's more, no one else had done anything like this in sixty years.

As Sherlock Holmes, another famous beekeeper, said, "Come, Watson, the game is afoot!" Over the next five years, during summers and school vacations, I went to a dozen national beekeeping conventions. I visited beekeepers in sixteen states. I interview giants in the field, like academics Marla Spivak, Tom Seeley, Dewey Caron, Sue Cobey, and Tom Rinderer, breeders like Binford Weaver, brokers like Joe Traynor, and producers like Richard Adee, the largest beekeeper in the country. The book became *Bees Besieged*, and was published in 2005 by Root Publications, the owner of *Bee Culture* magazine. Kim Flottum, its editor, added a poignant subtitle: *One Beekeeper's Bittersweet Journey to Understanding*. The next year, 2006, alas, a new crisis rolled over the industry, potentially as devastating as varroa mites. Annual hive losses went from around fifteen to twenty percent to thirty to thirty-five percent. No one could figure out the cause. So they called the mysterious condition CCD, colony collapse disorder. Aided by the Internet's ubiquity, the mixed malady caught the public's attention in ways varroa had not. The disorder quickly dated my book as journalism, but the work held up as history. Had I been a full-time agricultural reporter, I might have leapt on a sequel. But I was content to go back to my own bees, and throw myself into state and regional beekeeping organizations. Here, I felt invested in the future of billions of bees and thousands of people.

I joined the board of the Vermont Beekeepers Association and worked up to president. Then, I volunteered to represent Vermont on the regional Eastern Apiculture Society board that covers twenty states and three Canadian provinces. I was persuaded to become president and have Vermont host the annual summer conference. In 2012, I and seventy volunteers, including an invaluable aide-de-camp business consultant named Diane Meyerhoff, welcomed 750 beekeepers and a million bees to the University of Vermont campus in 2012. Among other things, such a roe allowed me to invite as speakers a number of the people I had interviewed for my book.

The conference was the second largest in history.

The Back Road to Boston

On a dark, snowy January afternoon back in 2002, forty of the Oriana Singers of Vermont straggled into the chapel of the First Congregational Church in Burlington. We doffed our mufflers, balaclavas, and coats and greeted each other like college reunionees, even though we had had our Christmas concert of Bach's Magnificat only four weeks before in the nave of this same church.

This was our first rehearsal of Bach's monumental three-hour-long *St Matthew Passion*, which we would perform in April in the Ira Allen Chapel at the University of Vermont. Until then, we would spend every Wednesday afternoon here between four thirty and six.

Our conductor was Prof. William Metcalfe and the accompanist was his wife Elizabeth, a professional pianist. Bill was a polymath of a teacher, the only professor in the history of the University of Vermont to chair three departments at different times: History, Music, and Canadian Studies. Under him, we singers had sung many of the major choral works of Bach, Haydn, Mozart, and others. With a slightly different mix of singers (including me), Bill had also formed an ensemble to perform most of the Gilbert and Sullivan operettas.

We were an eclectic mix of high school music teachers, professional singers, UVM professors, a retired cop, a stockbroker, a federal prosecutor, an emergency medical technician, etc. Bob Low, a UVM chemistry professor, and I had the oldest (albeit unwitting) shared musical experience. Forty years before, he and I sang in two joint concerts of the Princeton and Harvard glee clubs.

The *St. Matthew Passion* is an operatic retelling (without costumes and stage directions) of the familiar Good Friday story of Christ's last supper with his disciples, the walk in Gethsemane, his betrayal by Judas and denial by Peter, his deliverance to Pilate's judgment, his abandonment by the crowd, and his scourging, crucifixion, death, and burial. The *Passion* is scored for two orchestras, two four-part choruses, and a third chorus for the first half. Traditionally that third chorus is sung by boys, but in our rendition, one of our members, Aimee Bushey, who taught choral singing at a local high school, was training a chorus of her female students for the part.

About twenty minutes into the rehearsal, I suddenly realized that the concert would happen on the day before I was signed up to run the Boston Marathon. Yikes! This was *Boston*, the most celebrated road race in the world, a mecca for most distance runners. With its famous Heartbreak Hill, characters like Clarence DeMar (who won a record seven Bostons), the famous Johnny Kelley and Bill Rodgers, the infamous Rosie Ruiz, and the requirement to qualify in a certain time, the race had an almost magical quality for runners. I had run it three times before as well as twenty other marathons. Maybe I didn't need to run the race. I'd probably be wasted after all that emotional singing the day before. And even if I felt up to it physically, the timing was off. There was no way to sing an evening concert, or even a late afternoon concert, drive to Boston, get to Hopkinton, and start the race, even at noon. Back to singing.

But wait a minute. What if the concert was early Sunday afternoon? Chris might be willing to drive down with me, stay with friends in Concord, and get me to Hopkinton for the start. At the end of the practice, I rushed up to Bill to ask the concert time. I was in luck. The concert was at one thirty. Yippee!

I settled into overlapping routines. Formal music practices once a week and a few days weekly of practicing (or warbling, as Chris put it) on my own. The three-month preparation for Boston, on the other hand, was the same as for all my previous marathons. I tried to run six days a week, alternating long and short distances, increasing my weekly miles to fifty to sixty per week. When I ran alone, I would listen to music on an iPod or construct school lesson plans. The central event of my running week was an outing with a group of friends on Saturday mornings, in the hills outside Burlington. Rain, shine, or snow, we were out there for up to twenty miles, chatting, complaining, and aching together. We were roughly the same age (although I was both the oldest and the slowest), with roughly the same educational level, and political views. All of us had run multiple Bostons.

Ralph Swenson, an administrator in the University of Vermont Graduate College, was our guru, having run over fifty marathons, numerous fifty-milers, ten hundred-mile races, and four races up Mount Washington.

Other regulars included Phil Coleman, a fellow teacher from CVU, Rick Peyser, of Green Mountain Coffee Roasters, and Bob McDonald of the US Farmers Home Administration. In temperatures ranging from the thirties to ten below, we talked politics, books, sports, past races, the aches of the day, and in those early months of 2002, the "war on terror." Humor was both a diversion and a prod to keep us going, with the worst sin being not pride but self-pity. With Ralph and Phil both being Yalies, there were always scores to settle with my Harvard past.

Sometime during those early weeks, the book bug bit me again. Maybe, just maybe I could turn this dual experience into a book, something like *Music, Muscle, and Miles*. That was too cutesy. But the idea still simmered. I tried it out on Chris: "Why not? And here's a better title: *The Bach Road to Boston*. Clever, clever, as always!

So I settled in to write a more detailed journal each day, a dual diary of the singing and running for the three months. Only Chris knew of my secret ruminations. I didn't want the inevitable questions: What's it about? Who's the publisher? Etc. Having been burned once before, on the miners' book, I didn't want to be embarrassed again.

I dug into the two activities, their differences of course, but also their similarities, the tensions between self and selflessness, between the physical and the spiritual, and their respective rhythms. Ralph lent me a DVD of great Olympic runners, and I bought a used videotape of *Chariots of Fire* for further inspiration.

When the performance came, I was ready, we were ready. This concert became an augmented family affair. In addition to Bill and Elizabeth,

Boston Marathon Finish Line 2002

Back Road to Boston Illustration by Edward Koren

who played the harpsichord, their daughter-in-law, Emily Walhout, played the viola da gamba. Bill and Elizabeth's son, Scott, who directs his own choral group in Boston, added his tenor voice to Chorus II. Moreover, Vin Pelletier's daughter, Monique, a professional singer from New York City, had come to sing a number of the alto arias. The big-time professional countertenor Bill Hite came from Boston to sing the Evangelist's role. For us, it was like having Yo-Yo Ma play in our local string quartet.

My head was a thicket of emotions. Will I catch a cold? Will my legs hold up? Will I hit all the notes? After listening to the *Passion* dozens of times, I now shivered to be inside it.

The *Passion* opens with the antiphonal brilliance of three choruses and two orchestras.

Hite began his series of recitatives accompanied only by a solemn cello line. I used to think they were just boring inserts, but now I see how integral they are to the story. They are the story. The chorales, choruses, arias, and recitatives fit together in a moving mosaic of beauty and faith.

We were back two thousand years in those hot, dusty streets, sharing that last meal, sleeping in the garden, among the murderous crowd before Pilate, and weeping before the Cross. Here, in Burlington, our friends were Christ and Pilate, Judas and priests.

After the great chorus "O man, bewail thy sins so great," a lilting prayer of contrition that ends the first half, we took a break.

We marched through the second half in a flurry of roles, now accusers, now the crowd, now the disciples, now the priests. In one vicious chorus, we basses led the group to give derisive assent to Pilate's offer: "Lass ihn kreuzigen!" "Let him be crucified!"

The work ends not with the Resurrection but the prayerful entombment. "We lay ourselves with weeping prostrate / And cry to thee within the tomb ... Rest thou gently, gently rest. Rest thou gently, gently rest."

And, suddenly, it was over. The audience rose with wave upon wave of enthusiastic applause. On wobbly legs with no voice left, I stumbled down to the basement and out the door to meet Chris for our drive to Boston.

After a fitful sleep in Concord, Chris drove me out to Hopkinton. I knew the route, the corrals, the nervous hubbub of hundreds of already-sweaty runners, the invariable five-minute shuffle even to get to the starting line. But my focus was not on the scenery, human or otherwise, nor on the spectators, but to finish, pure and simple.

In the first five miles, we sorted out our own pace and place. Then, like spring ice, the pack broke up. We became groups of floes and then individual bergs bobbing eastward. On the wings of the runner's high, we sailed through Framingham and Natick. As we passed Wellesley College, the women were still cheering for us slowpokes. At Newton Center, the grind up Heartbreak Hill began. "All I have to do is finish" became my mantra.

Climbing the hill, I thought of Bach. He'll dull my pain. At the age of twenty, like a Baroque Deadhead, he hiked 220 miles in ten days from the town of Arnstadt in Central Germany to Lübeck on the Baltic Sea, to meet and hear the great Danish-German organist and composer Dietrich Buxtehude. That was almost a marathon a day for ten days! Stop whining.

At the top of the hill sat Boston College where a few students proffered cups of beer. I declined. Then we headed down the hill past the Chestnut Hill Reservoir, through Coolidge Corner, and through Kenmore Square, under the giant Citgo sign. The last five miles were almost silent, broken only by the scuffing of shoes and a few ragged cheers as the runners moved in their own cocoons of pain.

Right we turned onto the short Hereford Street, then left onto Boylston Street for the last slog to the big B.A.A. banner and digital clock and deafening cheers from spectators packed five-deep on both sides of the street. As I crossed the finish line, head down, arms held high, I couldn't resist repeating St. Paul's line to Timothy: "I have fought a good fight, I have finished my course, I have kept the faith."

I wove and wavered through the crowd for a couple of blocks, every muscle crying out, but not my spirits. And there was Chris, grinning with love.

So. The day was over in twenty-seven hours. But then the book took ten years to write! Well, I was fighting ego all the way. I had a lot of trouble finding the right tone that fit two such disparate experiences. Running and singing kept tripping over each other. All kinds of other activities were competing for my attention—other books, teaching, nonprofit board duties, our growing boys, the whole presumption of the project. Several times I wanted to give up. My agent did. "I can't sell merely a clever idea," she said.

I began to feel like the poet Paul Valéry, who said, "A poem is never finished, only abandoned." I was ready to abandon it without finishing it. Then, another running buddy, Dr. Joe Hagan, said, "Just tell a story. Don't overthink it. Practice on me." And that broke the logjam. Then I got two strong editors to help, Anita Selec and Emily Copeland. They were good literary mechanics, making sure this engine ran. I prevailed upon another cartoonist friend, Ed Koren, to do a witty cover, and that opened the door to a welcoming local publisher.

In the beginning, the two experiences seemed so different. What could Bach and Boston possibly have to do with one another? But then gradually, like Escher's tessellations, they began to merge as when his fish became half birds, and the half-birds became fish

On the simplest level, each took three months to prepare. Each had its own training rhythms. Each was a block of material to be mastered. Each had physical and cerebral elements. Each wove together the individual and the group, the solitary and the communal. Each was a rear guard action during the time of life that Clarence DeMar called the "slipping period."

Each inspired its own meditation, free-form and deliberate. I could put my mind in neutral and let it travel the globe. In motion, I was becalmed; in calmness, I roamed.

For me, unlike DeMar, neither endeavor was competitive. The cellist Yo-Yo Ma's remark on music applied equally to my running: "The reason for playing music is not to compare yourself to anyone, but to bring forth what is inside of you."

There was something else going on here. With this book, I would "hit for the cycle." In baseball terms, that means hitting a single, a double, a triple, and a home run in one game. In my life, I had already written books about three of my other hobbies, fishing, beekeeping, and home brewing. This book would cover the last two, singing and running.

In the end, I came to see that these two activities were sequences of my DNA, two parts of who I am as a human, both an individual and a member of a group, self-absorbed and selfless. My life was not a single note, in vocation or avocation. I was happy to play as many notes as I could, as long as they harmonized into a chord.

Chapter Thirteen

Talking at 50 Mph (2007–2019)

"And yet it is also true that one can write nothing readable unless one constantly struggles to efface one's own personality. Good prose is like a windowpane."
—George Orwell, "Why I Write"

A few months after retiring from teaching, I took up another kind of pedagogy; I went on the radio. Starting in the 1980s, Vermont Public Radio offered a distinctive series of short commentaries in which a cross section of Vermonters were invited to sound off about the human condition. One of them was Mike Martin, a French teacher at CVU as well as a jazz singer and musician. I liked Mike a lot. With another teacher, Robin Fawcett, we had chaperoned a school trip to France in 2000. "You should try a radio gig," he told me over beers. "You've had a mixed career in journalism, politics, and teaching, and a smorgasbord of other interests and experiences."

Well, I had done similar opinion pieces for several newspapers and for another local station, WJOY-AM. "OK, I'll give it a try," I said, and ended up writing and recording a hundred short pieces for VPR (now Vermont Public) between 2007 and 2019. (Find them by searching "Bill Mares" at www.vermontpublic.org.)

Writing is never easy, but I found I liked this form of short, personal five-hundred-word essays to be read aloud. It was a little like a school lesson plan—you had to have a main message, a beginning, and an ending. To say something coherent in five hundred words meant that every word must count. I would try to find the universal in a subject, connect it to my own life or to the world around me, and do so without leaving my thumbprint on the windowpane, to paraphrase George Orwell.

"If you want me to speak for an hour, I can do it tomorrow," Woodrow Wilson supposedly said. "If you want me to speak for thirty minutes, give me a week, but if you want only five minutes, I need a month." No matter how fine the grain, there is always more grinding to be done.

In my numerous revisions, I was mindful enough of a quote from William Strunk and E. B. White's classic, *The Elements of Style*, to repeat it: "Omit needless words, omit needless words, omit needless words." The process would start with an idea that I could try out on my wife, or one of my running buddies. If it passed that smell test, I'd send the thought to Betty Smith Mastaler at VPR headquarters for her green light. I'd begin by scribbling notes on a yellow pad. Then, like a dog with a bone, I'd gnaw on it for a few days before burying the first draft in the computer. Several days later I'd dig it up again. I'd gnaw some more until I could send a clean copy to Betty. If I was lucky, it would come back with "just a few tweaks." Sometimes she wanted major revisions, and we would go back and forth three or four times. Further polishing came when I read the piece aloud. It's amazing how many typos, non sequiturs, and other grammatical flaws appear in audible speech.

The scene then shifted to the VPR studio, where engineers Sam Sanders and Chris Albertine took their shots at my delivery and sometimes my grammar. Inside their headphones, their unfailing ears understood the average listener, who, they reminded me, must "understand you at fifty miles an hour." There was always a glitch, a stumble, or a gulp over some alliteration, allusion, or other phrasing that looked *so* smooth on paper but sounded rough in the voice. Fortunately, Sam and Chris could make their repairs electronically, sentence by sentence.

Once the piece was done, I was done. I almost never listened to myself live, except by accident. Unlike the bloggers of today, I didn't want dialogue or comment, not because there was no more to say, but because I wanted to move on to the next idea or experience. The only overt complaint I ever received was for a shot I took at the twin dictators Fidel Castro of Cuba and Hugo Chávez of Venezuela. One of Burlington's stalwart lefties took me to task for my criticism of these two worthies.

In the present Wild West of social media, it's quaint to think of those calm VPR commentaries moving slowly and peacefully across the plains. I hoped that my tone was not "There's no more to be said!" Nor did I want to imply the title of Chicago columnist Mike Royko's book *I May Be Wrong, But I Doubt It*. I just wanted to say something interesting.

In 2012, after I had done about a hundred commentaries, a local publisher, Wind Ridge Publishing, invited me to bring out a collection. We chose fifty-five pieces. I got blurbs from Representative Peter Welch and then-governor Peter Shumlin and a forward from Peter Gilbert, the executive director of the Vermont Humanities Council. We titled the book *3:14 and Out*, after the time limit for each commentary. Then I persuaded *New Yorker* cartoonist Ed Koren to draw a cover showing me running across a finish line with a microphone in hand.

Cover of 3:14 and Out *by Edward Koren*

Chapter Fourteen

Riding Authorial Shotgun (2009–2018)

Even after I stopped teaching in 2007, the literary tapeworm of writing books lived on. I never thought of writing a book about teaching. That just seemed too presumptuous, and I had nothing original to say. But "retirement" was a meaningless word since I had never stayed at a single job for the traditional thirty-thirty-five years straight. This next string of books became zippers of friendship and content I co-created with long-standing friends. Unlike those collaborations with Polk, Simmons, and Bryan, each of these three I'd known for decades and shared at least one pastime with—running, singing, or brewing.

My coauthors and I did not depend upon an equal knowledge base, but I knew that none of us alone would have or could have written books on these three topics. Together, yes!

My only ego demand was full equality on the book covers: none of this "Written with Bill Mares" or "As told to Bill Mares" stuff.

Brewing Change: Outside and Inside Green Mountain Coffee Roasters

In my last year of teaching, I began going to Latin America, partly to improve my Spanish and partly because after finishing writing my 2005 book *Bees Besieged*, I was curious about the effects of Africanized honeybees, or "killer bees," which had become ubiquitous in Latin America. There were hints that, after two decades of losses, countries like Mexico and Guatemala were seeing their honey production recover as the beekeepers learned to combat both bee aggression and the parasitic varroa mites.

I started in Panama, where I met up with Tom McCormack, a Pennsylvania beekeeper and airline mechanic who had begun a nonprofit to gather up used but serviceable prosthetic devices to donate to needy Panamanians. He also volunteered to help beekeepers in the northwest province of Chiriqui. There, he introduced me to Price Peterson, whose estate produced a world-class coffee named Esmeralda. I asked him if he knew my friend Rick Peyser, who worked for Green Mountain Coffee Roasters. "Of course I know him!" he exclaimed. Later in the conversation, he said, "You know, Rick is becoming quite an influential figure in the coffee industry. He's on track to become president of our trade organization, the Specialty Coffee Association of America." The modest Rick had told me a little bit about his service on the board of SCAA and other nongovernmental organizations, like Coffee Kids, the Fair Trade International, Save the Children, Heifer International, and Catholic Relief Services.

The next year, through Rick's connections, I went to Oaxaca, Mexico, for more Spanish and more beekeeping. I hitched up with a Mexican nongovernmental organization called CAMPO, which Green Mountain Coffee Roasters was supporting. CAMPO's chief beekeeper, Alfredo Contreras, opened my eyes on several fronts as I accompanied him on his rounds to remote mountain communities. He showed me how beekeeping had recovered from Africanization. The farmers learned how to work them with protective equipment, and to recognize that Africanized bees were somewhat more resistant to varroa mites than those they replaced.

Some local beekeepers had begun dreaming of selling honey in nearby

Beekeeping with Food4Farmers in Mexico

Me and Rick Peyser

towns and even abroad, thus adding to their income. But when they first went around to collect it, there was such a pent-up demand that most of the honey had already been sold at the village level. "Good problem to have," remarked Alfredo. CAMPO was now looking at the wider markets.

My preface to my 2012 book, *Brewing Change: Behind the Bean at Green Mountain Coffee Roasters*, begins this way: "The book is Rick's; the idea was mine."

Brewing Change

By 2007, I had known Rick for fifteen years. We had shared dozens of long Saturday morning runs as we prepared for marathons. We shared dog walks on Sundays. He had spoken several times about the coffee industry to my class in American foreign policy. We had kids about the same age. We shared a quietly activist Christian ecumenism—he went to Saturday afternoon Mass, while I went to Sunday Episcopal services. His favorite quote was by Stephen Grellet: "I shall pass through this world but once! Any good thing, therefore, that I can do or any kindness that I can show to any human being, let me do it now, for I shall not pass this way again." It went well with my favorite quote from St. Luke: "To whom much is given, much will be required" (Luke 12:48).

On one of our Saturday runs, I told him what Price Peterson had said about his influence, and how important he was to the philosophy and mission of Green Mountain Coffee Roasters. By then, I knew that Green Mountain donated approximately two and one-half percent of its pretax profits to domestic good works and two and a half percent to charities abroad, primarily in the coffee regions. As director of Social Advocacy and Supply Chain Community Outreach, Rick was responsible for distributing that second half, which grew from about $350,000 in 2006 to over $10,000,000 in 2012. He had become fluent in Spanish to communicate directly with coffee farmers.

In his work, Rick became appalled by the farmers' food insecurity, where even with higher prices given for fair trade or organic coffee, many coffee farmers could still not earn enough money to feed their families properly. (Those times were called "los meso flacos," or the thin months.) Natural disasters and climate change made their problems even worse. Rick set out to do something about this. He persuaded Green Mountain to commission a film about this food insecurity and, through contacts, got actress Susan Sarandon to do the narration.

I thought Rick had a good story to tell, and on one of our runs, I asked him if he wanted to write a book together.

"Sure, and when we're done, we'll climb Everest!"

Seriously, I told him. "You're a social entrepreneur changing the culture of the company and the lives of coffee farmers, and doing all this good work not from the top of Green Mountain but from the middle of the organization. I know you're modest, but I can help you get over the hump of ego and focus on what you are doing, not your own personality." I said that I had done a similar book about workplace democracy with an expert in that field.

"This will not be just another feel-good volume about gringos helping natives. Business schools will use it for examples of social entrepreneurship and, to use a latter-day term, of effective altruism. The industry will love it. The general public will love it. You're already giving talks at college campuses about your work." I even enlisted some of his Green Mountain co-workers to push the book idea.

After this barrage of friendly fire, Rick finally surrendered.

Now, it was simply a matter of finding the time for long interviews, transcriptions, edits, and finding a professional editor and a publisher. In a mere three years we were done. In the end, the process was easy. We set up regular meeting times each week. I recorded the conversations, transcribed them within two days, and sent them to Rick. He returned them in a week. Rick was a gem to work with. There was never an annoying or annoyed word. He supplied all the art, i.e., photographs, and blurbs from half a dozen heavies in the industry. The Saturday morning runs and Sunday afternoon dog walks gave us more time to work on the project.

I enjoyed being his amanuensis, his scribe. I would prod him with some journalistic questions, teasing out his story. I wanted to help him shine as brightly as possible without tarnishing his essential modesty, to convey his mission without bragging. We got help from those two good editors, Anita Selec and Emily Copeland. Bob Stiller, the president of Green Mountain, wrote the foreword. The book received industry-wide praise.

When the book was published in 2012, on the principle of "teaching a man to fish," Rick worked with Marcela Pino and Janice Nadworny to found Food 4 Farmers, a nonprofit dedicated to helping coffee farmers maintain sustainable livelihoods. Rick assembled a board of academics and employees in the coffee industry, and included me as a ringer.

My contribution to F4F was to persuade them to develop beekeeping programs in their target communities. I dragooned Prof. Dewey Caron of Oregon State University into being an adviser because he was already doing similar work in Latin America. He and I went to Mexico and Guatemala to visit some of the target coffee cooperatives to offer modest beekeeping advice.

Ten years later, I am still on the F4F board, and Rick and I are still walking together on Sunday afternoons, but with the next generation of dogs.

Grafting Memory

> On Fame's eternal camping-ground
> Their silent tents are spread,
> And Glory guards, with solemn round,
> The bivouac of the dead.
> —Theodore O'Hara, "Bivouac of the Dead"

I met Bill Lipke in the late 1970s when, as a reporter, I was sent up to the University of Vermont's art museum to write a story about part of its collection. Bill was then both a professor of art history and the museum director. After that introduction, we became neighbors and fellow singers in the Oriana Singers.

We also shared an interest in war memorials and monuments developed in the late 1970s, when we both read Paul Fussell's *The Great War and Modern Memory*—a powerful description of how a generation of poets struggled to

Better to Be Lucky than Smart!

Cover of Grafting Memory Written With Bill Lipke, 2015

Vermont Veterans Cemetery, Randolph, VT

World War I Gravestones, Thiepval, France

find the language to encompass the wretchedness and horror of the trenches and the epic slaughter of World War I. For Bill, it was building on a long academic interest in the period. I became hooked on the memoirs of poets Robert Graves, Edmund Blunden, Siegfried Sassoon, and others. I read diplomatic and military histories of the war, watched several TV series on the Great War. I made the war a central event in my classes in Western civilization, and set up a three-week reenactment of the Versailles Treaty negotiations, with parts for every student. I believed, with George Kennan, that World War I was the central event of the twentieth century.

In 1998, I and our younger son, Nick, with Chris's father (who had been a combat historian in World War II) traveled from Normandy to the Somme River, to Compiegne, to Verdun, the Maginot Line, Bastogne, and Waterloo, monuments to three wars, all in ten days. The acres of orderly gravestones in sylvan settings hid the torment, terror, and slaughter the war had brought. We carried those images home, the war imprinted on all our minds.

Back in Burlington, at our Oriana practices, Bill would periodically talk about his travel to Ottawa, Ontario, to work on a mysterious "memorial project." *What was that*, I asked. He explained that the memorial had been an assembly of Canadian artists' responses to World War I, part of a larger effort by Lord Beaverbrook to document Canada's role in the war through photos, film, paintings, and books. In fact, the Great War experience had helped

GAR Medallion, St. Albans, VT.jpg

Canada find its national identity. "Canada was born at Vimy Ridge," went the cliché about Canada's most famous action during the war.

Bill's interest in the Beaverbrook collection grew out of his PhD work about a group of artists known as the Vorticists, some of whose Canadian members were represented in the memorial collection. Vorticism was a London-based modernist art movement formed just before the war. It was partially inspired by Cubism, with familiar forms of representational art rejected in

Doughboy Statue in Wilmington, VT

favor of a geometric style with a hard-edged abstraction. Personally, Bill had a grandfather who had crossed the border to enlist in the Canadian army as well as an uncle who served in the American army and came home gassed.

Bronze Plaques with Names of Over 2,000 Residents of Burlington, VT, who Served in World War I

cultural history. I emailed him the next day and told him the subject was big enough for two books. As the hundredth anniversary of the war's outbreak approached, what better hook for such a book? He was less sure.

"Look," I said. "You can use all this material!" And then came my original, and brilliant, thought—compare the World War I memorials with those of the American Civil War, in whose sesquicentennial we were at that moment. I scolded him that it would be a crime against his profession and all the effort he'd already made not to finish, and in this novel, expanded fashion. "Plus, I'll help you!" I made an inventory of my potential contributions. I could add my journalist's and historian's eyes to his aesthetic and historical perspective. I knew how to collaborate on book projects. I loved the idea of interacting with history. Bill would lead, of course, but I was sure I could find a few original things to say. It would be a great ride.

After a week, Bill gave in, and away we went. Bill had already gathered a library full of materials on the Canadian experience. Together, we traveled across town greens in Vermont where granite sentinels still stood. We visited

Cornish, New Hampshire, where sculptor Augustus Saint-Gaudens had crafted his *54th Massachusetts Memorial*, and went on to Boston's Common. I went to Gettysburg, Antietam, and Washington, DC, to collect photographs. I found monuments from four wars.

We explored the different approaches to individual burials for officers and men, and the signal difference between the British practice of leaving their dead where they fell in cemeteries spread across France, Belgium, and beyond, and the American vow to bring home any of the dead whom their families desire. Ultimately, some seventy percent of the American dead were brought back to the States.

General George Stannard, Hero of the Battle of Gettysburg, Lakeview Cemetery, Burlington, VT

Cyprus Hills National Cemetery Dating from the Civil War, Brooklyn, NY

World War I Memorial, Tyne Cot Cemetery, Passchendaele, Belgium

I went to England and on to France with my grandnephew William Spooner to cover the Somme, Verdun, and Château-Thierry for three nations' cemeteries. I pored through files at the Imperial War Museums in London.

As a former photographer, I became interested in the early use of still cameras for war photos. I learned about the early use of training camp photos to simulate actual battle scenes. Elsewhere, artists used real photos of post-battle scenes as templates for some of their paintings. We didn't neglect our own city foits memorial legacies to the Civil War, or a plaque to the first Burlington resident to die in World War I and a World War II cannon, all set about in Battery Park. Grander still was the

Me at Fort Vaux, Verdun

basement discovery of twenty three-hundred-pound bronze plaques of the 2,100 World War I service members from Burlington in the city's 1929 Memorial Auditorium. Ninety-five names were starred, to mark the dead. I spearheaded a local committee to restore and rehang these massive treasures.

From Home Brew to House of Fermentology

> And malt does more than Milton can
> To justify God's ways to man.
> —A. E. Houseman, "A Shropshire Lad LXII"

In the mid-2000s, I would drive home from school by way of Magic Hat Brewing Company in South Burlington to pick up half-gallon growlers of my favorite Vermont beer, Blind Faith, a rich India pale ale. One of my former students who worked there knew I was a beekeeper. He told me that the head brewer, Todd Haire, was also a beekeeper and I should meet him. I promptly walked into the back shop where, in a tight little office with space for one, I found three scruffy brewers. Todd, a big friendly guy, introduced himself and apologized for the turmoil of the brewery's expansion. He said he had read my beer book, which made introductions easy. We talked bees and beers for a few minutes, and I left with a free six-pack of Blind Faith.

After a few more friendly visits, Todd and I decided to put our combined beehives together behind the brewery. I wanted to bring my hives back from suburban Shelburne, and Todd worried about bear destruction in his town of Hinesburg. The brewery was a good spot. Over three years, our apiary grew to a dozen hives, but then the brewery's own expansion ended our

Me and Todd Haire

"lease" and we both had to find other digs for the bees. But we stayed in touch.

Like me, Todd had grown up in Texas but he moved to New Jersey during high school. He was unable to go to college for lack of money after his father died. After running a yard-trimming crew, he switched to work in a beer packaging store. He began making home brews to mimic some of the beers in the store. He fell in love with brewing, and with a schoolteacher named Monica Lubic. She encouraged him to look for a real job in the brewing industry. First he needed some formal schooling, which he got at the Siebel Institute of Technology, in Chicago. Then he worked for breweries in New Jersey and Manhattan, before being hired by Magic Hat in 1998. That year, Magic Hat produced seven thousand barrels. Eleven years later, when Todd left as head of brewing operations, they were making 180,000 barrels. He then became head brewer at Switchback, another local brewery.

Fast forward to 2014. We were at the Vermont Brewers Association's annual festival on Burlington's waterfront, surrounded by thousands of tipplers. "Look around you at all the breweries in Vermont and across the country," Todd said. "Don't you think it's time to do another edition of *Making Beer*?"

Hmm! A good idea, I thought. But the problem was I didn't know anything about an industry that had grown to over five thousand breweries. I wasn't even making my own beer anymore, so good were the commercial products. What would be the message? But if I had a coauthor, who knew about styles and trends and hardware and mechanics, maybe I could come up with an original angle. How about Todd?

He didn't say no but reminded me that he was working full-time as head brewer at Switchback. And Monica wouldn't be joyful to see him take vacation time for beer treks. However, Todd had already begun experimenting with Belgian-style sour beers, with a small-scale dream of a different kind of brewery or blendary. A two-week trip to Belgian breweries had deepened his appreciation of their beer. What if we focused our research on some kind of microbrew shopping? We wouldn't commit to anything up front, just go and look. It would sharpen our focus and exclude ninety to ninety-five percent of the breweries out there Todd had produced the full range of beers from the lightest lagers to the heaviest stouts, except

Belgians. He came to believe, with beer guru Michael Jackson, that Belgian beers were the most complex in the world. Because the yeasts for Belgian beers could ruin lagers and ales, he had done his experimentation in his basement, using different yeasts he had cultured, and aging the products for six months or a year in carboys and a couple of oak barrels.

With Monica's and Chris's permission, we cobbled together trips around Vermont, one to the Boston area. But we needed more case studies. How about the state of Oregon, with over 230 breweries, which competed annually with Vermont for the most breweries per capita?

And so, in ten days in Oregon, we visited twenty breweries, big, medium, small, and tiny. That last was the two-barrel-sized Ale Apothecary brewery, in the woods far outside the town of Bend. The owner was Paul Arney, the son, grandson, and great-grandson of pharmacists. He produced about seventy-five barrels per year and sold most of it in 750-milliliter bottles. His capital investment was a fraction of a stand-alone brewery. Suddenly, I thought I might have a chance to fulfill the original dream of *Making Beer*—to actually build a brewery—with Todd's expertise, of course.

On the plane flight home, we dumped the home-brew-how-to perspective. First, I persuaded Todd to tell his own story in a separate chapter. Then we dumped the stand-alone brewery and brewpub models. We would build a blendary to make sour beers in the Belgian style, with the yeast Todd had been culturing for several years. (There was only one other such operation in Vermont.) The blendary wouldn't need the capital investment in kettles, fermentation tanks, and all that gleaming (expensive) stainless equipment. If we could find a place to rent, we could buy the boiled hops-malt wort, put it into our barrels, and then bottle it in a year or two. In effect, I was fulfilling my original dream through Todd.

As soon as we returned to Vermont, we got permission from Monica and Chris to begin what became an eighteen-month launch. We gathered our state and local permits. We found an empty bay at a local tire repair company. With Todd doing most of the work, we did the requisite renovations for fire codes, noise, power, and drainage. We bought our first batches of wort from two larger breweries, Fiddlehead and Zero Gravity. To our different batches, Todd added various fruits and his yeast. Then we waited fifteen months for the beer to age properly. In the middle of all this work, two of Todd's former brewers at Switchback, Bob Grim and Sam Keane, invited him to help start a new brewpub called Foam Brewers on Burlington's lakefront. He said yes, which meant that for about four months, he was working three brewing jobs!

Since Todd had been interested in fermented foods and meats for some time, we called our blendary the House of Fermentology. Every beer had "Dot" in the name, such as Blue Dot, Purple Dot, Perpetual Dot, Seurat Dot, etc., because as Todd said, "All great art begins with a single dot."

We sold all the beer at Foam, usually on a Saturday, with forty to fifty customers lined up for the noon sales. The first batches of forty-five twelve-bottle cases sold out in one hour, with a limit of two bottles to the customer. We told the thirsty public that to quench their thirst, these restrictions were the "tactic of scarcity," not "scare tactics."

We told our friends that HOF guaranteed its imbibers they required only three sips to reach enlightenment: After the first sip, the drinker gags and says the beer is "taking the enamel off my teeth." After the second sip, the reaction is "Hmm, this is an interesting mix of flavors." And after the third, it is "Where can I buy this stuff?"

To bring the original pair of hobbies back into sync, I taught a small cohort of Foam employees how to keep bees, first in the classroom and then with some hives set up near their brewhouse in the suburb of Charlotte. The most enthusiastic novice was Bobby Grim, one of the Foam co-owners. After a couple of years, we made him a partner in BTV Honey, which sold one thousand pounds annually, including some at Foam Brewers.

After a successful first five years, Todd and I sold the blendary to Foam Brewers. For me, going from the first two editions of *Making Beer* to opening a sour beer blendary in an auto body shop was like going from journalism to politics, from observation to action, even if Todd did ninety-five percent of the work. For Todd, it was the logical continuation of his chosen and enduring career. In early 2023, HOF was ranked on untappd.com the thirty-sixth brewery in the world, whatever that meant. The final title of our book became *Making Beer: From Homebrew to the House of Fermentology*.

My forty-five-year dream had come true!

In all these cases, I was delighted to help three friends arouse their sleeping egos to take on or finish the books that were in them, and to deepen my own interest in three blocks of knowledge. Here was Bill Lipke with boxes full of material he couldn't complete and me with the long interest in WWI. Here was Rick Peyser, so modest it never occurred to him to write a book about his professional life in coffee and me with a lifelong love of coffee. And with Todd, I was happy to extract from him his own story of growing professional brewing expertise and marry it to my own brewing origins in a St. Johnsbury cellar fifty years before.

Chapter Fifteen

Choruses of Coauthors (2013–2020)

In which our hero works with three coauthors to write three books in five years with threescore and ten contributors. A music metaphor works—after singing both literary solos and duets, he turns to choral directing.

In the summer of 2013, I was feeling like a hotshot, as a beekeeper, anyway. Our BTV Honey harvest had been good. The year before, the Vermont Beekeepers Association had hosted the annual Eastern Apicultural Society conference at the University of Vermont. As the Vermont representative on the board, I was the President of EAS that year and in charge, with the sterling help of seventy volunteers, we hosted over 750 attendees at the University of Vermont for the second-largest EAS conference in the fifty-year-old event.

Then, at the VBA summer meeting that year, I was named the first Vermont Beekeeper of the Year. I figured it was for my organizational work and the beekeeping teaching I had done for twenty years, not for my beekeeping skills.

At the end of the meeting, President Mike Willard asked for suggestions for future VBA meetings. Larry Karp, a mental health therapist and beekeeper for forty years, said, "Not so much a question but a suggestion—someone should do a history of beekeeping in this state. We have nationally known figures like Charlie Mraz, Mike Palmer, Kirk Webster, and Ross Conrad. We've contributed a lot to the national history as well."

All the nonwriters in the room huzzah'ed and whooped and said, "What a great idea!" "Cool!" The two writers (Ross Conrad and I) in attendance looked at each other quizzically.

A month later, I called Ross and said, "What about it? Want to do this together? We've both written books. We know the drill." Silence at the other end.

Ross Conrad of Middlebury had been a beekeeper for over twenty years. Ross learned his craft from the late Charles Mraz and his son Bill. Like me, he had been president of the Vermont Beekeepers Association. He was a regular contributor to *Bee Culture* magazine, and his book *Natural Beekeeping* had become a bestseller among bee books.

He was a strong advocate of "treatment-free" beekeeping, that is, using nonchemical methods to treat bees for diseases and varroa mites. He gave bee-related classes, lectures, and workshops throughout North America. His own company, Dancing Bee Gardens, sold honey and other bee-related products, like nucleus colonies and rental hives for local pollination.

Me with Co-Author Ross Conrad

Ross had one hundred hives; I had ten. This was his profession; I was a hobbyist. He had written a bestselling book on his techniques. My book, *Bees Besieged*, looked at the entire industry. As a pair, we had covered the waterfront.

Then Ross came back on the line. "This might work," he said cautiously. "I've even got a title: *The Land of Milk and Honey*." Yes, it was a biblical phrase, but also a long-gone road sign welcoming motorists to ADDISON COUNTY, VERMONT, THE LAND OF MILK AND HONEY. We were both excited about being the first state with a detailed history of its beekeeping industry. He wasn't sure of how much time he could devote to the research, working full-time as he was. I said, let's go get two or three or four other beekeepers from around the state to help us write several of the chapters. Done. We asked Kim Greenwood, a former president of the Vermont Beekeepers Association, Larry Karp, who had suggested the book originally, Scott

Wilson, former VBA secretary and owner of a small honey business, and Larry Solt, a retired music teacher and beekeeper who was writing his own book about Vermont town bands.

Ross's strengths were the early history, the current landscape, and the future. I shared the middle passages with the other four collaborators.

For my part, I dug into the records of the state Agency of Agriculture and Markets, the Vermont Historical Society, and the special collections department at the University of Vermont Library.

Our history buzzed with characters. We covered early Vermont inventors of hives, and found a hive dating from the 1830s with its patent signed by President Andrew Jackson. We discovered Augustin Manum, a Bristol harness maker who had survived the battle of Gettysburg and came home to become the largest beekeeper in Vermont in the 1880s. We wrote about Barre's Dr. DeForest Jarvis, whose 1959 book about the health benefits of honey and vinegar, called *Folk Medicine*, sold over a million copies. Then there was Charlie Mraz, who started a bee operation in Middlebury in 1931and built it up to eight hundred to nine hundred hives, He bred his own queens, but was perhaps more famous as a practitioner of apitherapy, or the use of beestings for a variety of maladies. He wrote a book on the subject, and when I went to see him just before he died, I asked if his suggested stinging points were related to those used with acupuncture needles. "The same!" he said.

We also covered the work of an ER doctor in Middlebury, Mike Kiernan, who founded Bee the Change. Their approach was to install arrays of plantings in and around solar fields to support a diverse array of pollinators.

We gave Mike Palmer plenty of ink, as well as Ross and Kirk Webster and the Mraz family. But we still didn't have enough to show the full flavor of Vermont beekeeping. So, we went looking for friends and a cross section of Vermont beekeepers who had day jobs as teachers, a baker, a band leader, a custodian, a bee equipment dealer, state employees, a bus driver, a therapist, a forester, etc. Then we asked them to write their own short beekeeping autobiographies, a page or two each.

Ross and I had some minor disagreements over some of the conclusions, probably born of our different philosophies of beekeeping, but not as severe as those with Simmons and the *Working* book. After all, as the wag once said, "Beekeepers are like lawyers—six beekeepers, seven opinions." In the end, Green Writers Press did a fabulous job of assembling the book, and we got wonderful blurbs from several national beekeeping giants, like Tom Seeley, Randy Oliver, Dewey Caron, Kim Flottum, and others.

The book arrived in the same month as Covid-19—February 2020.

The Full Vermonty

"You're Fired"

Me With Co-Author Jeff Danziger

Days after I had open-heart surgery, Donald Trump's election was the nightmarish present I received on my birthday in November 2016. Like millions of other Democrats (and some Republicans), I went into denial. How could sixty-three million people be so wrong? During the campaign, I had reread the Sinclair Lewis novel *It Can't Happen Here*, about a right-wing presidential victory. Little did I expect that this book, written and set in Vermont in 1935, could be so prescient.

Now we had a presidential buffoon, a man of willful ignorance, bigotry, and prejudice, a malignant narcissist who lacked all curiosity, compassion, and humility. Upon further reflection I saw that the Republicans had done it with the help of Russian hacking, the antiquated electoral college, widespread gerrymandering, and appeals to the worst human instincts.

Adding to my ill humor, I went through a bad post-op patch. To treat a heart-lining infection, the doctors put me on steroids. They made me miserable. I couldn't sleep. I couldn't eat much. I felt as if my brain were detached from my body, and floating up somewhere in the ether. If this was life, I was ready to leave.

However, as I emerged from my own Slough of Despond, I didn't lose my dismay over Trump's election. I didn't want just to stew in my own juices. I couldn't march against him because of my heart. I had no complaints about our Vermont congressional delegation. I dutifully wrote checks to the ACLU and 350.org. But these weren't enough. What could I, a single voter, do?

I sought comfort with my friends in Vermont and beyond. I called Jeff Danziger, my cartoonist buddy whom I had known for forty years and who had illustrated two of my books and three of those with Frank Bryan. Jeff split his time between Vermont and New York City. With his biting political cartoons, he daily afflicted the comfortable and comforted the afflicted.

While we commiserated, he asked, "Why not another book before dementia sets in?"

"Hmm. That's what Rachel Maddow said on MSNBC a few weeks ago: 'Think what you do well, and do it for the country.' I can write humor. But I'll only do it with you!"

"There's a title I've always loved," said Jeff. "*The Full Vermonty! Vermont in the Age of Trump.*"

"Excellent! Let's go. Desperate times demand desperate measures."

So I started writing a few essays, like "Who's Afraid of the Big Bad Wolf?"

and "Donald Trump as the Ultimate Invasive Species." Then I said maybe we could get Steve Terry, a former news editor and aide to Sen. George Aiken, to write a foreword. Jeff agreed.

Meanwhile, Jeff was doodling out eight to twelve cartoons, showing Trump in the most buffoonish light.

We turned our energies to scouring the hills and hollows for ideas. Vermont had withstood the Revolution, a New York invasion, and the New Hampshire Land Grants and would assuredly survive the next few years under the Washington axis of evil, a.k.a. the Trump administration, the Republican leadership in Congress, the conservatives on the Supreme Court, and Putin's gang in Moscow.

We were the first state to outlaw slavery. We banned billboards and went to great lengths to protect our natural resources. Vermont has a history of speaking truth to tyranny, from Matthew Lyon to Ralph Flanders. We're little but we're loud. Look how we elected a New Yorker, Bernie Sanders, to carry our message nationwide.

Trump may see himself as a Western version of Vladimir Putin, but we don't. He's just a bully used to stiffing banks (Vermonters make their payments), stiffing his subcontractors (we pay them, because we're related to most of them), and treating women poorly (we just know better). We'll be damned if we're going to let a man who dyes his hair, cheats workers (and on his wives), and has his products made in China dictate to us how life should be.

We made a good start, with some lists, quizzes, cartoons, and a cover. We thought about seceding from the Union but that is not our style. Frank Bryan, Jeff, and I had already written about this in the 1980s.

Vermonters fight back, always have and always will. But then it dawned on us that the task was too large, and the enemy too fearsome, to do it alone. As in most hostage situations, and this was the biggest one in the nation's history, we needed backup.

So, one day, driving across the state from St. Johnsbury, Chris and I began making a list of other wise, witty, and like-minded friends who could join our posse of writers and artists. We looked for folks with the right kind of grudge against Trump. As we scoured the hills and hollows, the list grew, and in a month's time, our duet became a chorus. There was Dr. Harry Chen, Dr. Joe Hagan, my walking buddy, musician Bob Stannard, writer Julia Alvarez, former governor Madeleine Kunin, ex-CIA operative Haviland Smith, fellow high school teacher Mike Martin, fellow author of *Out of Order* Don Hooper, etc. Hallelujah!

Chris likened my recruitment work to our succession of border collies, whose preternatural instinct was herding sheep, and, absent sheep, humans.

With each new companion, my health improved.

I wrote nine to ten of the essays, like the following:

> "High Noon at Highgate"
>
> So, the federal government is not the only entity that can build a wall. Fortunately we'll only need one about 45 miles long across the boundary with Massachusetts. In the north, we have our friends the Quebecois. On the east, we have the Connecticut River. On our west we're guarded by Lake Champlain.
>
> Our wall will be built with hedgerows of kale genetically modified to be eight feet tall. It will be a bipartisan effort from our Republican governor Phil Scott, a contractor, and Democratic lieutenant governor David Zuckerman, an organic farmer. (Sorry, David, this GMO is in a good cause!)
>
> Vermont will become a refuge for folks from both blue and red states fleeing from polluted waters, fouled air, and never-ending Trump rallies.
>
> Each year we will admit a certain number of people with needed skills, giving preference to disillusioned Trump supporters. Our own EB-5 program will be scandal-free.
>
> For the rest, because we don't want to be inhospitable (after all, Vermont was called the Beckoning Country back in the 1960s), we will invite, even encourage, them too, to "invest" in Vermont. Tom Salmon, a good governor in tough times, famously said, "Vermont is not for sale." Well, we'll have to revise that for our own Time of Troubles. We will encourage those folks who don't get admitted to buy some land in

Vermont. "Get a place in Vermont!" will be our slogan.

That place would be one hundred square inches, slightly bigger than a hand- or boot print. Thus there would be about sixty thousand plots in an acre. With 6.1 million acres in the state, there's a real land bank, thirty billion pieces of Vermont. We could sell one to every person on earth and still have enough for ourselves. Our Green Card will be a deed of ownership.

The mind boggles at the thought of it.

I Could Hardly Keep from Laughing

Don Hooper and I met in 1985, during our first term as state representatives, me from Burlington, Don from Brookfield. We never served on the same committee, and Don stayed around Montpelier longer than I did, but we shared an affection for the Capitol's denizens and ghosts. We knew a lot of the same people around the state, but he was far more politically active than was I.

In 1991, along with my UVM-professor buddy Frank Bryan, we parleyed that fondness into a collection of true and almost-true stories about local and state politics in Vermont. I wrote a narrative about two fictional custodians, Vern and Chet, who collected stories for *Out of Order: The Very Unofficial Vermont State House Archives*. Don did the art, created Vern and Chet, and captured past pols and their pratfalls in wacky cartoons. I wrote the stories and Frank oversaw the final product, which sold modestly.

I went on to teach high school and write other books, and Don went on to higher office, becoming Vermont's secretary of state. During his term, he wrote a booklet on easing barriers to voting, *Doing Democracy*. From there, he became the New England regional representative for the National Wildlife Federation.

For the next twenty-five years, Don continued, like Edward Gibbon, to "scribble, scribble, scribble" and send to friends an irregular stream of cartoons from a host of fictitious card companies such as "This Dog Won't Hunt Card Company," of "Troll the Droll Publishing," not so mysteriously located at his home, while becoming bosom buddies with the celebrated *New Yorker* cartoonist Ed Koren, also a resident of Brookfield.

We stayed in touch, and when cartoonist Jeff Danziger and I assembled our twenty-voice Vermont response to Donald Trump's 2016 election, *The Full Vermonty*, Don was a contributor.

In early 2018, Don and I met in the Three Penny Taproom in Montpelier to catch up, and to survey all the good we had done with *The Full Vermonty*. "What's the next book," he asked. Quickly as lightning, I said, "A history of Vermont humor, but only if you'll do it with me." I had begun a fitful search for old stories, but Don's cartoons might brighten an anthology of something old, something current, something loving, even something original. After a few days of thought, he said yes. He sharpened his colored pencils and a Vesuvius of cartoons began to pour forth. During one stretch of almost three months, he mailed me almost a cartoon a day. Chris and I would judge them and then put the weekly winners on the icebox door.

In two years we were done.

We got other ideas along the

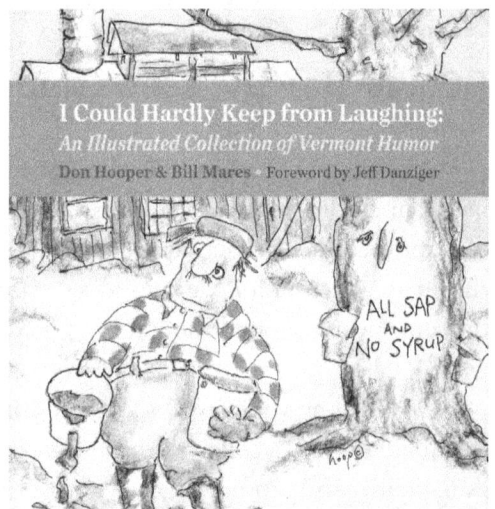

I Could Hardly Keep From Laughing

Me and Co-Author Don Hooper

way. We changed our theme from a history to a collection of humor, the better to reflect its evolution, as we stumbled into modern groves and troves of humor. Humor moved out of the barn and off the country store steps into school gyms and town halls and onto stages, even formal comedy clubs. Best of all, it included women, thanks to Dan Bolles, who had written a big article about women comedians.

Don added some stories of his own, but his great talent was his illustrations, whose primitive brilliance he sprayed onto the page like a fire hose. In truth, Don's cartoons were so original and profuse that there was nothing to do with the cover but put his name first.

Chapter Sixteen

Public Service/Private Joy (1965-present)

"Let humble Allen, with an awkward shame,
To do good by stealth, and blush to find it fame."
—Alexander Pope

"The man who seeks God in isolation from fellow believers is likely to find, not God, but the Devil, who will bear an embarrassing resemblance to himself."
—R. H. Tawney

Time, Talent, Treasure

For me, the boundary between work and nonwork has been more porous than for many. This was also true with my public service. My impulses were three: the Bible, Chris's example, and the panoply of opportunities to serve in this small, welcoming state.

I started slowly, with work on a cluster of traditional local boards. They were in the category of community service in which you give something back, something outside your private interests. My first nonprofit work was to be a board member for the Fairbanks Museum in St. Johnsbury, our first home in Vermont. The museum is half of the extraordinary dual philanthropy of the Fairbanks family, who also gave the library to the town. The museum has a marvelous collection of taxidermy animals, rocks, ethnography, a planetarium, and a weather station in a beautiful Richardsonian Romanesque–style sandstone building. There I served with local lawyers, doctors, insurance folk, my beekeeping mentor Arnold Waters, and others.

In Burlington, I joined the Vermont Council on World Affairs, which grew out of my life of study and travel. Their simple motto was "Bringing Vermont to the world and the world to Vermont." The Fletcher Free Library held a wonderful collection to serve all ages with books and programs, and when I told my mother I would join that board, she said, "Ah, books, the next best thing to friends."

While in the legislature, I applied for one of the two legislative slots on the Vermont Bicentennial Commission. With uncharacteristic ambition, I wormed myself into the vice chair's seat. Perhaps I got the job because of my contribution to a collection about the anniversary, an essay with the (now) insensitive title of "The Vermont Mind: Adventures in Schizophrenia." I helped choose a license plate we sold to pay our expenditures. Along with my hero Bill Gray, the commission chair, I traveled the state, gave speeches, and encouraged local celebrations. I even oversaw a sold-out debate between my buddy Frank Bryan and Supreme Court Justice John Dooley, on whether Vermont should secede from the Union.

The bees created a class of nonprofit work by themselves. After keeping them as a solitary hobby for twenty years, I felt the call to help others learn this cherished craft. I joined the board of the Vermont Beekeepers Association and was president for a few years. I began teaching night classes in beekeeping at the high school where I taught history, and day workshops at my beeyard in Burlington. For five years I wrote a biweekly column called The Flight Path for the state Department of Agriculture newsletter. I helped lobby the legislature about pesticide threats to bees.

Regionally, I became president of the Eastern Apicultural Society and with seventy volunteers hosted a summer conference in 2012 for 750 people from twenty states and three Canadian provinces.

Building on my VPR commentary experience, I joined the Speakers Bureau of the Vermont Humanities Council and gave talks on beekeeping history and home brewing all around the state. As I said in my bees peroration:

> To work with bees is a perfect expression of citizen science, exploring, taking good notes, figuring out what ails them. Working with bees is to use all your senses: smell, hearing, taste, touch, and sight. In addition to the fine taste of honey, I love the sweet and sour smells of nectar, curing honey, warm wax, and the burlap smoldering in my smoker. Sure, it can

be hard work at times. Hauling 90-pound "supers" is heavy lifting, but that load is in refined gold.

I enjoy the praise of friends who like my honey. I love winning prizes with my honey. I delight in selling my honey. But I never forget that the bees painted the picture; I merely hung it on the wall. As Bridport beekeeper Kirk Webster says, "The bees are the color; everything else is black-and-white."

Friendship, some hero worship, and my coauthorship with Rick Peyser on his life story spawned another long-term civic activity. I became one of the first board members of Food 4 Farmers, the nonprofit organization Rick founded to deliver both aid and technical assistance to coffee-farming families in Latin America. My principal contribution was to help them get into beekeeping as a local income-producing supplement for the farmers.

In 2016, my journalism background led me to invite myself onto the board of a revolutionary statewide digital newspaper, *VTDigger*, founded by Anne Galloway, a newspaper reporter-editor who had lost her job at a local daily newspaper. All over the country, local newspapers were crashing. Donald Trump's election set off more alarm bells about objective news coverage. *The Washington Post* captured the crisis with its ominous slogan: "Democracy dies in darkness." Now, here in Vermont, I had a chance to join the fight to preserve hard-hitting news coverage. My sub-rosa dream was to help *VTDigger* be a national model for statewide nonprofit journalism. I would remain on the board for nine years.

At my Episcopal parish, I served in several capacities—lay reader, vestry member, choir member, and sometime lay preacher, which benefited from all the radio commentaries I had done. Work at the local food shelf was similarly multifarious—washing pots, stacking shelves, sorting food donations, grinding coffee. Besides Americans, I got to know refugees from France, Senegal, the Congo, and Somalia. My best friend was a Bosnian, Midhat Hadzic, with whom I could talk about public affairs in general and Balkan history in particular. Which brings me to the other great bookend of my life, Chris and my own family. Very little of my last fifty years' accomplishments would have happened without her. She has been my best friend.

Chris was the ravishing blonde I had dreamed about since high school. Every good and generous thing in our marriage has her mark on it. I have been the mercurial partner, she the steady calm presence in every storm. She is an organizational genius wedded with a balanced judgment. I held grudges; she forgave. I raced to finish my jobs; she was devoted to a good task well completed.

As my first editor, she was acute, smarter, and in some ways more learned than I. She is a puzzle master, gobbling up thousand-piece jigsaw puzzles, daily crosswords, sudoku, and other games. She collects all kinds of things, like windup toys, model boats, musical postcards, mystery stories, and all the Anthony Trollope novels.

Her historic painted theater scenery project, Curtains Without Borders, and the book she wrote, *Suspended Worlds*, are the apotheosis of all her talents: people, history, art, technology, politics, technique, and promotional writing. Just imagine the awesome memory it took to keep seven hundred different curtains in mind. How many can say they are the world's expert in one field?

Here's what her publisher, David Godine, wrote about her book in his memoir, *Godine at Fifty*:

> Talk about esoteric. When Chris Hadsel first approached me with her proposal for a book on what seemed to be a hopelessly remote corner of the art world, I was less than enthusiastic. But when she came to the office, showed us the photos, and told us the backstory of what Curtains Without Borders has done to preserve and protect these fragile, wonderful, and often bizarre canvas backdrops, I couldn't resist. Yes, it's a small corner of the art world, but never has a small corner been more thoroughly, thoughtfully, and beautifully explored.

Chris is also a great lover of gardens and birds, books, and our succession of border collies: Tree Bear, Digger, Toby, Juno, and Augie, all memorable, to use her favorite word. The range of her public service is legion, far broader than mine. The Vermont Symphony Orchestra, Planned Parenthood, Vermont Humanities Council, UVM Lane Series, the St. Johnsbury Athenaeum, Fairbanks Museum, Vermont Governor's Institutes, Burlington School Board.

Raised an Episcopalian like me, she does more good by *not* going to church than I do by going. She is altogether a Gibraltar of intelligence, kindness, and tough love.

"Happy families are all alike; every unhappy family is unhappy in its own way." Based upon our own experience, Tolstoy's famous opening line to *Anna Karenina* just seems silly.

For the first five years of our marriage, we didn't want to have children because there were so many places to go and work to be tried. For the next five, we fussed with infertility doctors. So, when the two boys came, we made up for lost time. Chris and I both came from accomplished families. We both had "every advantage." We figured our job was to expose the kids to a large number of healthy experiences, figuring the unhealthy ones they'd find for themselves. We set about building a family without being what our friend Ben Mason called "overly aggressive parents."

Well, we learned what every other parent learns: Parenting is fun, but it's hard work. My mother quoted Kahlil Gibran to me and I quoted him to myself in the more frustrating moments of child-rearing:

> You may strive to be like them, but seek not to make them like you.
>
> For life goes not backward nor tarries with yesterday.
>
> You are the bows from which your children as living arrows are sent forth.

But then I thought, Gibran was just a bachelor mystic; what did he know?

Just as our parents had launched us into books at an early age, we read to our kids: *Curious George*, *Babar*, *The Jungle Book*, Uncle Wiggily, Thornton W. Burgess, the Moomins, Tintin, and Asterix. They learned to read early, before cell phones, thank God. Then came *Redwall*, Narnia, the Hardy Boys, etc. I created Toe Bear, a tiny creature who lived between the toes of unsuspecting children like Nick, while Chris invented for Tim the endless adventures of Uncle Wiggily's monkey pals Jacko and Jumpo Kinkytail.

Of course, Tim and Nick had their rebellious "pout-burgers," as we called them. Daddy had his "eruptions." Nick could howl like a wolf and fight back with a host of witticisms. Of his toothbrush, he threatened, "I'm not afraid to use this!" And as I was about to light my pipe in the car once, he said, "Don't even think of it!"

Nick's first complete sentence also emerged on a car trip. As he sat in the passenger seat happily eating a bagel, I leaned over and took a bite. Outraged, he hissed, "Buy your own bagel, Daddy!"

Tim was more taciturn but once at the age of three put his filial thoughts into art with A Mean Dad drawing. Later he would coin his own version of Woody Allen's career lesson "Eighty percent of life is showing up" by saying, "You have to be at the table!" Chris was always the honest broker, adjudicating complaints from both boys and me.

Each had some athletic success. Tim was a ranked junior tennis player in New England, and Nick was all-conference on his high school football team.

I think our greatest gift to them was to encourage the habit, love, and practice of travel. It was as if **the centripetal force of going places actually brought our family closer.** Life in foreign parts was a "museum of life" and we let them choose the exhibits they liked.

Early on, we all went to the YMCA camp in Estes Park, Colorado. Four years later, we took another family trip to the Northern Plains and Montana, to visit my father's roots around Helena, then to Colorado and the Grand Canyon. Starting when Tim was five, Chris took one boy to England almost every year, and once the three of them went to the original Norwegian home of the Hadsel clan in the Lofoten islands, north of the Arctic Circle. Both boys went to the Czech Republic, Tim to study and Nick to visit.

In general, we found it easier to travel with the boys singly. On one such trip I took Tim to southern France where, among lots of Provençal sites, we stayed with Bill Polk. The next year, Nick, Chris's father, and I toured battlefields in France and Belgium from Normandy to the Somme and Verdun.

During college, both boys took flight to study abroad for two semesters each in two different countries. That's when I likened parenting to the falling away of the first rocket stage and the ignition of their own next stage.

After graduating from the University of Richmond, Tim returned to Thailand, where he had spent a semester studying, and has lived there for seventeen years and counting. He married a wonderful Thai woman, and in a succession of international work, went through five passports and 160 pages of travel documents. After his graduation from George Washington University, Nick worked in Argentina for five years, becoming fluent in

Spanish before returning to Vermont. He married, and with his wife took their daughter on three trips abroad before she was three.

I was flattered beyond words to be asked to marry them both, Tim on top of the hill where Chris and I had been married and Nick in Burlington's Intervale, not twenty yards from one of my beeyards. And then to have Nick and Chelsea name their first child after my mom, Delia, made for more teary pride.

Presiding at Nick and Chelsea's Wedding in Burlington

Presiding at Tim and Natt's Wedding on the Hill in St. Johnsbury

Just as Texas was a great place to be from, so Vermont has been a great place to be. As Frank Bryan said, the proximity of its town and state governments helps to sustain a society of better human scale.

In no other state could I have done the range of things I've done. Vermont allowed me to know an incredible range of people and participate in a great range of activities—politics, beekeeping, fishing, politics, sports, and singing. If you are at all gregarious, you can get to know just about anyone in the state, where the custom is two or three degrees of separation, not the proverbial six or seven. You can know people from across the state and approach anyone from the governor and congressional delegation on down. When you throw a stone into the social pond, its waves radiate out through even more groups and individuals. Between us, Chris and I knew people in every county and corner of the state.

As "real Vermonters," the boys feel the same way. Tim went to kindergarten with Nate Anderson, whose aunt Chris O'Donnell I taught with at Champlain Valley Union High School, and Nate's sister Sarah was one of my students. Twenty years later Tim ended up working for Nate in two different companies in Asia. When Nick went to buy a house, he went through Nancy Farley, who shares a Texas upbringing with me, and who in a former life working for a Vermont publisher, helped edit one of my books. She is married to a man who was godfather to Nick's best friend through high school and college.

Then there is the quirkiness factor. Vermont just seems to have more eccentrics than other places. That offbeat charm makes the state more interesting still. Yet, paradoxically, all that personal individuality invites greater participation and engagement at all levels.

Probably a little presumptuously, I thought of ending this memoir with St. Timothy: "I have fought the good fight; I have finished the race; I have kept the faith." But funnier and more humble is the note sent to me after my first speech on the statehouse floor by Keith Wallace,

Chris in Magic Summer of 1969

a retired dairy farmer and fellow legislator: "You have fulfilled the three requirements of good public speaking: Stand up and be recognized; speak up and be heard; sit down and be appreciated."

Chris and Bill in 2000

Acknowledgments

TO CHRIS, FOREVER!

AND A HEARTY THANKS TO: Joe Mares, Delia Mares, Jan Mares, Rick Peyser, John Donnelly, Emily Copeland, Jeff Danziger, Don Hooper, Sue Miller, Ralph Swenson, Marty French, Jack Downing, John Tweedle, Dick Foster, Chuck Lewis, Jim Welch, Connie Metz, Reeve Lindbergh, Nat Tripp, Joe Hagan, Sheryl Rapée-Adams, editor, and Eddie Vincent, book designer.

About the Author

Raised in Texas, educated at Harvard, Bill Mares is a former journalist, state representative, and high school teacher. He has authored or co-authored 19 books on subjects ranging from the US Marines to desert travel, from war memorials to brewing beer, from beekeeping to Vermont humor. For pleasure and work, he has traveled to over sixty countries. From 2007 to 2018 he wrote over two hundred commentaries for Vermont Public Radio. He has served on the boards of VTDigger, the Vermont Beekeepers Association, the Fairbanks Museum, the Vermont Council of World Affairs, the Vermont Brewers Association, and Food4Farmers. He lives in Burlington with his wife of 52 years, Chris Hadsel. They have two sons. Visit his website www.bill-mares.com.

We Grow Our Books in Montpelier, Vermont

Learn more about our titles in Fiction, Nonfiction, Poetry and Children's Literature at the QR code below or visit www.rootstockpublishing.com.

www.ingramcontent.com/pod-product-compliance
Lightning Source LLC
Chambersburg PA
CBHW070133080526
44586CB00015B/1671